CURRENT ECONOMIC ISSUES
16TH EDITION

READINGS IN ECONOMICS, POLITICS,
AND SOCIAL POLICY FROM
DOLLARS & SENSE

EDITED BY JAMES M. CYPHER, ALEJANDRO REUSS, CHRIS STURR,

AND THE *DOLLARS & SENSE* COLLECTIVE

CURRENT ECONOMIC ISSUES, 16TH EDITION

Copyright © 2012 by Economic Affairs Bureau, Inc.

All rights reserved. No portions of this book may be reproduced, stored in a retrieval system, or transmitted in any form or by any means, electronic, mechanical, photocopying, recording, or otherwise, except for brief quotations in a review, without prior permission from Economic Affairs Bureau.

Article 8.3 originally appeared in *The Nation* magazine. Used with permission.

ISBN: 978-1-878585-91-2

Published by:
Economic Affairs Bureau, Inc. d/b/a *Dollars & Sense*
1 Milk Street, Boston, MA 02109
617-447-2177; dollars@dollarsandsense.org.
For order information, contact Economic Affairs Bureau or visit: www.dollarsandsense.org.

Current Economic Issues is edited by the *Dollars & Sense* collective, which also publishes *Dollars & Sense* magazine and the classroom books *Real World Macro*, *Real World Micro*, *The Economic Crisis Reader*, *Real World Globalization*, *Real World Latin America*, *Real World Labor*, *Real World Banking and Finance*, *The Wealth Inequality Reader*, *The Economics of the Environment*, *Introduction to Political Economy*, *Unlevel Playing Fields: Understanding Wage Inequality and Discrimination*, *Striking a Balance: Work, Family, Life*, and *Grassroots Journalism*.

The 2012 *Dollars & Sense* Collective:
Betsey Aron, Arpita Banerjee, Leibiana Feliz, Ellen Frank, Shirley Kressel, John Miller, Linda Pinkow, Paul Piwko, Smriti Rao, Alejandro Reuss, Dave Ryan, Dan Schneider, Bryan Snyder, Chris Sturr, and Jeanne Winner.

Co-editors of this volume: James M. Cypher, Alejandro Reuss, and Chris Sturr

Cover design: Chris Sturr
Cover photo: Former PT Kizone workers protest in Jakarta, Indonesia, June 2012. Credit: United Students Against Sweatshops (usas.org).

Production: Chris Sturr

Printed in U.S.A.

CONTENTS

CHAPTER 1 • THE ONGOING CRISIS
1.1 Inequality, Power, and Ideology   *Arthur MacEwan*   1
1.2 Unemployment: A Jobs Deficit or a Skills Deficit?
    John Miller and Jeannette Wicks-Lim   12
1.3 Why the United States is Not Greece
    John Miller and Katherine Sciacchitano   18
1.4 Greece and the Eurozone Crisis by the Numbers   *Gerald Friedman*   25
1.5 Resistance to Austerity Grows in Europe   *Marjolein van der Veen*   28

CHAPTER 2 • DEFICITS AND FISCAL POLICY
2.1 Government "Living Within Its Means"?   *John Miller*   35
2.2 The Ideological Attack on Job Creation   *Marty Wolfson*   38
2.3 Jobs, Deficits, and the Misguided Squabble over the Debt Ceiling
    Tim Koechlin   43
2.4 Don't Drive Off the Fiscal Cliff   *Heidi Garrett-Peltier*   50
2.5 Why Do They Oppose More Stimulus?   *Arthur MacEwan*   52

CHAPTER 3 • TAXATION
3.1 No Fooling—Corporations Evade Taxes   *John Miller*   55
3.2 Transaction Tax: Sand in the Wheels, Not in the Face   *John Miller*   59
3.3 Taxing the Rich, from Right to Left   *John Miller*   62
3.4 What's Wrong with a Flat Tax?   *Arthur MacEwan*   66
3.5 The "Obamacare" Tax Hike and Redistribution   *John Miller*   68
3.6 Taxes and Economic Growth   *Arthur MacEwan*   70

CHAPTER 4 • MONEY, BANKING, AND FINANCE
4.1 Abolishing the Fed Is No Solution to a Real Problem   *Arthur MacEwan*   73
4.2 How Have Banks Managed to Repay the Bailout?   *Arthur MacEwan*   77
4.3 The JOBS Act and Green Slime   *William K. Black*   79
4.4 Private Equity Moguls and the Common Good   *John Miller*   82
4.5 Is China's Currency Manipulation Hurting the U.S.?   *Arthur MacEwan*   86
4.6 Libor Liability   *Max Fraad Wolff*   88

CHAPTER 5 • SOCIAL POLICY
5.1 Universal Health Care: Can We Afford Anything Less?   *Gerald Friedman*   91
5.2 Different Anti-Poverty Regime, Same Single-Mother Poverty
    Randy Albelda   98
5.3 The Big Lie About the "Entitlement State"   *Alejandro Reuss*   106
5.4 Go Ahead and Lift the Cap   *John Miller*   109
5.5 Hard Work at an Advanced Age   *Amy Gluckman*   113
5.6 Putting the Screws to Generation Screwed   *John Miller*   115

CHAPTER 6 • THE ENVIRONMENT

6.1 The Phantom Menace: Environmental Regulations Are Not "Job-Killers"
   Heidi Garrett-Peltier   121
6.2 Way Beyond Greenwashing   *Jonathan Latham   123*
6.3 The Costs of Extreme Weather   *Heidi Garrett-Peltier   131*
6.4 Living Up to Renewable Fuel Standards   *Heidi Garrett-Peltier   133*
6.5 Keep It in the Ground   *Elissa Dennis   135*

CHAPTER 7 • LABOR, UNIONS, AND WORKING CONDITIONS

7.1 How High Could the Minimum Wage Go?   *Jeannette Wicks-Lim   139*
7.2 Campus Struggles Against Sweatshops Continue
   Sarah Blaskey and Phil Gasper   142
7.3 Florida Tomato Pickers Demand "Fair Food"   *Dan Schneider   145*
7.4 Wrong about Right-to-Work   *John Miller   147*
7.5 Wal-Mart Makes the Case for Affirmative Action   *Jeannette Wicks-Lim   151*
7.6 Unions and Economic Performance   *Arthur MacEwan   153*

CHAPTER 8 • SPOTLIGHT—PUBLIC-SECTOR WORKERS

8.1 America's Public-Sector Workers Under Attack   *Gerald Friedman   155*
8.2 State Workers Face a Compensation Penalty   *Ethan Pollack   159*
8.3 The Betrayal of Public Workers   *Robert Pollin and Jeffrey Thompson   161*
8.4 Teachers, Secretaries, and Social Workers: The New Welfare Moms?
   Randy Albelda   167
8.5 Making Labor Pay: Why We Need Universal Pensions
   Katherine Sciacchitano   169

CHAPTER 9 • POVERTY AND WEALTH

9.1 The 99%, the 1%, and Class Struggle   *Alejandro Reuss   177*
9.2 No Thanks to the Super-Rich   *Alejandro Reuss   179*
9.3 The Great Recession in Black Wealth   *Jeannette Wicks-Lim   183*
9.4 How Important Is *Citizens United*?   *Arthur MacEwan   185*
9.5 Who Are the "47%"? And Why Don't They Pay (Income) Taxes?
   Gerald Friedman   187
9.6 Famine Myths   *William G. Moseley   190*

CHAPTER 10 • RESISTANCE AND ALTERNATIVES

10.1 Rank-and-File Economics   *Katherine Sciacchitano   197*
10.2 Full Employment as the Answer for Europe   *Robert Pollin   206*
10.3 The Case for a National Infrastructure Bank   *Heidi Garrett-Peltier   209*
10.4 Saving Energy Creates Jobs   *Heidi Garrett-Peltier   211*
10.5 Turning Toward Solutions   *Richard D. Wolff   213*
10.6 Greetings from the New Economy   *Abby Scher   216*

CONTRIBUTORS   *223*

Chapter 1

THE ONGOING CRISIS

Article 1.1

INEQUALITY, POWER, AND IDEOLOGY
Getting It Right About the Causes of the Current Economic Crisis

BY ARTHUR MacEWAN
March/April 2009; updated November 2012

It is hard to solve a problem without an understanding of what caused it. For example, in medicine, until we gained an understanding of the way bacteria and viruses cause various infectious diseases, it was virtually impossible to develop effective cures. Of course, dealing with many diseases is complicated by the fact that germs, genes, diet, and the environment establish a nexus of causes.

The same is true in economics. Without an understanding of the causes of the current crisis, we are unlikely to develop a solution; certainly we are not going to get a solution that has a lasting impact. And determining the causes is complicated because several intertwined factors have been involved.

The current economic crisis was brought about by a nexus of factors that involved: a growing concentration of political and social power in the hands of the wealthy; the ascendance of a perverse leave-it-to-the-market ideology which was an instrument of that power; and rising income inequality, which both resulted from and enhanced that power. These various factors formed a vicious circle, reinforcing one another and together shaping the economic conditions that led us to the present situation. Several other factors were also involved—the growing role of credit, the puffing up of the housing bubble, and the increasing deregulation of financial markets have been very important. However, these are best understood as transmitters of our economic problems, arising from the nexus that formed the vicious circle.

What does this tell us about a solution? Economic stimulus, repair of the housing market, and new regulation are all well and good, but they do not deal with the underlying causes of the crisis. Instead, progressive groups need to work to shift each of the factors I have noted—power, ideology, and income distribution—in the other direction. In doing so, we can create a *virtuous* circle, with each change reinforcing the other changes. If successful, we not only establish a more stable economy, but we lay the foundation for a more democratic, equitable, and sustainable economic order.

A crisis by its very nature creates opportunities for change. One good place to begin change and intervene in this "circle"—and transform it from vicious to virtuous—is through pushing for the expansion and reform of social programs, programs that directly serve social needs of the great majority of the population (for example: single-payer health care, education programs, and environmental protection and repair). By establishing changes in social programs, we will have impacts on income distribution and ideology, and, perhaps most important, we set in motion *a power shift* that improves our position for preserving the changes. While I emphasize social programs as a means to initiate social and economic change, there are other ways to intervene in the circle. Efforts to re-strengthen unions would be especially important; and there are other options as well.

Causes of the Crisis: A Long Time Coming

Sometime around the early 1970s, there were some dramatic changes in the U.S. economy. The twenty-five years following World War II had been an era of relatively stable economic growth; the benefits of growth had been widely shared, with wages rising along with productivity gains, and income distribution became slightly less unequal (a good deal less unequal as compared to the pre-Great Depression era). There were severe economic problems in the United States, not the least of which were the continued exclusion of African Americans, large gender inequalities, and the woeful inadequacy of social welfare programs. Nonetheless, relatively stable growth, rising wages, and then the advent of the civil rights movement and the War on Poverty gave some important, positive social and economic character to the era—especially in hindsight!

In part, this comparatively favorable experience for the United States had depended on the very dominant position that U.S. firms held in the world economy, a position in which they were relatively unchallenged by international competition. The firms and their owners were not the only beneficiaries of this situation. With less competitive pressure on them from foreign companies, many U.S. firms accepted unionization and did not find it worthwhile to focus on keeping wages down and obstructing the implementation of social supports for the low-income population. Also, having had the recent experience of the Great Depression, many wealthy people and business executives were probably not so averse to a substantial role for government in regulating the economy.

A Power Grab

By about 1970, the situation was changing. Firms in Europe and Japan had long recovered from World War II, OPEC was taking shape, and weaknesses were emerging in the U.S. economy. The weaknesses were in part a consequence of heavy spending for the Vietnam War combined with the government's reluctance to tax for the war because of its unpopularity. The pressures on U.S. firms arising from these changes had two sets of consequences: slower growth and greater instability; and concerted efforts—a power grab, if you will—by firms and the wealthy to shift the costs of economic deterioration onto U.S. workers and the low-income population.

These "concerted efforts" took many forms: greater resistance to unions and unionization, battles to reduce taxes, stronger opposition to social welfare programs, and, above all, a push to reduce or eliminate government regulation of economic activity through a powerful political campaign to gain control of the various branches and levels of government. The 1980s, with Reagan and Bush One in the White House, were the years in which all these efforts were solidified. Unions were greatly weakened, a phenomenon both demonstrated and exacerbated by Reagan's firing of the air traffic controllers in response to their strike in 1981. The tax cuts of the period were also important markers of the change. But the change had begun earlier; the 1978 passage of the tax-cutting Proposition 13 in California was perhaps the first major success of the movement. And the changes continued well after the 1980s, with welfare reform and deregulation of finance during the Clinton era, to say nothing of the tax cuts and other actions during Bush Two.

Ideology Shift

The changes that began in the 1970s, however, were not simply these sorts of concrete alterations in the structure of power affecting the economy and, especially, government's role in the economy. There was a major shift in ideology, the dominant set of ideas that organize an understanding of our social relations and both guide and rationalize policy decisions.

Following the Great Depression and World War II, there was a wide acceptance of the idea that government had a major role to play in economic life. Less than in many other countries but nonetheless to a substantial degree, at all levels of society, it was generally believed that there should be a substantial government safety net and that government should both regulate the economy in various ways and, through fiscal as well as monetary policy, should maintain aggregate demand. This large economic role for government came to be called Keynesianism, after the British economist John Maynard Keynes, who had set out the arguments for an active fiscal policy in time of economic weakness. In the early 1970s, as economic troubles developed, even Richard Nixon declared: "We are all Keynesians now."

The election of Ronald Reagan, however, marked a sharp change in ideology, at least at the top. Actions of the government were blamed for all economic ills: government spending, Keynesianism, was alleged to be the cause of the inflation of the 1970s; government regulation was supposedly crippling industry; high taxes were, it was argued, undermining incentives for workers to work and for businesses to invest; social welfare spending was blamed for making people dependent on the government and was charged with fraud and corruption (the "welfare queens"); and so on and so on.

On economic matters, Reagan championed supply-side economics, the principal idea of which was that tax cuts yield an increase in government revenue because the cuts lead to more rapid economic growth through encouraging more work and more investment. Thus, so the argument went, tax cuts would reduce the government deficit. Reagan, with the cooperation of Democrats, got the tax cuts—and, as the loss of revenue combined with a large increase in military spending, the federal budget deficit grew by leaps and bounds, almost doubling as a share of GDP over the course of the 1980s. It was all summed up in the idea of keeping the government out of the economy; let the free market work its magic.

Growing Inequality

The shifts of power and ideology were very much bound up with a major redistribution upwards of income and wealth. The weakening of unions, the increasing access of firms to low-wage foreign (and immigrant) labor, the refusal of government to maintain the buying power of the minimum wage, favorable tax treatment of the wealthy and their corporations, deregulation in a wide range of industries, and lack of enforcement of existing regulation (e.g., the authorities turning a blind eye to offshore tax shelters) all contributed to these shifts.

Many economists, however, explain the rising income inequality as a result of technological change that favored more highly skilled workers; and changing technology has probably been a factor. Yet the most dramatic aspect of the rising inequality has been the rapidly rising share of income obtained by those at the very top (see figures), who get their incomes from the ownership and control of business, not from their skilled labor. For these people the role of new technologies was most important through its impact on providing more options (e.g., international options) for the managers of firms, more thorough means to control labor, and more effective ways—in the absence of regulation—to manipulate finance. All of these gains that might be associated with new technology were also gains brought by the way the government handled, or didn't handle (failed to regulate), economic affairs.

Several sets of data demonstrate the sharp changes in the distribution of income that have taken place in the last several decades. Most striking is the changing position of the very highest income segment of the population. In the mid-1920s, the share of all pre-tax income going to the top 1% of households peaked at 23.9%. This elite group's share of income fell dramatically during the Great Depression and World War II to about 12% at the end of the war and then slowly fell further during the next thirty years, reaching a low of 8.9% in the mid-1970s. Since then, the top 1% has regained its exalted position of the earlier era, with 21.8% of income in 2005. Since 1993, more than one-half of all income gains have accrued to this highest 1% of the population.

Figures 1 and 2 show the gains (or losses) of various groups in the 1947 to 1979 period and in the 1979 to 2005 period. The difference is dramatic. For example, in the earlier era, the bottom 20% saw its income in real (inflation-adjusted) terms rise by 116%, and real income of the top 5% grew by only 86%. But in the latter era, the bottom 20% saw a 1% decline in its income, while the top 5% obtained a 81% increase.

The Emergence of Crisis

These changes, especially the dramatic shifts in the distribution of income, set the stage for the increasingly large reliance on credit, especially consumer and mortgage

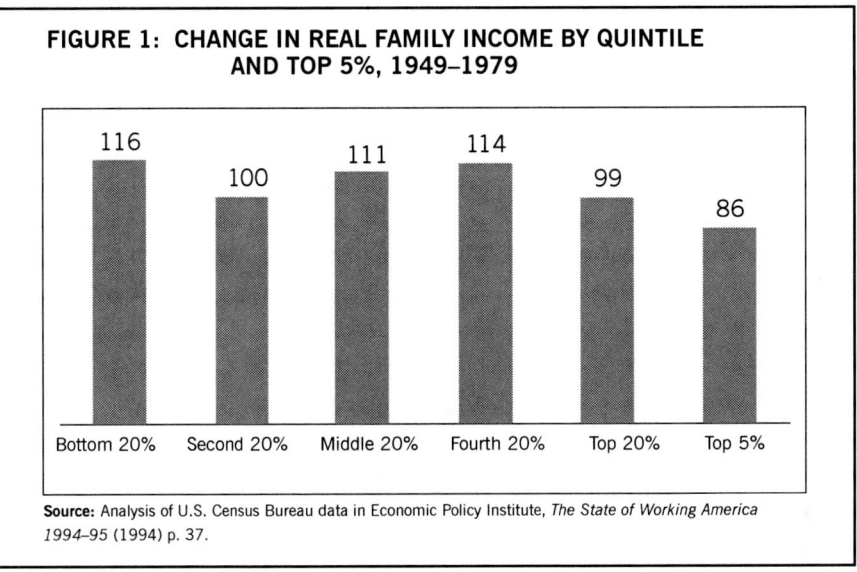

credit, that played a major role in the emergence of the current economic crisis. Other factors were involved, but rising inequality was especially important in effecting the increase in both the demand and supply of credit.

Credit Expansion

On the demand side, rising inequality translated into a growing gap between the incomes of most members of society and their needs. For the 2000 to 2007 period, average weekly earnings in the private sector were 12% below their average for the 1970s (in inflation-adjusted terms). From 1980 to 2005 the share of income going to the bottom 60% of families fell from 35% to 29%. Under these

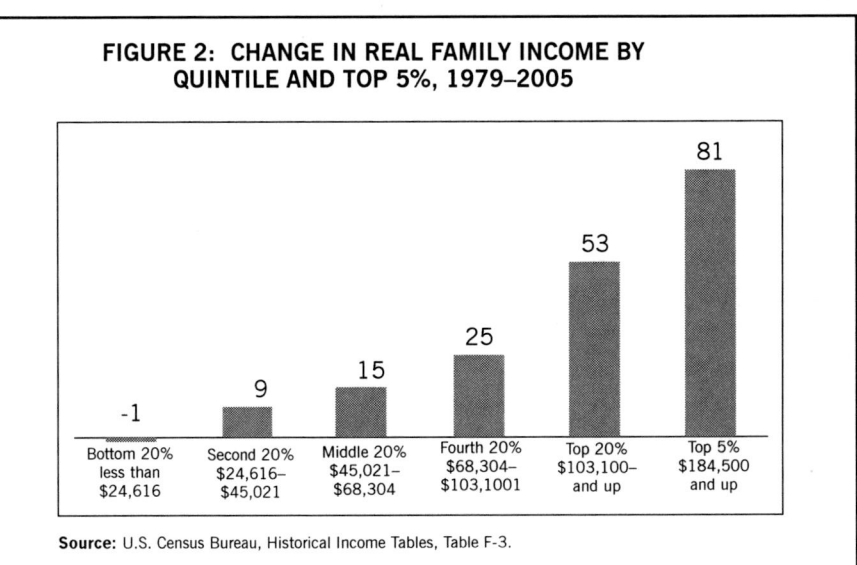

circumstances, more and more people relied more and more heavily on credit to meet their needs—everything from food to fuel, from education to entertainment, and especially housing.

While the increasing reliance of consumers on credit has been going on for a long time, it has been especially marked in recent decades. Consumer debt as a share of after-tax personal income averaged 20% in the 1990s, and then jumped up to an average of 25% in the first seven years of the new millennium. But the debt expansion was most marked in housing, where mortgage debt as a percent of after-tax personal income rose from 89% to 94% over the 1990s, and then ballooned to 140% by 2006 as housing prices skyrocketed.

On the supply side, especially in the last few years, the government seems to have relied on making credit readily available as a means to bolster aggregate demand and maintain at least a modicum of economic growth. During the 1990s, the federal funds interest rate averaged 5.1%, but fell to an average of 3.4% in the 2000 to 2007 period—and averaged only 1.4% in 2002 to 2004 period. (The federal funds interest rate is the rate that banks charge one another for overnight loans and is a rate directly affected by the Federal Reserve.) Corresponding to the low interest rates, the money supply grew twice as fast in the new millennium as it had in the 1990s. (And see the box on the connection of the Fed's actions to the Iraq War.)

The increasing reliance of U.S. consumers on credit has often been presented as a moral weakness, as an infatuation with consumerism, and as a failure to look beyond the present. Whatever moral judgments one may make, however, the expansion of the credit economy has been a response to real economic forces—inequality and government policies, in particular.

The Failure to Regulate

The credit expansion by itself, however, did not precipitate the current crisis. Deregulation—or, more generally, the failure to regulate—is also an important part of the story. The government's role in regulation of financial markets has been a central feature in the development of this crisis, but the situation in financial markets has been part of a more general process—affecting airlines and trucking, telecommunications, food processing, broadcasting, and of course international trade and investment. The process has been driven by a combination of power (of large firms and wealthy individuals) and ideology (leave it to the market, get the government out).

The failure to regulate financial markets that transformed the credit expansion into a financial crisis shows up well in three examples:

The 1999 repeal of the Glass-Steagall Act. Glass-Steagall had been enacted in the midst of the Great Depression, as a response to the financial implosion following the stock market crash of 1929. Among other things, it required that different kinds of financial firms—commercial banks, investment banks, insurance companies—be separate. This separation both limited the spread of financial problems and reduced conflicts of interest that could arise were the different functions of these firms combined into a single firm. As perhaps the most important legislation regulating the financial sector, the repeal of Glass-Steagall was not only a substantive change but was an important symbol of the whole process of deregulation.

The failure to regulate mortgage lending. Existing laws and regulations require lending institutions to follow prudent practices in making loans, assuring that borrowers have the capacity to be able to pay back the loans. And of course fraud—lying about the provisions of loans—is prohibited. Yet in an atmosphere where regulation was "out," regulators were simply not doing their jobs. The consequences are illustrated in a December 28, 2008, *New York Times* story on the failed Washington Mutual Bank. The article describes a supervisor at a mortgage processing center as having been "accustomed to seeing babysitters claiming salaries worthy of college presidents, and schoolteachers with incomes rivaling stockbrokers'. He rarely questioned them. A real estate frenzy was under way and WaMu, as his bank was known, was all about saying yes."

One may wonder why banks—or other lending institutions, mortgage firms, in particular—would make loans to people who were unlikely to be able to pay them back. The reason is that the lending institutions quickly combined such loans into packages (i.e., a security made up of several borrowers' obligations to pay) and sold them to other investors in a practice called "securitization."

Credit-default swaps. Perhaps the most egregious failure to regulate in recent years has been the emergence of credit-default swaps, which are connected to securitization. Because they were made up of obligations by a diverse set of borrowers, the packages of loans were supposedly low-risk investments. Yet those who purchased them still sought insurance against default. Insurance sellers, however, are regulated—required, for example, to keep a certain amount of capital on hand to cover possible claims. So the sellers of these insurance policies on packages of loans called the policies "credit-default swaps" and thus were allowed to avoid regulation. Further, these credit-default swaps, these insurance policies, themselves were bought and sold again and again in unregulated markets in a continuing process of speculation.

The credit-default swaps are a form of derivative, a financial asset the value of which is derived from some other asset—in this case the value of packages of mortgages for which they were the insurance policies. When the housing bubble began to collapse and people started to default on their mortgages, the value of credit-default swaps plummeted and their future value was impossible to determine. No one would buy them, and several banks that had speculated in these derivatives were left holding huge amounts of these "toxic assets."

Bubble and Bust

The combination of easy credit and the failure to regulate together fueled the housing bubble. People could buy expensive houses but make relatively low monthly payments. Without effective regulation of mortgage lending, they could get the loans even when they were unlikely to be able to make payments over the long run. Moreover, as these pressures pushed up housing prices, many people bought houses simply to resell them quickly at a higher price, in a process called "flipping." And such speculation pushed the prices up further. Between 2000 and 2006, housing prices rose by 90% (as consumer prices generally rose by only 17%).

While the housing boom was in full swing, both successful housing speculators and lots of people involved in the shenanigans of credit markets made a lot of money. However, as the housing bubble burst—as all bubbles do—things fell apart. The packages of loans lost value, and the insurance policies on them, the credit-default swaps, lost value. These then became "toxic" assets for those who held them, assets not only with reduced value but with unknown value. Not only did large financial firms—for example, Lehman Brothers and AIG—have billions of dollars in losses, but no one knew the worth of their remaining assets. The assets were called "toxic" because they poisoned the operations of the financial system. Under these circumstances, financial institutions stopped lending to one another—that is, the credit markets "froze up." The financial crisis was here.

The financial crisis, not surprisingly, very quickly shifted to a general economic crisis. Firms in the "real" economy rely heavily on a well-functioning financial system to supply them with the funds they need for their regular operations—loans to car buyers, loans to finance inventory, loans for construction of new facilities, loans for new equipment, and, of course, mortgage loans. Without those loans (or with the loans much more difficult to obtain), there has been a general cut-back in economic activity, what is becoming a serious and probably prolonged recession.

What Is to Be Done?

So here we are. The shifts in power, ideology, and income distribution have placed us in a rather nasty situation. There are some steps that will be taken that have a reasonable probability of yielding short-run improvement. In particular, a large increase in government spending—deficit spending—will probably reduce the depth and shorten the length of the recession. And the actions of the Federal Reserve and Treasury to inject funds into the financial system are likely, along with the deficit spending, to "un-freeze" credit markets (the mismanagement and, it seems, outright corruption of the bailout notwithstanding). Also, there is likely to be some re-regulation of the financial industry. These steps, however, at best will restore things to where they were before the crisis. They do not treat the underlying causes of the crisis—the vicious circle of power, ideology, and inequality.

Opportunity for Change

Fortunately, the crisis itself has weakened some aspects of this circle. The cry of "leave it to the market" is still heard, but is now more a basis for derision than a guide to policy. The ideology and, to a degree, the power behind the ideology, have been severely weakened as the role of "keeping the government out" has shown to be a major cause of the financial mess and our current hardships. There is now widespread support among the general populace and some support in Washington for greater regulation of the financial industry.

Whether or not the coming period will see this support translated into effective policy is of course an open question. Also an open question is how much the turn away from "leaving it to the market" can be extended to other sectors of the economy. With regard to the environment, there is already general acceptance of the principle that the government (indeed, many governments) must take an active role in regulating economic activity. Similar principles need to be recognized with regard to health care, education, housing, child care, and other support programs for low-income families.

The discrediting of "keep the government out" ideology provides an opening to develop new programs in these areas and to expand old programs. Furthermore, as the federal government revs up its "stimulus" program in the coming months, opportunities will exist for expanding support for these sorts of programs. This support is important, first of all, because these programs serve real, pressing needs—needs that have long existed and are becoming acute and more extensive in the current crisis.

Breaking the Circle

Support for these social programs, however, may also serve to break into the vicious power-ideology-inequality circle and begin transforming it into a virtuous circle. Social programs are inherently equalizing in two ways: they provide their benefits to low-income people and they provide some options for those people in their efforts to demand better work and higher pay. Also, the further these programs develop, the more they establish the legitimacy of a larger role for public control of—government involvement in—the economy; they tend to bring about an ideological shift. By affecting a positive distributional shift and by shifting ideology, the emergence of stronger social programs can have a wider impact on power. In other words, efforts to promote social programs are one place to start, an entry point to shift the vicious circle to a virtuous circle.

There are other entry points. Perhaps the most obvious ones are actions to strengthen the role of unions. The Employee Free Choice Act may be a useful first step, and it will be helpful to establish a more union-friendly Department of Labor and National Labor Relations Board. Raising the minimum wage—ideally indexing it to inflation—would also be highly desirable. While conditions have changed since the heyday of unions in the middle of the 20th century, and we cannot expect to restore the conditions of that era, a greater role for unions would seem essential in righting the structural conditions at the foundation of the current crisis.

Shifting Class Power

None of this is assured, of course. Simply starting social programs will not necessarily mean that they have the wider impacts that I am suggesting are possible. No one should think that by setting up some new programs and strengthening some existing ones we will be on a smooth road to economic and social change. Likewise, rebuilding the strength of unions will involve extensive struggle and will not be accomplished by a few legislative or executive actions.

Also, all efforts to involve the government in economic activity—whether in finance or environmental affairs, in health care or education, in work support or job training programs—will be met with the worn-out claims that government involvement generates bureaucracy, stifles initiative, and places an excessive burden on private firms and individuals. We are already hearing warnings that in dealing with the financial crisis the government must avoid "over-regulation." Likewise, efforts to strengthen unions will suffer the traditional attacks, as unions are portrayed as corrupt and their members privileged. The unfolding situation with regard to the auto firms' troubles has demonstrated the attack, as conservatives have blamed the United Auto Workers for the industry's woes and have demanded extensive concessions by the union.

Certainly not all regulation is good regulation. Aside from excessive bureaucratic controls, there is the phenomenon by which regulating agencies are often captives of the industries that they are supposed to regulate. And there are corrupt unions. These are real issues, but they should not be allowed to derail change.

The current economic crisis emerged in large part as a shift in the balance of class power in the United States, a shift that began in the early 1970s and continued into the new millennium. Perhaps the present moment offers an opportunity to shift things back in the other direction. Recognition of the complex nexus of causes of the current economic crisis provides some guidance where people might start. Rebuilding and extending social programs, strengthening unions, and other actions that contribute to a more egalitarian power shift will not solve all the problems of U.S. capitalism. They can, however, begin to move us in the right direction. ❑

Inequality, Power, and Ideology: An Afterword
November 2012

When this article was written in early 2009, the U.S. economy was in a severe recession, which came to be called the Great Recession. The economic downturn—defined in terms of a drop-off in total output, or gross domestic product (GDP)—had begun at the end of 2007. Although the recession came to a formal end by June 2009, when GDP started to grow again, economic conditions continued to be very poor. With slow economic growth, unemployment remained high, falling below 8% only in late 2012, and many people simply gave up looking for work and were not even counted among the unemployed.

Several factors contribute to an explanation of the weak recovery from the Great Recession. When economic downturns are brought about by financial crises, they tend to be more lasting because the machinery of the credit system and the confidence of lenders have been so severely damaged. Also, while the Great Recession developed in the United States, it spread to much of the rest of the world. Conditions in Europe, especially, have hampered full recovery in the United States.

The continuing economic malaise, however, also has its bases in the political conditions of Washington, in the weakness of the federal government's response to the Great Recession. While it is possible to debate the extent to which the weak response has been the responsibility of the recalcitrant role of Republicans in Congress versus the limited actions of President Obama, there is no doubt regarding the several aspects of that weak response:

- ·The fiscal stimulus implemented at the beginning of 2009, the American Recovery and Reinvestment Act (ARRA), was too small. This action did stem the decline of the economy, probably preventing things from getting much worse. But given the severity of the downturn, the ARRA was insufficient to reestablish growth that would have moved the United States strongly back toward full employment.

- ·Programs to relieve the dreadful damage done to millions of homeowners have been minimal, leaving families in dire straits and leaving the housing market in the doldrums.

- ·The Wall Street Reform and Consumer Protection Act, the Dodd-Frank bill, was enacted in 2010. Yet it was a weak bill, failing to deal with the most serious problems in the financial sector—for example, leaving several banks "too big to fail." Also, many of its provisions were sufficiently vague to allow the Wall Street firms to use their influence to blunt its impact.

- ·The huge bailout of the financial sector, the Troubled Asset Relief Program (TARP) and other actions of the Federal Reserve, probably did make an important contribution to preventing an even worse financial crisis. But TARP was a tremendous boon to the bankers who had been instrumental actors in bringing about the crisis. There were other actions that could have been taken. Moreover, the continuing weak response of the economy to the Fed's continued efforts to stimulate economic growth demonstrated the insufficiency of monetary policy to deal with a severe economic downturn.

Even if the government's actions had been more forceful, the underlying causes of the crisis remain unaddressed—economic inequality, power, and ideology remain largely as they were as the crisis emerged. Figure 3 shows that from 2005 through 2011, all groups have seen their incomes decline. However, with those at the bottom suffering the most severe decline, income inequality has increased. Also, there is no indication that the power of the elite has been curtailed. Indeed, with the evisceration of campaign finance regulations (the Citizens United Supreme Court decision in particular), money and power are increasingly tied firmly together.

What of ideology? The outcome of the 2012 election suggests that a majority of the electorate rejects the leave-it-to-the-market ideology that has supported inequality and the concentration of political power and that led into the crisis. Whatever the limits of the Obama administration, it portrayed itself with rhetoric of social responsibility and promised some regulation of markets. Regardless of the limited extent to which reality in the subsequent years will match this rhetoric, the actions of a majority of the electorate suggest that there are some possibilities for positive change. Moreover, when the Occupy Wall Street (OWS) movement appeared in late 2011, it forced a discussion of basic issues of inequality, power, and ideology onto the public agenda. Whatever happens to OWS, it is likely that these issues will continue to be well recognized.

The sorts of changes advocated in this article, changes that would affect the underlying causes of the economic crisis, continue to be necessary. They also continue to be possible.   *—Arthur MacEwan*

An elaboration of the points in this afterword is contained in the book that grew out of the original article: *Economic Collapse and Economic Change: Getting to the Roots of the Crisis*, by Arthur MacEwan and John A. Miller, M.E. Sharpe Publisher, 2011.

Article 1.2

UNEMPLOYMENT: A JOBS DEFICIT OR A SKILLS DEFICIT?
BY JOHN MILLER AND JEANNETTE WICKS-LIM
January/February 2011

Millions of Americans remain unemployed nearly a year and a half after the official end-date of the Great Recession, and the nation's official unemployment rate continues at nearly 10%.

Why? We are being told that it is because—wait for it—workers are not qualified for the jobs that employers are offering.

Yes, it's true. In the aftermath of the deepest downturn since the Great Depression, some pundits and policymakers—and economists—have begun to pin persistently high unemployment on workers' inadequate skills.

The problem, in this view, is a mismatch between job openings and the skills of those looking for work. In economics jargon, this is termed a problem of "structural unemployment," in contrast to the "cyclical unemployment" caused by a downturn in the business cycle.

The skills-gap message is coming from many quarters. Policymaker-in-chief Obama told Congress in February 2009: "Right now, three-quarters of the fastest-growing occupations require more than a high school diploma. And yet, just over half of our citizens have that level of education." His message: workers need to go back to school if they want a place in tomorrow's job market.

The last Democrat in the White House has caught the bug too. Bill Clinton explained in a September 2010 interview, "The last unemployment report said that for the first time in my lifetime, and I'm not young ... we are coming out of a recession but job openings are going up twice as fast as new hires. And yet we can all cite cases that we know about where somebody opened a job and 400 people showed up. How could this be? Because people don't have the job skills for the jobs that are open."

Economists and other "experts" are most likely the source of the skills-gap story. Last August, for instance, Narayana Kocherlakota, president of the Federal Reserve Bank of Minneapolis, wrote in a Fed newsletter: "How much of the current unemployment rate is really due to mismatch, as opposed to conditions that the Fed can readily ameliorate? The answer seems to be a lot." Kocherlakota's point was that the Fed's monetary policy tools may be able to spur economic growth, but that won't help if workers have few or the wrong skills. "The Fed does not have a means to transform construction workers into manufacturing workers," he explained.

The skills-mismatch explanation has a lot to recommend it if you're a federal or Fed policymaker: it puts the blame for the economic suffering experienced by the 17% of the U.S. workforce that is unemployed or underemployed on the workers themselves. Even if the Fed or the government did its darndest to boost overall spending, unemployment would be unlikely to subside unless workers upgraded their own skills.

The only problem is that this explanation is basically wrong. The weight of the evidence shows that it is not a mismatch of skills but a lack of demand that lies at the heart of today's severe unemployment problem.

High-Skill Jobs?

President Obama's claim that new jobs are requiring higher and higher skill levels would tend to support the skills-gap thesis. His interpretation of job-market trends, however, misses the mark. The figure that Obama cited comes from the U.S. Department of Labor's employment projections for 2006 to 2016. Specifically, the DOL reports that among the 30 fastest growing occupations, 22 of them (75%) will typically require more than a high school degree. These occupations include network systems and data communications analysts, computer software engineers, and financial advisors. What he fails to say, however, is that these 22 occupations are projected to represent less than 3% of all U.S. jobs.

What would seem more relevant to the 27 million unemployed and underemployed workers are the occupations with the *largest* growth. These are the occupations that will offer workers the greatest number of new job opportunities. Among the 30 occupations with the largest growth, 70%—21 out of 30—typically do not require more than a high school degree. To become fully qualified for these jobs, workers will only need on-the-job training. The DOL projects that one-quarter of all jobs in 2016 will be in these 21 occupations, which include retail salespeople, food-preparation and food-service workers, and personal and home care aides.

In fact, the DOL employment projections estimate that more than two-thirds (68%) of the jobs in 2016 will be accessible to workers with a high school degree or less. Couple this with the fact that today, nearly two-thirds (62%) of the adult labor force has at least some college experience, and an alleged skills gap fails to be convincing as a driving force behind persistent high unemployment.

Labor Market Musical Chairs

To understand the data discussed here, try picturing the U.S. labor market as a game of musical chairs, with a few twists. At any time, chairs (job openings) can be added to the circle and players can sit down (get hired). When the music stops at the end of the month, not all the chairs are filled. Still, many people—far more people than the number of empty chairs—are left standing.

Each month, the Bureau of Labor Statistics reports on what happened in that month's game of labor market musical chairs in its various measures of unemployment and in the Job Openings and Labor Turnover Survey (JOLTS). Here's how the BLS scorecard for labor market musical chairs works.

- **Job openings** is a snapshot of the number of jobs available on the last day of the month—the number of empty chairs when the music stops.

- **Hires** are all the new additions to payroll during the month—the number of people who found a chair to sit in while the music was playing. Because many chairs are added to the circle and filled within the same month, the number of hires over a month is typically greater than the number of openings available on the last day of that month.

- **Unemployed persons** are those who looked for a job that month but couldn't find one—the number of people who played the game but were left standing when the music stopped at the end of the month.

Low-Skill Workers?

If employers were having a hard time finding qualified workers to fill job openings, you'd think that any workers who are qualified would be snapped right up. But what the unemployment data show is that there remains a substantial backlog of experienced workers looking for jobs or for more hours in their existing part-time jobs in those major industries that have begun hiring—including education, healthcare, durable goods manufacturing, and mining.

Most telling are the *underemployed*—those with part-time jobs who want to work full-time. Today there are more underemployed workers in each of the major industries of the private economy than during the period from 2000 to 2007, as Arjun Jayadev and Mike Konczal document in a recent paper published by the Roosevelt Institute. Even in the major industries with the highest number of job openings—education and health services, professional and business services, transportation and utilities, leisure and hospitality, and manufacturing—underemployment in 2010 remains at levels twice as high or nearly twice as high as during the earlier period (measured as a percentage of employed workers).

Purveyors of the mismatch theory would have a hard time explaining how it is that underemployed workers who want full-time work do not possess the skills to do the jobs full time that they are already doing, say, 20 hours a week.

More broadly, workers with a diverse set of skills—not just construction workers—lost jobs during the Great Recession. Workers in manufacturing, professional and business services, leisure and hospitality, transportation and utilities, and a host of other industries were turned out of their jobs. And many of these experienced workers are still looking for work. In each of the 16 major industries of the economy unemployment rates in September 2010 were still far higher than they had been at the onset of the Great Recession in December 2007. In the industries with a large number of (cumulative) job openings during the recovery—education and health services, professional and business services, and manufacturing—experienced workers face unemployment rates twice what they were back in December 2007.

There are plenty of experienced workers still looking for work in the industries with job openings. To be faithful to the data, Kocherlakota and the other mismatch proponents would need to show that experienced workers no longer possess the skills to work in their industry, even though that industry employed them no more than three years ago. That seems implausible.

Statistical Errors

Still, the statistical oddity that Bill Clinton and many economists have pointed to does seem to complicate the picture. If the number of job openings is rising at a good clip yet the number of new hires is growing more slowly and the unemployment rate is stagnant, then maybe employers *are* having trouble finding qualified folks to hire.

Once you take a closer looks at the numbers, though, there is less here than meets the eye.

First, the *rate* at which job openings and new hires numbers change over time is not the right place to look. What we really need to know is how the number of unfilled job posts compares to the number of qualified workers employers hire over the same month. If employers in today's recovery are having a hard time finding workers, then the job openings left unfilled at the end of the month should be relatively high compared to the number of newly hired workers that month. In other words, if the number of positions left unfilled at the end of the month relative to the number of new hires rises *above* what we've seen during past recoveries, this would mean that employers are finding it harder to fill their positions with the right workers this time around.

But it turns out that the ratio of unfilled job openings to new hires is approximately the same during this recovery as in the recovery from the 2001 recession. In September 2010, fifteen months into the current economic recovery, the ratio of job posts left unoccupied at the end of the month to the number of monthly new hires stood at 69%—very close to its 67% level in February 2003, fifteen months into the last recovery. In other words, today's employers are filling their job openings with the same rate of success as yesterday's employers.

Comparisons that focus on the unemployment rate rather than on the number of new hires are even less meaningful. As hiring picks up at the beginning of an economic recovery, workers who had given up the job search start looking again. This brings them back into the official count of the unemployed, keeping the unemployment rate from dropping even as both job openings and new hires rise.

Where Mismatches May Matter

The skills-mismatch theory does not go very far toward explaining stubbornly high U.S. unemployment. Still, there are unquestionably some unemployed and underemployed workers whose job prospects are limited by "structural" factors.

One kind of structural unemployment that does seem to fit the contours of the Great Recession to at least some degree is that caused by a mismatch of geography: the workers are in one part of the country while the jobs they could get are in another. The housing crisis surely has compromised the ability of unemployed workers to unload their single largest asset, a house, and move to another part of the country. Plus, job losses have been particularly heavy in regions where the housing crisis hit hardest.

But at the same time, lost jobs have been widespread across industries and there is little real evidence of geographic mismatch between job openings and unemployed workers. As labor economist Michael Reich reports, "economic decline and the growth of unemployment have been more widespread than ever before, making it unclear where the unemployed should migrate for greater job opportunities."

Even where there is a skills mismatch, that doesn't mean the government shouldn't get involved. On the contrary, government policies to boost economic demand can help significantly. When demand is high, labor markets become very tight and there are few available workers to hire. Workers previously viewed as "unemployable" get hired, get experience and on-the-job training, and see their overall career prospects brighten.

And, of course, government can fund expanded job-training programs. If the economy continues to slog along with low growth rates and persistent unemployment, the ranks of the long-term unemployed will rise. As they go longer and longer without work, their skills will atrophy or become obsolete and they will face a genuine skills-mismatch problem that will make job-training programs more and more necessary.

Not Enough Jobs

The reality of the situation—the widespread job losses and the long, fruitless job searches of experienced workers—make it clear that today's employment problem is a jobs deficit across the economy, not a skills deficit among those looking for work.

While it's true that any given month ends with some number of unfilled job openings, the total number of jobs added to the economy during this recovery has simply been inadequate to put the unemployed back to work. In fact, if every job that stood open at the end of September 2010 had been filled, 11.7 million officially unemployed workers would still have been jobless.

This recovery has seen far fewer job openings than even the so-called "jobless" recovery following the 2001 recession. Economists Lawrence Mishel, Heidi Shierholz, and Kathryn Edwards of the Economic Policy Institute report that cumulative job openings during the first year of this recovery were roughly 25% lower than during the first year of the recovery following the 2001 recession—that's 10 million fewer jobs. Even in the industries generating the most job openings in the current recovery—education and health services, professional and business services, leisure and hospitality, and manufacturing—the cumulative number of job openings has lagged well behind the figure for those industries during the first year of the recovery from the 2001 recession. (Only the mining and logging category, which accounted for just 0.5% of employment in 2007, has had more job openings during the first year of this recovery than during the first year of the 2001 recovery.)

Why has the pick-up in jobs following the Great Recession been worse than usual? The simple answer is that the recession was worse than usual. The sharp and extreme decline of output and employment in the Great Recession has severely dampened demand—that is, people have not had money to buy things. With the resulting lack of sales, businesses were not willing to either invest or hire; and this in turn has meant a continuing lack of demand.

If businesses have barely resumed hiring, it has not been for lack of profits. By the middle of 2010, corporate profits (adjusted for inflation) were about 60% above their low point at the end of 2008, well on their way back to the peak level of mid-2006. Also, in early 2010 non-financial firms were sitting on almost $2 trillion in cash. There was no lack of ability to invest and hire, but there was a lack of incentive to invest and hire, that is, a lack of an expectation that demand (sales) would rise. As is well known, small businesses have generally accounted for a disproportionately large share of job growth. Yet, since the onset of the Great Recession, small business owners have consistently identified poor sales as their single most important problem—and thus, presumably, what has prevented them from expanding employment.

The Role of Demand

Regardless of the lack of evidence to support it, the skills-mismatch story has seeped into media coverage of the economy. Take, for example, National Public Radio's recent Morning Edition series titled "Skills gap: holding back the labor market." In one segment, reporter Wendy Kaufman presents anecdotes about employers turning down record numbers of applicants and leaving job openings unfilled. Economist Peter Capelli then comes on and remarks, "You know, a generation ago you'd never expect that somebody could come into a reasonably skilled, sophisticated position in your organization and immediately make a contribution. That's a brand new demand." Now, that comment does not point to today's workers possessing fewer skills or qualifications. Rather, it suggests that employers have raised the bar: they are pickier than in the past.

That makes sense. We've seen that employers are successfully filling positions at about the same rate as in the recent past. What's different this time around is that employers have had up to six unemployed workers competing for every job opening left vacant at the close of the month. This is by far the highest ratio on record with data back to 2000. During the 2001 recession, that ratio rose to just over two unemployed workers for each opening. (In the first years of the "jobless recovery" following the 2001 recession, the ratio continued to rise, but it remained below three to one.) Clearly, these numbers favor the alternative explanation. Unfortunately, Kaufman doesn't even consider it.

That's too bad. Recognizing that a lack of demand for goods and services is to blame for the severe crisis of unemployment puts the focus squarely back on the federal government and on the Fed, which could help to remedy the problem —*if* they had the political will to do so. Millions of unemployed workers, organized and armed with an accurate diagnosis of the problem, could create that political will—unless they are distracted by a wrong-headed diagnosis that tries to blame them for the problem. ❑

Sources: Bureau of Labor Statistics Table A-14, Unemployed persons by industry and class of workers, not seasonally adjusted, historical data (bls.gov); Lawrence Mishel, Heidi Shierholz, and Kathryn Anne Edwards, "Reasons for Skepticism About Structural Unemployment," Economic Policy Institute, Briefing Paper #279, September 22, 2010 (epi.org); Arjun Jayadev and Mike Konczal, "The Stagnating Labor Market," The Roosevelt Institute, September 19, 2010 (rooseveltinstitute.org); Bureau of Labor Statistics, Job Openings and Labor Turnover (JOLTS) Highlights, September 2010 (bls.gov); Michael Reich, "High Unemployment after the Great Recession: Why? What Can We Do?," Policy Brief from the Center on Wage and Employment Dynamics, Institute for Research on Labor and Employment, University of California, Berkeley, June 2010 (irle.berkeley.edu/cwed); Narayana Kocherlakota, President Federal Reserve Bank of Minneapolis, "Inside the FOMC," Marquette, Michigan, August 17, 2010 (minneapolisfed.org); Lawrence Mishel and Katherine Anne Edwards, "Bill Clinton Gets It Wrong," Economic Policy Institute, Economic Snapshot, September 27, 2010 (epi.org); "Remarks of President Barack Obama—Address to Joint Session of Congress," February 24, 2009 (whitehouse.gov); "The Skills Gap: Holding Back the Labor Market," Morning Edition, National Public Radio, November 15, 2010 (npr.org).

Article 1.3

WHY THE UNITED STATES IS NOT GREECE

BY JOHN MILLER AND KATHERINE SCIACCHITANO
January/February 2012

For almost two years, we've been hearing a new battle cry in the war against government spending: unless the United States slashes deficits we will become Greece, Europe's poster child for fiscal insolvency and economic crisis. The debt crisis in the eurozone, the 17 European countries that share the euro as their common currency, is held up as proof positive of the perils that await the United States if it continues its supposedly fiscally irresponsible ways.

Take the Heritage Foundation, the Washington-based think tank that specializes in providing red meat for anti-government pro-market arguments. Heritage introduces its 2011 chart on the rising level of government debt (to GDP) with this dire warning: "Countries like Greece and Portugal have suffered or are anticipating financial crises as a result of mounting debt. If the U.S. continues federal deficit spending on its current trajectory, it will face similar economic woes."

Even for those who understand that cutting deficits right now will only weaken a still-fragile recovery, and that weakening the recovery will only increase deficits, getting past the argument that "a eurozone crisis is on its way" is no easy task.

What follows is a self-defense lesson on why the United States is not Greece—or Europe. The U.S. economy is far larger and more productive than Greece. The United States has many more tools in its macro-economic policy box than countries in the eurozone. And while calls for austerity have kept the United States from undertaking government spending and investment large enough to support a robust economic recovery, at least thus far, the United States hasn't undertaken the same self-defeating austerity measures Europe has. If we learn the right lessons from what is happening in the eurozone now, we never will.

Central Banks and Deficit Spending

When economic activity plummeted during 2008 and 2009 in the United States, Europe, and throughout the world, coordinated stimulus spending of nations across the globe prevented the collapse of world output from becoming another Great Depression. Today, deficit spending remains critical as working people continue to struggle through an economic recovery that has done little to create jobs or to lift wages, but much to restore profits.

Governments finance deficit spending by borrowing. Governments sell bonds—promissory notes—to domestic and foreign investors as well as other government agencies, and then use the proceeds to pay for spending in excess of their tax revenues. In the United States, domestic investors, foreign investors, and government agencies hold near equal shares of government bonds issued by the Treasury and receive the interest paid on those bonds.

The Federal Reserve ("the Fed"), the U.S. central bank, can buy U.S. government bonds as well. The Fed can also create money (sometimes metaphorically called "printing money") simply by entering an appropriate credit on its balance sheet and spending it. When the Fed uses this newly created money to purchase bonds directly from the government, it is financing the government deficit. Economists call the Fed's direct purchase of government bonds "monetizing the deficit." By such direct purchases of bonds that finance the deficit, the Fed can fund government spending in an emergency, should it choose to do so. Monetizing the deficit also significantly expands the money supply, which pushes down interest rates, which can also help stimulate the economy.

In the current crisis, the Fed did precisely that. By purchasing government bonds, the Fed financed public-sector spending, and by pushing down interest rates, it encouraged private-sector borrowing. In doing so, the Fed supported a market recovery, but also helped to keep unemployment from rising even higher than it did.

In seeking to lower unemployment, the Fed was exercising what is known as its "dual mandate" under the law to promote both low inflation and low unemployment.

Nevertheless, the Fed's decision to inject more money into the economy has come under heavy fire from those who worry more about inflation than unemployment, and who think that "printing money" is always inflationary. Neither continued low inflation rates nor persistently high unemployment were enough to change the thinking of these inflation-phobes. Back in August, Rick Perry, the Texas governor and candidate for president in the Republican primary, went so far as to insist that if the Fed "prints more money between now and the election" (in November 2012) it would be "almost treasonous."

The central banks of most other countries have much the same abilities as the Fed has to inject money into their economies and to buy government debt. As with the Fed, they may or may not choose to use this power. But the power is unquestionably there.

Europe's Central Bank Is Different

The 17 countries in the eurozone, however, relinquished their ability to print money, expand their money supplies, and lower interest rates when they adopted the euro as their common currency. Only the European Central Bank—known as the ECB—can authorize the "printing of euros," and the ECB maintains control over the money supply of the eurozone.

Unlike the Fed, the ECB does not have a dual mandate to pursue low employment as well as low inflation. The ECB's authority is limited to maintaining low inflation, known as "price stability," which the ECB defines as an inflation rate below 2%.

And the ECB is prohibited from directly buying government bonds. The ECB is authorized to buy government bonds only on the "secondary" bond market, when original purchasers resell them.

The result of these policies is that eurozone countries must sell their bonds on the open market. That leaves them entirely dependent on private bond buyers (i.e., lenders), whether from their own country or other countries, to finance their government deficits. Governments must offer their bonds for sale with rates of returns (or interest rates) that will attract those bonds buyers. Each uptick in the interest rate adds to the debt burden of these countries, and makes deficit spending to stimulate the economy that much more expensive.

Another way a country can stimulate its economy is by increasing exports. Typically, individual countries' currencies (when not fixed to the value of a dominant currency such as the U.S. dollar) lose value, or "depreciate," when an economy falls into a crisis, such as the crisis Greece is in now. As the value of its currency depreciates, a country's exports become cheaper, and that boosts export sales and domestic production and aids recovery. While currency fluctuations can open the door to speculative excesses, the falling value of a country's currency is yet another way to help turn around a flagging economy not available to the eurozone economies. The problem is that all countries in the eurozone have the same currency. So individual countries can't let their currencies depreciate. Nor can they take steps countries outside the eurozone can take to intentionally lower their exchange rates to become more competitive, known as devaluing.

Similarly, central banks outside the eurozone routinely stimulate economies by pushing down key interest rates at which banks lend to each other. This helps lower other interest rates in the economy, such as rates for business and consumer loans, and can lead to the expansion of borrowing and spending. But the ECB targets one interest rate for lending between banks for the whole eurozone. It is not possible to set one interest rate for Germany to fight inflation, and a second, lower, rate in Greece or Italy to stimulate growth.

Without the ability to use separate exchange rates or interest rates to stimulate lagging economies, the crisis-ridden eurozone had but one public policy left to get their economies going again: expansionary fiscal policy. But even that remaining policy option was constrained. The ECB was not about to ease the burden of increased government spending (or the cost of tax cuts) by directly buying government bonds. Eurozone guidelines prohibit budget deficits that exceed 3% of GDP, or national debt in excess of 60% of their GDP. And there is no central fiscal authority with deep pockets to turn to. Contrast this with the United States, where states also share the same currency and the Fed targets one interest rate, but where states can turn to the federal government for assistance in times of economic stress.

In effect, the eurozone countries were left to confront the global downturn and the sovereign debt crisis with one policy hand tied behind their back, and a couple of digits lopped off the other. Market pressure on interest rates made it yet more difficult for eurozone countries to get out of trouble by undertaking countercyclical, or stimulus, spending when economies slowed.

In the few cases where eurozone authorities have provided loans to indebted countries, they have insisted on austerity measures ranging from slashing government spending to public- and private-sector wage cuts as the pre-condition for providing relief. But since cutting government spending in a downturn leads to both a fall in demand and rise in unemployment, this emergency lending is making it even harder for eurozone countries to recover.

No wonder the global downturn hit the most vulnerable eurozone countries so hard, turning their sovereign (or government) debt as toxic as the mortgage-based securities that sparked the initial global downturn. This is what we're seeing played out with the Greek debt crisis.

Greek Austerity

When the 2008-2009 global collapse pushed down GDP and trade, and pushed up budget deficits around the world, Greece already had a large trade deficit and high government debt. Greece had consistently run government deficits greater than 5% of its GDP, and had carried government debt that just about matched its GDP for nearly a decade, both clear violations of eurozone guidelines. Nonetheless, Greek banks, and then banks elsewhere in Europe (including Germany and France), readily lent money to the Greek government, buying their bonds, which regularly yielded a handsome 5% rate of return (the rate of interest on a ten-year government note), and which presumably carried limited risk as the sovereign debt of a developed country unlikely to default.

But as the Greek economy tumbled downward, Greece had to raise its interest rates to above 12% to sell the additional debt it needed to stay afloat. By the summer of 2010, Greece was pushed to the point of default—not being able to pay its lenders.

The European Union and the IMF gave Greece a $140 billion loan so debt payments to the banks could continue. But both the IMF and the European Union insisted on austerity to reduce deficits and ensure repayment. Greece was forced to agree to sharp cuts in government spending, public employment, and wages and benefits of public employees; to tax increases; and to privatization of government assets. The banks that had happily lent Greece money well beyond the allowable eurozone limits escaped without having to write down the value of their loans to the Greek government.

The Greek economy, on the other hand, dropped like a stone. In the year that followed, Greece lost more output than the United States had during the Great Recession. Unemployment rates reached 18.4%, over one-third of young people were unemployed, and more than one-fifth of the population was poverty stricken. The austerity measures did trim the Greek budget deficit. Nonetheless the ratio of public debt to GDP continued to rise as Greek output plummeted.

One year later, Greece was on the brink of default again. The interest rate on Greek government bonds had skyrocketed to above 20% on ten-year government bonds, only adding to Greece's already unsustainable debt burden.

In October 2011 the IMF and the European Union granted an additional $173 billion loan to Greece in return for a new round of austerity measures. More public-sector workers lost their jobs, public pensions were cut further, and the privatization program expanded. The austerity measures were "equivalent to about 14 percent of average Greek take-home income," according to the *Financial Times*, the authoritative British newspaper, or an impact about "double that brought about by austerity measures in the other two eurozone countries subject to international bail-out programmes, Portugal and Ireland."

Also as part of the price for its debt reduction, Greece would have to accept monitoring of its fiscal affairs by the European Union. Greek Prime Minister George Papandreou, forced to cancel a referendum on the second round of austerity cuts, resigned in favor of a "government of national unity" headed by Lucas Papademos, a former banker sure to listen to the markets.

This time, banks and other holders of Greek government bonds seemed not to have escaped unharmed. The value of their bonds were to be written down to 50% of their face value, meaning they could still insist on repayment of half the amount lent, although the market value of those bonds was surely far less than that. In addition, the agreement was "voluntary," and it is yet to be seen if the agreement will be enforced.

As 2011 came to a close with this second round of austerity measures and the near collapse of the Greek economy, the Greek government was paying out a crippling 35% interest rate to attract buyers for their ten-year bonds.

Vortex Europe

European banks are the main buyers of European debt. French and German banks hold large quantities of Greek bonds.

So does the ECB, which began buying Greek bonds and other sovereign debt on the secondary (or resale) market in 2010. It resumed the practice in late 2011 to ease pressures on interest rates. Ordinarily, this bond-buying would also stimulate the economy by increasing the money supply, since the ECB creates the money it uses to buy the bonds. But the ECB also "sterilizes" its bond buying by contracting the money supply in the same amount as its purchases. This eliminates any possibility of inflation, but also negates the stimulus effect.

The bottom line is that because of the extensive holdings of Greek and other government debt within the European banking system, a Greek default would cause substantial losses in the European banking system and destabilize it.

In the last weeks of 2011, the ECB did extend a financial lifeline to banks – exactly what it had refused to give to the Greek government. To help buffer them against sudden losses, the ECB offered the banks $638 billion in three-year loans with the bargain basement interest rate of 1%. The majority of eurozone banks, some 523 of them, took out loans. The ECB's backdoor bailout, as a Wall Street Journal editorial called it, was twice the combined size of the two rescue packages for Greece. The banks, unlike governments, would not have to turn to the bond markets for funding if a Greek default occurred. And like banks bailed out in the United States, no requirements were placed on them to continue lending—in Europe's case, to continue lending to governments.

While the ECB move shored up the banks for now, it won't protect them from the large losses that will come with an outright default by Greece or another of the crisis-ridden southern eurozone countries. Such large losses would in turn force countries to bail out banks again, as they did in 2008, to avoid the prospect of cascading banking failures. Because the ECB is prohibited from directly buying European government debt, a new round of bailouts would raise the specter of increasing government deficits, of rising interest rates, and of additional countries defaulting, a sequence that could induce a depression-like downturn.

As a result, private lenders are now insisting on higher interest rates on government bonds not just in Greece, but throughout much of Europe. These interest rate rises began in weaker economies with higher debt levels, including the Italian and Spanish economies, both of which are far larger than the Greek economy. Interest-rate hikes have even spread to France and (very briefly) to Germany, the eurozone's two largest economies. The spikes in rates not only increase the likelihood of default, they put real roadblocks in the way of the spending and investment needed for recovery and long-term growth.

The danger is not only to Europe. The European Union is the largest economy in the world, accounting for nearly 20% of global economic activity. Every region of the world that trades with Europe will be affected by a slowdown there. The eurozone is the largest export market for both the United States and China. The default of any European country would cause losses and instability throughout the global economy. The U.S. financial system would also be sharply affected, for European global banks provide much of the credit for the U.S. economy.

To stem the bleeding, many in Europe and beyond have urged and continue to urge the ECB to step up and find a way to act as most normal central banks would in the situation: inject money into these economies by buying government debt in unlimited quantities. That in turn would lower interest rates, and give countries time to rebuild and restart growth. Germany, the largest and the dominant economy in Europe, continues to block this option on the grounds that printing money is not only inflationary but a "moral hazard" and makes borrowing too easy. At the last European summit, Germany successfully insisted instead on a "fiscal stability union" that will require balanced budgets (before taking interest payments into account). In other words, austerity for workers.

Rejecting Austerity

Austerity won't work for Europe: Europe needs growth, and austerity can't produce growth. Austerity also can't work because the proposed cure—budget cuts—assumes the disease is government spending. But excessive social spending by its government did not cause Greece's debt problems. In 2007, the year before the crisis hit, Greece's social expenditures relative to the size of its economy stood at 21.3% of GDP, lower than the social expenditures in France (28.3% of GDP) and Germany (25.2% of GDP), the two countries most responsible for orchestrating the austerity measures that have slashed social spending in Greece.

Europe didn't have a government debt crisis before the subprime collapse of 2008. It had countries like Germany in the north with large permanent trade surpluses, and countries in the south like Greece with large permanent trade deficits. Fixing these trade deficits and imbalances can't be done by pushing down wages. In fact, repressive wage and labor policies, especially as practiced in Germany, are what lie at the heart of those imbalances that made the weaker southern eurozone countries so vulnerable to the crisis that followed.

Rather, what's needed is government investment and coordination throughout Europe. A public investment program could modernize the infrastructure of the southern eurozone economies and boost the productivity of their workforce by improving workers' health and education.

A recession—or worse—in Europe will slow down growth and raise budget deficits in the United States as well. It will create political pressure for austerity exactly when we need more investment and more stimulus spending.

If this happens, it will be more important than ever to remember that Europe is in the position it is in, first, because it insisted on austerity for Greece and, second, because Europe has a central bank that is prohibited from financing government deficits and whose sole policy mandate is to limit inflation. Without the insistence on austerity, and without having relinquished these basic tools of economic policy—both of which the United States retains—the mess in Europe could never have happened. The United States is not and will never be Greece.

Yet like the crisis in Europe, the crisis in the United States isn't temporary or fleeting. The outcome will determine what kind of jobs and economic security people will have for a long time to come. It will have a huge effect on public-sector unions. And it will affect democracy itself, especially if we stay silent. Austerity in Europe is being imposed from above. There's no reason to let it be imposed here. ❑

Sources: C. Lapavitsas, et al., "Breaking Up? A Route Out of the Eurozone Crisis," Research on Money and Finance, RMF Occasional Report, November 2011; Heiner Flassbeck and Friederike Spiecker, "The Euro—A Story of Misunderstanding," Intereconomics, 2011; "The ECB's Backdoor Bailout," *Wall Street Journal*, December 24, 2011; George Irvin and Alex Izurieta, "Fundamental Flaws in the European Project," Economic & Political Weekly, August 6, 2011; C.P. Chandrasekhar, "The Crisis in Europe," *The Frontline*, Jul. 30-Aug. 12, 2011; Robert Skidelsky, "The Euro in a Shrinking Zone," Project Syndicate, December 12, 2011; David Enrich, "European Banks Rush to Grasp Lifeline," *Wall Street Journal*, December 22, 2011; Paul Krugman, "Bernanke's Perry Problem," *New York Times*, August 25, 2011; Paul Krugman, "Currency Warnings that Europe Ignored," Krugman & Co., November 22, 2011; Andre Leonard, "The Republican plot to turn the U.S. into Greece," Salon.com, July 18, 2011; Sally Giansbury et al.," Greek austerity plans threaten growth," *Financial Times*, October 17, 2011; James Bullard, "The Fed's Dual Mandate: Lessons of the 1970s," The 2010 Annual Report of the Federal Reserve Bank of St. Louis, April 2011.

Article 1.4

GREECE AND THE EUROZONE CRISIS BY THE NUMBERS
BY GERALD FRIEDMAN
July/August 2012

With its surging debt and sinking economy, Greece has been held up as the poster-child for the need for fiscal discipline and austerity. Instead, it should be seen as a case study in the danger of neoliberal financial integration. Greece's economic problems stem from its joining the eurozone, a single-currency region where monetary policy is managed by a largely independent European Central Bank (ECB). The ECB is based in Frankfurt, Germany, and is committed to maintaining stable prices without regard for levels of unemployment or economic growth. Within the eurozone, Greek industry has been unable to compete with its German competitors. If Greece had retained an independent currency, it could have maintained balanced trade and supported domestic industries and employment by devaluing its currency. Membership in the European Union and the eurozone, though, prevents Greece from adjusting its currency value or otherwise imposing trade restraints, even in the face of a rising tide of German imports which have devastated much of Greek industry.

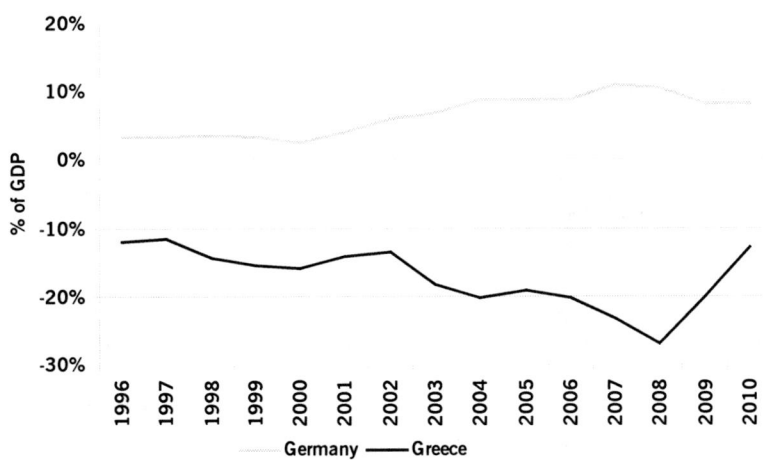

ANNUAL TRADE BALANCE, PERCENTAGE OF GDP, GERMANY AND GREECE, 1996-2010

Greece's trade deficits were financed by borrowing, including deposits in Greek banks from Germany and other northern European countries. When the financial crisis began in 2008, however, these countries sought to pull their deposits out of Greek banks and reduce their lending. If Greece had an independent central bank, as it did before joining the euro, that bank would provide liquidity to replace these financial flows and thus guarantee the stability of the Greek banking system. But Greece gave up its own independent monetary authority when it joined the eurozone. Instead, the ECB has used the Greek financial crisis as a tool to drive down Greek wages and living standards.

Binding southern Europe with Germany has allowed Germany to run extraordinary trade surpluses with these other countries. For seven years after 2001, capital flows from Germany balanced German trade surpluses. However, Germany's trade surplus soared with the establishment of the euro in 2002. Most of this surplus was with its eurozone partners, who, without independent currencies, could not adjust to balance their trade.

Greece had a trade deficit even before joining the eurozone, but its deficit soared after it adopted the euro. Germany's surplus and Greece's deficits were balanced with borrowing when Greek banks accepted large deposits from Germans and others.

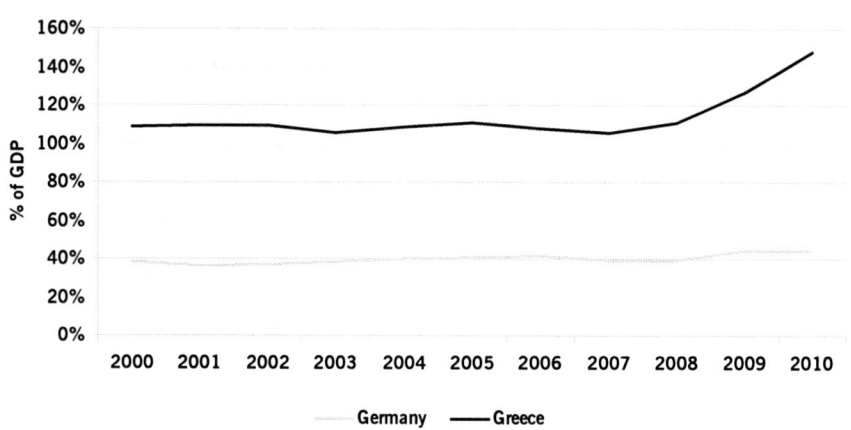

CENTRAL GOVERNMENT DEBT, PERCENTAGE OF GDP, GERMANY AND GREECE, 2000-10

Throughout the 2000s, the Greek government had a relatively high debt burden but remained stable before the economic crisis. Due to falling tax revenues and increased need for government services during the crisis, Greece experienced a sharp rise in its government deficit. Forcing austerity on Greece to stabilize its financial system has led to soaring unemployment. This has led to falling tax revenues and rising expenditures for unemployment relief, which have actually increased the government deficit.

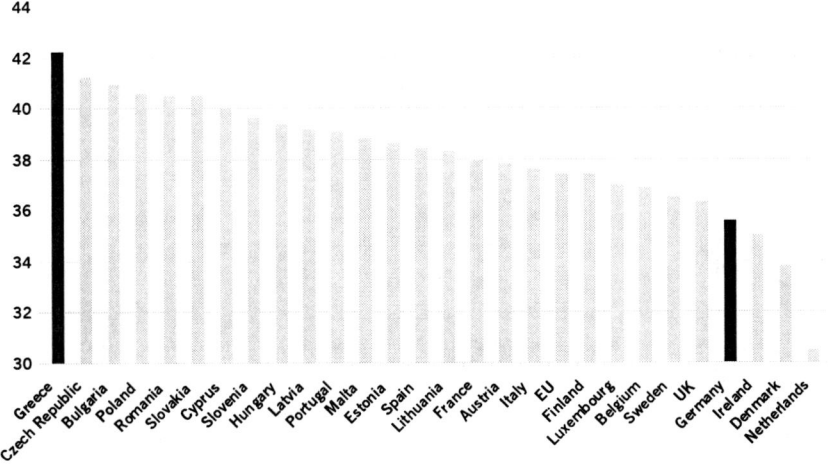

AVERAGE USUAL HOURS WORKED (WEEKLY), EU MEMBERS, 2011

Greece's recent economic troubles come despite the country's work ethic. Relatively poor compared with others in the European Union, Greeks work more hours per week than workers in any other EU member country. By contrast, the relatively affluent Germans work about six hours a week less than the Greeks, and have many more vacation days. ❑

Sources: OECD.stat data base for gross domestic product, government deficits, and unemployment. Eurostat data base for hours worked. International Monetary Fund for trade data.

Article 1.5

RESISTANCE TO AUSTERITY GROWS IN EUROPE
Popular sentiment shifts in Germany's ally-in-austerity, the Netherlands.

BY MARJOLEIN VAN DER VEEN
July/August 2012; updated November 2012

The Netherlands made world news when its government collapsed on April 21, 2012. The day before it was revealed that an additional 12 billion euro (nearly $15 billion) would be needed in 2013 to meet the rules of the Maastricht Treaty, the treaty that led to the creation of the euro. This was on top of 18 billion euro in cuts (nearly $22.5 billion) over four years that the government had already started implementing. The governing right-wing coalition then collapsed when the right-wing populist PVV party of Geert Wilders refused to support additional austerity.

Resistance to austerity shocked those who saw the Netherlands as Germany's chief ally in pushing European countries to adopt austerity programs. Under the Maastricht Treaty, each country's deficits can be no higher than 3% of GDP, and debt no higher than 60% of GDP. Because the Netherlands' budget deficit was 4.6% of GDP and its debt was 70.2% of GDP, it had to submit a budget to Brussels by April 30 to meet the Maastricht thresholds. Failure to do so would entail a penalty of 1.2 billion euro (nearly $1.5 billion), the possible downgrading of its bonds, and a potential rise in interest rates at which it could borrow.

The collapse of the Dutch government briefly took the spotlight away from Greece and Spain, where the crisis has hit the hardest. By the spring of 2012, the unemployment rate had reached depression levels of 24.4% in Spain and 18.8% in Greece, compared to 5.5% in the Netherlands and 10.8% for the EU as a whole. While Dutch unemployment is not as bad as elsewhere, the economy remains precarious and slipped back into recession during the last half of 2011, mainly because falling housing prices from a bursting housing bubble continue to dampen consumer spending. The Netherlands had one of the largest housing bubbles (depending on which measurement is used) and the highest level of mortgage debt in Europe. The additional proposed cuts were projected to harm the economy further, with real GDP declining by 0.75% in 2012, possibly putting the economy into a "triple-dip" recession. Also of concern is the on-going euro crisis, uncertainties regarding pensions (some of which are tied up in Spanish banks), and the likely damage to exports with a slowing global economy.

Growing frustration with austerity has fueled support for anti-austerity political parties. As in France and Greece, anti-austerity support in the Netherlands is split between the left (the Dutch labor party and Socialist party) and the far-right (the populist party of Geert Wilders). The Socialist Party made remarkable gains in the polls during the summer months, doubling its support since the last election, and was even leading the governing pro-business VVD party in the polls at one point. Following the victory of the Socialists in France, some hoped a victory for the Socialist Party could help chart a new course for Europe and challenge the austerity policies forced upon Greece and other European countries in crisis.

The Menu of Cuts

The initial cuts of 18 billion euro (about $22.5 billion, about 3% of GDP) over four years were deep and wide-ranging. Public transportation would have been cut by 40%. Cuts to programs that employ disabled workers would have scrapped 70,000 out of 100,000 jobs. In education, 300 million euro (about $370 million) would have been cut from programs for special-needs kids, resulting in 5,000 teachers and coaches losing their jobs. University students would be penalized with fines of 3,000 euro (about $3,700) per year for taking longer to finish their studies. In the health sector, the budget for professional interpreters would have been cut, and co-payments would have been introduced. Arts programs faced a 25% cut, and taxes on tickets to many cultural events would have risen from 6% to 19%. Foreign development assistance would have been cut almost 25%. In addition, the pension age would have been raised to 66 in 2019, and a value-added tax (VAT—a type of sales tax) raised from 6% to 7% (and from 19% to 21% for luxury goods).

Dutch workers actively resisted with strikes and public protests. On March 7, teachers held the largest one-day strike since 1982, with 50,000 teachers filling a stadium in Amsterdam. A one-day strike of workers with disabilities brought 15,000 people to The Hague on March 22. On April 25, about 600 health care workers protested wage cuts, the deterioration of quality in health care, and the "flexibilization" of labor contracts (making it easier to hire and fire workers). Transportation workers and students also had days of protests. While there was no general strike, as in Spain or Greece, protests nonetheless succeeded in slowing down the cuts. The new budget accord brokered after the government collapse pared back and even eliminated some cuts (e.g. for special needs education, development assistance, and public transportation).

After the government collapse on April 21, VVD leaders scrambled to broker an agreement with the opposition, such as the Green-Left party, in order to close the additional budget hole. On April 26, a new budget accord was produced that relied on a two-year freeze on public sector wages, and an increase in the VAT by 2%. Also, the increase in the retirement age would be phased in as early as 2013. The package contained

---

Three Ways to Reduce the Deficit/GDP Ratio

There are three ways a government can reduce its deficit/GDP (or debt/GDP) ratio:

(1) Cutting government spending
(2) Raising taxes
(3) Boosting GDP

GDP may be boosted through government spending, in such a way that GDP grows more than the deficit and brings the deficit/GDP ratio down.
    Austerity policies usually focus only on the first way—cutting government spending. Typically, these spending cuts end up hurting poor and working classes most. Elites tend to studiously ignore other ways of reducing the deficit/GDP ratio (such as raising taxes on the wealthy and corporations). Even though the causes of the crisis lay mostly with the banks, the burden of the crisis is shifted onto the shoulders of working people.

other measures, such as scrapping a mortgage deduction for new homebuyers, elimination of rental subsidies, cuts in travel subsidies, some "sin" and luxury taxes, a doubling of the bank tax, a tax on high incomes, and a series of new environmental taxes and subsidies. While these spending cuts and tax increases were more progressive and bore a little more heavily on higher income households, they would still have a contractionary effect on the economy, and could drive the Dutch economy back into recession.

Why did Dutch government deficit exceed the Maastricht thresholds and lead to this belt tightening? First, the crisis of 2008-09 caused tax revenues to fall and government expenditures on unemployment insurance to rise. Then there was the bank bailout, to the tune of 30 billion euro (about $37 billion), with another 200 billion euro (around $250 billion) in loan guarantees. The government also implemented expansionary fiscal policies, all of which led to rising deficits.

In some cases deficits and debt may be problematic (especially the rising cost of borrowing, as in Greece, Spain, and Italy), but only after the recession is over and full employment is restored should governments turn to reducing deficits and debt.

"Expansionary Austerity"?

The standard view in economics is that trying to reduce a deficit during a recession leads to a slowdown of the economy, thereby worsening the recession. But in 2009, Harvard economists Alberto Alesina and Silvia Ardagna proposed that austerity could actually be expansionary by raising confidence and expectations of lower taxes, spurring private investment and encouraging consumers to spend. Examples were taken from obscure cases (e.g. Denmark in 1982-86) and then used to inform austerity programs in Europe and elsewhere.

Another reason for thinking austerity could be expansionary is that it would help boost net exports. The eurozone countries cannot devalue their currency to make exports competitive—unless they break from the euro, a prospect with costs attached. An alternative is "internal devaluation," which reduces wages and prices. Austerity would help achieve "internal devaluation," as cutbacks in government spending and resulting layoffs and wage freezes would contribute to driving down real wages overall. Lower labor costs then reduce the price of exports, enabling exports to become competitive and expand the economy.

There are several problems with these "expansionary austerity" theories. First, expectations of higher taxes have not significantly discouraged business investment;

The Role of the European Central Bank (ECB)

Running deficits to stimulate growth may bear the risk of raising interest rates. When European countries gave up their national monetary policy tools to join the eurozone, they gave up the ability for their central banks to accommodate expansionary fiscal policies with monetary policy. One solution lies with the European Central Bank (ECB), which could step in by buying government bonds (even if only in the secondary market). Last December, the ECB started injecting money into private banks to allow them to buy government bonds, though it has still resisted directly buying government bonds in a major way, insisting on using the ESM to solve the crisis. The ECB also should include lowering unemployment in its mandate, which is currently focused solely on keeping inflation low.

in many countries taxes have already been lowered over several decades of neoliberalism. More significant in discouraging business investment was insufficient aggregate demand due to the economic collapse. Falling household wealth and income have dampened consumer spending, and with so much excess capacity (empty factories, office buildings, and unused equipment), firms are reluctant to expand investment and build up even more productive capacity. The low interest rates provided by central banks were not enough of an incentive to invest. Nor were consumers likely driven to spend by expectations of lower taxes. Rather, the austerity cutbacks led to lower consumer confidence and spending, as households became worried about their jobs and incomes and about the value of their houses and pensions.

The policy of "internal devaluation" was also wrong-headed. If the crisis was contained to only one country, then promoting export competitiveness through devaluation might work. However, when the crisis is global, all countries can't simultaneously export themselves out of it. The squeeze on real wages and incomes only exacerbates problems of insufficient aggregate demand. Plus, it can initiate a competitive race to the bottom, as each country and trading partner tries to devalue to maintain its competitive position for its exports.

Austerity Was Contractionary

So how did the theory of "expansionary austerity" hold up? By 2011 and 2012, after two years of austerity in Europe, country after country experienced slowdowns or recessions and rising unemployment. Not only did GDP growth decline, the austerity policies did little to reduce debt as tax revenues fell with slumping economies. The failures of the austerity policies imposed on European countries were finally recognized by the S&P ratings agency in January 2012, when it downgraded the debt of nine European countries, including France, Spain, Italy and Portugal, although not the Netherlands. As Paul Krugman noted in a blog post, an S&P FAQ stated:

We also believe that the agreement [the latest euro rescue plan] is predicated on only a partial recognition of the source of the crisis: that the current financial turmoil stems primarily from fiscal profligacy at the periphery of the eurozone. In our view, however, the financial problems facing the eurozone are as much a consequence of rising external imbalances and divergences in competitiveness between the EMU's core and the so-called "periphery". As such, we believe that a reform

---

The European Stabilization Mechanism (ESM)

The ESM is a 500 billion euro permanent bailout fund established in March 2012. It places rules on borrowing countries' structural deficits (that part of the deficit that is not the result of cyclical downturns), imposing a maximum structural deficit of 0.5% of GDP (unless a country has a debt to GDP ratio of less than 60%, in which case it is allowed a maximum structural deficit of 1%). Failure to meet these thresholds results in fines or other penalties. At the June EU summit, European governments agreed to use the ESM to directly bail out banks in Spain and Italy, and exempted these countries from complying with the austerity requirements imposed on other countries such as Greece. In what amounts to a victory for the banks, the ESM funds for Spain's banks would not have seniority over private claims, meaning that shareholders would be paid back before taxpayers.

process based on a pillar of fiscal austerity alone risks becoming self-defeating, as domestic demand falls in line with consumers' rising concerns about job security and disposable incomes, eroding national tax revenues.

Not only did austerity policies decrease GDP and tax revenues, and thereby increase government deficits and debt, they also had a terrible effect on workers, who were thrown into unemployment and slipped into poverty. Even those fortunate to keep their jobs were often worked more intensely, as employers expected the same amount of work from smaller numbers of people, and as fear of layoffs compelled workers to comply. The public at large also faced negative consequences from austerity. Cutbacks in employment and services often meant an inferior quality of service provided (whether in public transportation, health care, education, etc.), which in some cases could even jeopardize the safety of consumers or the public (e.g. more train accidents, medical mishaps, faulty economic theories, etc.).

Other Agendas

If austerity policies have been shown to fail, why are they still being implemented by policymakers? Undoubtedly there are other agendas at stake. The economic crisis is being used to push through "structural reforms," at a time when workers and their political parties are thought to be weak. (Ironically, the greatest need for structural reforms remains in financial markets, not labor markets.) In Greece, the bailouts have included vast privatization of state assets. The cuts to public education, healthcare, and transport will merely open these sectors to private corporations producing on a for-profit basis. At a time when existing markets are becoming saturated and private investors find it more difficult to find new investment opportunities, investors are eyeing these public services as new profit opportunities.

In the Netherlands, business interests are eager to weaken unions and push through labor-market flexibility and an increase in the retirement age. With unions in a state of disarray, they are imposing wage freezes and reductions aimed at boosting profits. Business also seeks to institutionalize austerity measures with the new fiscal pact signed in March, the European Stabilization Mechanism (ESM).

Alternatives to Austerity

There are several alternatives to austerity. First, as long as unemployment remains high, the focus should be on reviving the economy. Growth could lower the debt/GDP ratio if growth in GDP is larger than additional debt. Growth promotion should ideally be done in a way that is environmentally sustainable and does not add to CO_2 emissions. A green "New Deal" program could create jobs through public investment in renewable energy, energy efficiency and conservation, public transportation, and other investments that are geared toward reducing poverty and future climate change emissions.

Second, deficits can be reduced through tax increases, rather than spending cuts. Since raising taxes will slow down the economy, attempts to balance budgets should wait until economies have fully recovered and full employment restored. Then, taxes should be levied on those institutions responsible for the crisis in the first place (i.e. the banks). Workers and ordinary people should not have to pay for the crisis they did not cause. Tellingly, the total package of Dutch austerity cuts now amounts to 30 billion euro (about $37 billion), which is precisely the amount of the Dutch bailout of the banks! Taxes could be raised on financial speculation, capital gains, dividends, profits of financial institutions, and executive compensation packages. Loopholes could be eliminated and taxes raised on foreign corporations with head offices in the Netherlands, which has become a tax haven for foreign corporations taking advantage of an effective tax rate of 5%.

Lessons and Implications for the Future

Deficit cutting is misguided during periods of high unemployment, and likely to worsen the economy while providing only a weak remedy to budget deficits. What has happened in Europe is an important lesson for the United States, which is engaging in austerity at the state level as states try to balance their budgets. The U.S. federal government should also heed the lessons from Europe, as it too is facing possible fiscal contraction when various tax cuts and spending programs expire on Dec. 31, 2012.

The Dutch case is important as an indicator of the changing mood in Europe. Overall the Dutch elections resulted in a shift leftwards. While the pro-business VVD party won the election with 41 seats, the Labor Party came in second with 38 seats. Two weeks before the election, the Socialist Party dramatically slid in the polls, as support switched over to the Labor party. While at one point the Socialist Party had reached 39 seats in the polls, on election day it garnered only 15 seats. The far-right PVV party lost 9 seats and ended up also with 15 seats. The remaining seats were distributed among a couple other parties. The international press welcomed the election results as a shift towards the center and towards stability.

A coalition government was formed between the VVD and the Labor Party, but the governing agreement they brokered continued with austerity, only in a slightly more softened form. Overall, the deficit will be cut by 16 billion euros (or about $20.3 billion). The tax deduction for mortgage interest will be gradually reduced, but to compensate wealthy households the top marginal income tax rate will be reduced from 52 to 49%. Health care premiums will be progressively tied to income, but some 5 billion euros (about $6.35 billion) will still be cut from the health sector. Students will lose scholarships, the development assistance budget will face severe cuts, and other measures will adversely impact immigrants. The retirement age will be raised to 66 in 2018 and 67 in 2021, and labor laws will make it easier for businesses to fire workers. No sooner had the ink dried on the agreement than support for both the VVD and Labor parties began to fall. How long this coalition government will be able to last remains to be seen. ❑

Sources: "Short-term Forecasts June 2012," June 14, 2012 (cpb.nl); "Details miljardenakkoord op een rij," April 26, 2012 (rtl.nl); Paul Krugman, "Bleeding Britain," *New York Times* blog, November 30, 2011; Paul Krugman, "Fiscal Fantasies," *New York Times* blog, June 18, 2010; Paul Krugman, "S&P on Europe," *New York Times* blog, January 14, 2012.

Chapter 2

DEFICITS AND FISCAL POLICY

Article 2.1

GOVERNMENT "LIVING WITHIN ITS MEANS"?
Claims about budget balancing are baloney.

BY JOHN MILLER
November/December 2011

> "Government has to start living within its means, just like families do. We have to cut the spending we can't afford so we can put the economy on sounder footing, and give our businesses the confidence they need to grow and create jobs."
> —President Barack Obama, weekly radio address, July 2, 2011

> "If the US was a business, it would be a failing business. That's the problem. You have to spend less than you make. Business 101."
> —Boston-area car dealer Ernie Boch, Jr., quoted in "From some of the richest, two cheers for higher taxes," *Boston Globe*, August 21, 2011

Turn on any of the television or radio gab shows and it won't be long before you hear someone proclaim that government must live within its means just as families do and businesses must.

Barack Obama gave this analogy the presidential seal of approval in a radio address in early July. In August, Ernie Boch, Jr., the Boston-based auto dealership magnate, added his two cents to Warren Buffett's call to hike taxes on the rich: he would pay more taxes only if the government balanced its budget just as his and every other business must do.

But the truth is neither families nor businesses balance their books in the sense of forgoing borrowing. And even if they did, to insist that government do the same would extinguish whatever remains of economic growth and job creation, not ignite them.

Family and Business Red Ink

Few families balance their budgets the way the guardians of financial rectitude are now demanding of government. Nearly all families spend more than they earn and borrow to do so. When a family takes out a car loan, a student loan, or a mortgage on a house, it's spending money it doesn't have.

Is borrowing the road to ruin? Not if the debt is affordable. That depends not just on the size of the debt relative to the income available to service that debt, but also on how the family spends the borrowed money. For instance, assuming the size of the debt is manageable, borrowing to pay for education is justified if the education improves the family's earning potential and so helps provide the income necessary to service the debt.

The same holds true of businesses. They borrow to invest and operate, especially in the United States where corporations finance the bulk of their investments by borrowing rather than by issuing stock. While exact numbers are not available about the privately held Boch auto dealerships, rest assured that Boch's company borrows to put the cars on his lot that he sells to the public or to build yet another dealership. That borrowing allows Boch's and other businesses to spend more than they are taking in—Business 101.

Families and businesses in the United States do quite a bit of borrowing and quite a bit more borrowing than they had in the past. Today families rely on credit to meet their needs—for everything from food to fuel, from education to entertainment, and especially housing. Total household debt stood at 92.5% of GDP in 2010, more than thirty percentage points higher than its level two decades earlier, 60.2% in 1990. And as their debt rose, families shelled out more and more of their income to make payments on that debt. In the first quarter of 2011, household payments on consumer and mortgage debt consumed 11.5% of disposable personal income.

Businesses, too, have increased their reliance on debt to finance their operations. Total debt of non-financial businesses was 53% as great as GDP in 1980, but reached 74.3% in 2010.

Those figures surely put the lie to the claim that families and businesses balance their budgets year in and out without relying on borrowing to spend beyond their income.

Government's Red Ink

Still it's true that federal government debt has increased steadily and rapidly over the last decade as the government has consistently run budget deficits. The ratio of the outstanding debt of the federal government to the country's GDP rose from 32.5% in 2001 to 62.1% in 2010.

However, payments on that rising debt are less of a burden on the federal government budget than debt payments are on family budgets. The U.S. government can perpetually refinance its debt in ways that are not open to the richest family or the largest business. Its debt burden, then, consists of the net interest payments on its debt, which will amount to 9.5% of federal revenues in 2011. That's two percentage points less than the proportion of their income that families devoted to making their debt payments—interest payments and payment on the principal—in the beginning of 2011.

Moreover, a good share of federal spending has gone to investments that are aimed at increasing its (and U.S. families') future income—similar to a household taking out an education loan or a business borrowing to expand its operation. A recent study conducted by the Brookings Institution, the Washington-based think tank, found that in 2008 the federal government spent $253.8 billion on non-defense investments in infrastructure, mostly transportation, research and development, and education and training, all expenditures that will boost the productivity of the economy and help to provide the tax revenue to service the debt. That investment spending equaled a little more than half of the $453.6 billion budget deficit in 2008.

Political Will

The aversion to the federal government deficits and borrowing fostered by pundits and politicians who pronounce that governments must balance their budgets like families and businesses do, even as the economy falters, is not only at odds with the facts. It has made us worse off by blocking government spending just when it is most needed. When family budgets are tight, and spending constrained with so many out of work and with the overhang of mortgage debt, it falls to government to provide the spending necessary to get the economy going. Government spending can put people to work and provide the income that will loosen tight family budgets, so they too can buy what businesses produce.

What's needed is to reverse the austerity budgets favored by conservative politicians in the United States and Europe today. More government spending and tax cuts targeted at working people, beyond what President Obama has proposed in his recent jobs bill, will surely make the budget deficit yet larger and drive up government debt. But that ratio of government debt to GDP, currently 62.1%, is still far below the 1946 record peak of 109% at the end of World War II, which was followed by the two of the strongest decades of economic growth in U.S. history.

It has happened before, and during even worse economic conditions than today's stagnation. In a Pittsburgh campaign speech in October 1932, some three years into the Great Depression, presidential candidate Franklin Delano Roosevelt promised that he would slash federal expenditures by 25% and balance the federal budget. But once in office, FDR reneged on his promise to balance the budget and initiated the New Deal. When he returned to Pittsburgh during his 1936 campaign for reelection, FDR declared, "to balance the budget in 1933, or 1934, or 1935 would be a crime against the American people."

Without massive government spending and without the political will to brand balancing the government budget as a "crime against the American people," today's crisis will likely drag on for a decade as economic hardship mounts for more and more of us. ❑

Sources: Barack Obama, Weekly Radio Address, July 2, 2011; Erin Ailworth, "From some of the richest, two cheers for higher taxes," *Boston Globe*, Aug. 21, 2011; Congressional Budget Office, *The Budget and Economic Outlook: Fiscal Years 2011 to 2021*, January 2011; Emilia Istrate and Robert Puentes, "Investing for Success," Metropolitan Policy Program at Brookings, Dec. 2009; Arthur MacEwan and John Miller, *Economic Collapse, Economic Change: Getting to the Roots of The Crisis*, M.E. Sharpe, 2011; Address of Gov. Franklin D. Roosevelt, Pittsburgh, Pa., Oct. 19, 1932; Franklin D. Roosevelt, "Address at Forbes Field, Pittsburgh, Pa.," Oct. 1, 1936, The American Presidency Project.

Article 2.2

THE IDEOLOGICAL ATTACK ON JOB CREATION
Responding to Anti-Government Arguments

BY MARTY WOLFSON

> "Government doesn't create jobs. It's the private sector that creates jobs."
> —presidential candidate Mitt Romney, speaking at Wofford College, Spartenburg, S.C., January 18, 2012

It is jarring to hear pundits say that the government can't create jobs. It is even more jarring to hear the same refrain from someone whose job was created by the government! Perhaps Mr. Romney has forgotten, or would like to forget, that he used to have a government job as governor of Massachusetts.

But surely those currently on the government payroll have not forgotten, like the chairman of the House Republican Policy Committee, Rep. Tom Price (R-Ga.). He used the same talking points, "The government doesn't create jobs. It's the private sector that creates jobs," speaking on MSNBC's "Andrea Mitchell Reports" last June.

Rep. Price apparently thinks he doesn't have a real job, but what about teachers, firefighters, police officers, and school cafeteria workers? And what about the 2 to 4.8 million jobs—in both the public and private sectors—the U.S. Congressional Budget Office estimated were created by the 2009 U.S. economic stimulus package?

The "government doesn't create jobs" mantra is part of a coordinated right-wing campaign to *prevent* the government from creating jobs and promoting the interests of working families, and to instead encourage a shift in the distribution of income towards the wealthy. It is supported by ideologically motivated arguments and theories from conservative economists and anti-government think tanks. In what follows, these arguments are addressed and criticized, in the hopes of clearing away some of the confusion undermining a vigorous government program to put people back to work.

The Argument That Government Spending Can't Increase Jobs

A Senior Fellow at the Cato Institute says the idea that government spending can create jobs "has a rather glaring logical fallacy. It overlooks the fact that, in the real world, government can't inject money into the economy without first taking money out of the economy." This argument is wrong for several reasons.

First, the government *can* inject money into the economy. It does so whenever it finances its spending by selling bonds to the Federal Reserve. In this case, money is created by the Federal Reserve when it buys the bonds. It creates a reserve account on its books; money is thus created without any reduction in money elsewhere in the economy.

Alternatively, the government can finance its spending by taxes or by selling bonds to the public. This is the case envisioned by the Cato analysis. The argument is that the money spent by the government is exactly balanced by a reduction in money in the pockets of taxpayers of bond buyers. However, if the taxpayers' or the bond buyers' money would otherwise have been saved and not spent, then there is a net injection into the economy of funds that can put people to work.

The argument made by the Cato Institute is actually a variation of another theory, known as "crowding out." In this theory, government spending creates competition for real resources that "crowds out," or displaces, private investment; private companies are unable to obtain the workers and capital they need for investment, so that any jobs due to government spending are offset by a decrease of jobs in the private sector.

This theory is valid only when there is full employment because there would be no idle resources, labor or capital, to put to use. In that case, though, neither the government nor the private sector would be able to create net new jobs. In contrast, in a situation of unemployment, it is precisely because the government can access otherwise idle resources that it can create jobs.

And, of course, that is exactly the situation we are in. As of March, the official unemployment rate stood at 8.2 %. Adjusted for underemployment, e.g., by counting those discouraged workers who have dropped out of the labor force and those workers who are working part-time but would like to work full-time, the more accurate unemployment rate was 14.5%.

The Argument That Cutting Government Spending Creates Jobs

Consistent with anti-government ideology, conservative economics asserts not only that government spending can't create jobs, but also that cutting government spending creates jobs. Here's how the argument goes: less government spending will reduce the government deficit; smaller deficits will increase the confidence of businesses that will invest more and in that way create more jobs. According to John B. Taylor, an economist affiliated with Stanford's conservative Hoover Institution, "Basic economic models in which incentives and expectations of future policy matter show that a credible plan to reduce gradually the deficit will increase economic growth and reduce unemployment by removing uncertainty and lowering the chances of large tax increases in the future." (Interestingly, an analysis by economist Robert Pollin of the Political Economy Research Institute at the University of Massachusetts-Amherst finds that Taylor's empirical model concludes that the stimulus bill was ineffective—but only because it included too much in tax cuts as opposed to direct government spending.)

This assertion is based more on wishful thinking than empirical validity, and has been criticized by Paul Krugman as depending on belief in a "confidence fairy." But it is not just liberal economists like Krugman who are critical of this theory. A confidential report prepared for clients by the investment bank Goldman Sachs concluded that a $61 billion cut in government spending from a bill passed by the House of Representatives in February 2011 (but not enacted into law) would lead to a decline in economic growth of 2%. And economist Mark Zandi, formerly an advisor to Republican presidential candidate John McCain, concluded that this $61 billion reduction in government spending could result in the loss of 700,000 jobs by 2012.

Ben Bernanke, chairman of the Board of Governors of the Federal Reserve System, stated that "the cost to the recovery [of steep reductions in government outlays now] would outweigh the benefits in terms of fiscal discipline." Even the International Monetary Fund, in its semiannual report on the world economic outlook, concluded that "the idea that fiscal austerity triggers faster growth in the short term finds little support in the data."

Also, in a review of studies and historical experience about the relationship between budget-cutting and economic growth, economists Arjun Jayadev and Mike Konczal concluded that countries historically did not cut government spending and deficits in a slump and that there is no basis to conclude that doing so now, "under the conditions the United States currently faces, would improve the country's prospects."

The Argument That Private Spending Is Always Better than Public Spending

Another way that right-wing economics tries to discredit the idea that the government can create jobs is to assert that private spending is always to be preferred to public spending. There are several rationalizations for this view.

One is that private spending is more efficient than public spending. This ideological refrain has been repeated consistently, and gained a following, over the past thirty years. But repetition does not make it correct. Of course, the proponents of this argument can point to examples of government mismanagement, such as that following Hurricane Katrina. However, government bungling and inefficiency by an administration that did not believe in government does not prove the point. A much more grievous example of inefficiency and misallocation of resources is the housing speculation and financial manipulation—and eventual collapse that brought us to the current recession—due to a deregulated private financial system. Yet for free-market ideologues, this somehow does not discredit the private sector.

Some people think that economists have "proven" that "free" markets are efficient. The only thing that has been proven, however, is that you can arrive at any conclusion if your assumptions are extreme enough. And the assumptions that form the basis for the free-market theory are indeed extreme, if not totally unrealistic and impossible. For example: orthodox free-market economics assumes perfectly competitive markets; perfect information; no situations, like pollution, in which private decision-makers do not take account of the societal effects of their actions; even full employment. But none of these assumptions hold true in the real world. Also, the distribution of income is irrelevant to the conclusions of this theory. The distribution of income is simply taken as given, so that the results of the theory are consistent with a relatively equal distribution of income as well as a very unequal distribution. As economist Joseph Stiglitz has said, "Today, there is no respectable intellectual support for the proposition that markets, by themselves, lead to efficient, let alone equitable outcomes."

A second reason for supposing that private spending is to be preferred to public spending is the notion that public spending is less worthwhile than private spending. This means, for many people, reducing government spending as much as possible. For example, Grover Norquist, founder and president of Americans for Tax Reform and author of the anti-tax pledge signed by many members of Congress, said that he wanted to "shrink [the government] down to the size where we can drown it in the bathtub." The anti-tax, anti-spending crusade has in many cases been successful in reducing government budgets, on the national as well as the local level. This has resulted in a significant decrease in government services. Although some people are attracted to the view that government spending should always be reduced, they probably at the same time don't want to drive on roads and bridges that aren't repaired and they probably want fire trucks to arrive if their house is on fire. Perhaps, too, they wouldn't automatically prefer twelve kinds of toothpaste to schools, parks, and libraries.

The Argument That Government Spending Is Wasteful

Another argument contends that public spending is wasteful. Discussions of government accounts generally do not take account of public investment, so all public spending is essentially treated as consumption. As such, it is considered unproductive and wasteful by those who wish to disparage government spending. In other words, the government budget does not make a distinction between long-term investments and other spending as corporate budgets do.

One implication of treating all government spending as consumption is the notion that the federal government should maintain a balanced budget. To put this in accounting terms, on this view government accounts are considered to only have an income statement (which shows current revenues and current expenditures), not a balance sheet (which shows assets and liabilities).

Corporations, in contrast, maintain balance sheets. They don't balance their budgets in the way that the budget hawks want the government to do. Private investment in plant and equipment, for example, is accounted for on the asset side of the balance sheet; borrowing to finance this investment is accounted for on the liability side. Interest on the debt is accounted for on the income statement, and it is only the interest, not the outstanding debt balance, that has to be covered by current revenues. The assumption behind this accounting is that borrowing to finance

---

The Ryan Budget: A Path to Prosperity?

On March 29, the House of Representatives passed Rep. Paul Ryan's budget proposal, called the "FY2013 Path to Prosperity Budget." It would be a disaster for working Americans. It shreds the safety net; according to the Center for Budget and Policy Priorities, 62% of Ryan's trillions in spending cuts come from programs affecting low-income Americans. The vast majority of tax cuts would go to corporations and upper-income Americans. Yet Ryan claims that his budget brings the "size of government to 20 percent of [the] economy by 2015, allowing the private sector to grow and create jobs." But an independent analysis by Ethan Pollack, a researcher at the Economic Policy Institute, concludes that Ryan's budget would result in the loss of 4.1 million jobs by 2014.

productive investment will generate the revenue to pay off the borrowing.

In other words, corporations borrow on a regular basis to finance investment. So they only attempt to balance their current expenditures and revenues and not their capital budget.

Much confusion about private and public spending, and also about budget deficits, could be avoided if discussion focused on a federal government balance sheet. In that way, current spending that needs to be balanced with current revenue could be separated from long-term investments that will increase the productivity of the American economy. Such investments, in areas like infrastructure and education, can increase future economic growth and income, and thus generate more tax revenue to pay off the debt. Just like a private company's investments, they are legitimately financed by borrowing.

Government Can Indeed Create Jobs

The main point, though, is this: whether financed by borrowing or taxes, whether consumption or investment, government spending that increases the demand for goods and services in the economy is not wasteful. It has the ability to employ underutilized resources and create jobs.

Ultimately, a job is a job, whether created by the private or public sector. A job has the potential to enable workers to support themselves and their families in dignity. We should not let ideological arguments keep us from using every available means to promote the basic human right of employment. ❑

Sources: Congressional Budget Office, "Estimated Impact of the American Recovery and Reinvestment Act on Employment and Economic Output From April 2010 Through June 2010," August 2010; Daniel J. Mitchell, "The Fallacy That Government Creates Jobs," The Cato Institute, 2008; John B. Taylor, "Goldman Sachs Wrong About Impact of House Budget Proposal," Economics One blog, February 28, 2011; Paul Krugman, "Myths of austerity," *The New York Times*. July 1, 2010; Jonathan Karl, "Goldman Sachs: House Spending Cuts Will Hurt Economic Growth," The Note, 2011; Mark Zandi, "A federal shutdown could derail the recovery," Moody's Analytics, February 28, 2011; Pedro da Costa and Mark Felsenthal, "Bernanke warns against steep budget cuts," Reuters, February 9, 2011; International Monetary Fund, *World Economic Outlook: Recovery, Risk, and Rebalancing*, 2010; Arjun Jayadev and Mike Konczal, "When Is Austerity Right? In Boom, Not Bust," *Challenge*, November-December 2010, pp. 37-53; Joseph Stiglitz, Foreword, in Karl Polanyi, *The Great Transformation: The Political and Economic Origins of Our Times*, 2001; David Aschauer, "Is Public Expenditure Productive?" *Journal of Monetary Economics*, 1989, pp. 177-200; Robert Pollin, "US government deficits and debt amid the great recession: what the evidence shows, *Cambridge Journal of Economics*, 2012, 36, 161-187; Kelsey Merrick and Jim Horney, "Chairman Ryan Gets 62 Percent of His Huge Budget Cuts from Programs for Lower-income Americans," Center on Budget and Policy Priorities, March 23, 2012; Paul Ryan, The Path to Prosperity, March 20, 2012; Ethan Pollack, "Ryan's Budget Would Cost Jobs," The Economic Policy Institute, March 21, 2012.

Article 2.3

JOBS, DEFICITS, AND THE MISGUIDED SQUABBLE OVER THE DEBT CEILING

BY TIM KOECHLIN
August 2011

These are obviously very grim economic times. One in six Americans who would like full-time work is unable to find a full-time job. Millions of Americans have lost their homes, and many millions more are "underwater"—they owe more than their homes are worth. The pain has been felt by nearly every household in the United States. Some have been hit harder than others. The unemployment rate for African Americans is double the rate for whites; since 2007, the median wealth of Black and Hispanic households has fallen by more than half. The distributions of wealth and income in the United States—the most unequal among industrialized countries before the crash of 2008—have become even more unequal.

In the midst of all of this suffering, U.S. corporate profits are at an all-time high. In 1980, the richest 1% of income earners in the United States claimed about 12% of all income; in 2008, they earned nearly one quarter of all income. The share of the top .1% has increased even faster. The U.S. economy and the human beings it ought to serve are suffering, first and foremost, from a *jobs deficit*. Closing this gap—creating and facilitating the creation of good jobs—should be the very top priority of Congress and the White House. At this point, it is not. Indeed, Republicans (enabled by President Obama) are currently doing what they can to make things worse.

The absurd squabble over the debt ceiling and the national debt is distracting, destructive, and almost entirely beside the point. The budget deficit is not the most pressing economic problem facing the United States—not by a long stretch. Whatever comes of these negotiations, it will not address the jobs deficit, and it will not improve the lives of the overwhelming majority of U.S. families. Indeed, it is likely to make things worse.

Let's be clear: the Republican approach to the economy and the budget is deeply misguided, wrong-headed, mean-spirited, and irresponsible. Their approach is as familiar as it is appalling: more tax cuts for the rich; more tax cuts for corporations; and cuts in social programs, including Medicare and Social Security. This tack is unconscionable. It is also bad economic policy, that is, it will not promote growth and it will not create jobs. Nobel Prize winner Paul Krugman is exactly correct when he concludes that "the G.O.P... has gone off the deep end."

President Obama's approach is less troubling for sure, and clearly preferable to the appalling Republican strategy. But this is a very low bar. President Obama has, unfortunately, embraced the faulty premise that deficit reduction should be a top priority. As a result, the President is prepared to make substantial spending cuts at precisely the wrong moment—when the economy needs demand, and people need help. And, alas, Mr. Obama has demonstrated a disturbing willingness to pursue cuts in Medicare and Social Security.

An intelligent response to this crisis has to reflect an understanding of its causes. Cutting spending during a recession is like blood-letting an anemic patient, or invading Iraq in an attempt to disempower Osama bin Laden.

Our best hope on this issue is that the president and Congress will be forced to "kick the can down the road." We can only hope that whenever we re-encounter the can, saner heads will prevail—or, more to the point, that the balance of political forces will have changed enough that we won't have to endure a repeat performance.

Some Good Ideas and Some Bad Ideas about the Economic Crisis, Economic Policy, and the Federal Budget

1. *Cutting spending in the middle of a recession is a terrible idea.* It will destroy jobs, and undermine the economy's already feeble momentum. Intelligent spending—extending unemployment benefits, block grants to states and municipalities, spending on green infrastructure, and keeping college affordable, for example—will create jobs today, lighten the load of those who are in the most economic trouble, and facilitate growth and competitiveness in the long run. Serious, enforceable, well-funded efforts to liberate homeowners from their enormous debt burden would help to re-ignite consumer spending and the housing market.

This is indeed the worst crisis since the Great Depression. How did and why did the Great Depression finally come to an end? After nearly a decade of mass unemployment (peaking at 25%), the U.S. government increased its *debt-financed spending* massively to pay for the war; that is, it ran enormous budget deficits. War spending put people to work; these newly employed workers spent their income, and this spending created jobs for others. In fact, during the war, the U.S. economy suffered from *labor shortages*. The U.S. government and corporations actively recruited women into professions and trades that had previously been off limits—women in large numbers "manned" the factories and shipyards.

An implication of this argument and this history is that *the primary problem facing the U.S. economy is not the budget deficit*. Indeed, in the short run, substantial *budget deficits are likely to accelerate the recovery.*

The National Debt is often characterized as "a burden to future generations." In fact, deficit spending—and the long-run growth and opportunities that it can facilitate—can be *a gift to our children* and grandchildren. Debt-financed investments today can leave them with a more prosperous, productive, sustainable economy, an economy that can provide them with educational, economic and personal opportunities that would not otherwise have been possible.

Notice, also, that, during a period of economic stagnation, budget deficits and government spending can be good for *business*. Rising demand means rising revenues, and this provides businesses with an incentive to hire workers. With adequate demand, it will be profitable for many businesses to increase hiring.

2. *The current debt ceiling "crisis" is utterly unnecessary; it is an irresponsible political maneuver by the Republicans.* Since 1962, the debt ceiling has been raised 74 times (including 18 times under President Reagan). With one exception—Newt Gingrich's government shut down in 1995—this has been trivial and routine. If Congress simply voted to raise the debt ceiling—allowing the Treasury to pay its

bills, as it is mandated to do by the Constitution—there would be no crisis. If the Republicans want to make changes in economic policy or shrink the federal government that is their prerogative. But this is not a reasonable or responsible way to make policy. It is an especially irresponsible way to make major decisions about the government's long-standing commitment to provide health coverage and minimal economic security to elderly Americans.

3. *The Republicans do not care about reducing the deficit.* Their objective is to cut taxes—especially for the rich—and dismantle what's left of the New Deal. Indeed, they have a long history of enthusiastically supporting enormous budget deficits and squandering surpluses (see the presidencies of Reagan and George W. Bush). Representative Paul Ryan's proposed ten-year budget—which got *unanimous* support from House Republicans in April—proposes trillions in tax cuts (over ten years), cuts which will overwhelmingly benefit corporations and the rich. Note: tax cuts do not reduce deficits! Ryan's plan also includes massive cuts to programs that benefit the poor and the middle class (most notably Medicare and Medicaid). According to the non-partisan Congressional Budget Office (CBO), Ryan's plan would reduce the deficit by $155 billion over 10 years—a meager $15 billion per year. The Republican plan is rooted in politics, ideology, and mendacity. There is no evidence at all that it is rooted in a commitment to "fiscal responsibility."

4. *Taxes in the United States are extraordinarily low.* Taxes in the United States are lower (as a share of GDP) than any other industrialized country. As a share of GDP, U.S. corporate taxes are lower than every industrialized country but Iceland. Tax rates for corporations and the wealthy have fallen substantially over the past 30 years. In the three decades following World War II—when taxes on the wealthy and corporate profits were considerably higher—the U.S. economy performed better: higher average growth rates, lower average rates of unemployment, and a much more equal distribution of income. Tax cuts for the rich are unfair, and trickle-down economics—the notion that giveaways to corporations and the rich will stimulate growth and employment—simply does not work.

5. If political pressures compel us to focus on the deficit at this moment, *our first step should be to tax the rich more heavily.* Refusing to extend President Bush's tax cuts (which will expire in 2013) for the top 5% income earners would raise government revenue by more than two trillion dollars over ten years. Spending cuts (if we must) should be back loaded—that is, they should occur disproportionately down the road, so that they do not undermine our efforts to get out of the current economic malaise.

6. *The U.S. federal budget deficit (and the national debt) is not analogous to overspending by a household.* The U.S. government—despite a national debt that is $14 trillion and growing—will not go bankrupt. Budget deficits can be problematic for sure; but at this moment, the benefits of debt financed government investment overwhelm the costs. (More on this below.)

7. *Republicans have been working diligently to disempower the Government's ability to regulate Wall Street's excesses, and protect consumers.* Their current target is the brand-new Consumer Financial Protection Bureau. If they are successful, another financial crisis is inevitable.

8. *This economic crisis is a devastating indictment of neoliberalism,* the free-market ideology that has framed economic policy debates since Ronald Reagan. The

financial meltdown of 2008 revealed (yet again!) that financial markets do not regulate themselves. The deep and ongoing recession that followed reflects the fact that depressed economies do not have a reliable mechanism for restoring full employment, prosperity and growth. The "invisible hand" cannot do it alone. In early 2009, many of us imagined that this ideology was on its last legs. Even Alan Greenspan—the once-legendary Federal Reserve Chairman, the "Maestro" of monetary policy, and a devoted protégé of the libertarian icon Ayn Rand—acknowledged before Congress that the model on which his worldview and policy recommendations had been premised—the view that unfettered markets (including financial markets) are efficient and stable—had failed. Of course it had! How could anyone continue to argue that *laissez-faire* works? But bad ideas can be resilient—especially when they are promoted by well-funded think tanks.

The Logic of a Recession: What Happened to All of the Jobs?

The catalyst to this current economic disaster was an unregulated financial system that ran amok—as unregulated financial systems inevitably do. Financial panics and crises are a chronic part of let-it-rip capitalism. If financial markets are not regulated adequately, this tendency will eventually manifest itself. The historical record is overwhelmingly clear about this.

The financial system crashed in October, 2008—although the strains had been mounting for years. Major financial institutions failed; housing prices collapsed and foreclosures spiked; the Dow Jones Industrial Average fell by nearly half, and banks stopped lending money. Investors panicked—with good reason. Consumers, spooked by shrinking retirement accounts, plummeting home prices, layoffs, a pervasive sense of economic chaos and, of course, declining incomes, cut their spending. The U.S. economy shed nearly two million jobs over the last third of 2008, and another four million in 2009.

The essential logic of a recession is not terribly complicated. When businesses experience declining demand, they shed workers (or decelerate hiring). These laid-off workers in turn cut their spending, because they must. In some cases, their increasingly nervous neighbors begin to reduce their spending also—they put off buying a new car, taking a trip, or re-modeling the kitchen. Thus the process accelerates—car dealerships, airlines, hotels, and contractors (etc.) are forced to lay workers off. *These* newly unemployed workers spend less, and so on. Tax revenues fall, forcing state and local governments to fire teachers and cops and to cut social spending when it is needed most. At some point, apparently healthy businesses begin to worry that their demand projections are overly optimistic; many decide to put off investment in plant and equipment. Because of this "multiplier" process, "shocks" to the economy have the potential to accelerate. According to a recent *Wall Street Journal* article, "The main reason U.S. companies are reluctant to step up hiring is scant demand, rather than uncertainty over government policies, according to a majority of economists in a new *Wall Street Journal* survey."

Insufficient demand explains the jobs deficit, not "high" corporate taxes, not regulation, not immigration, not "uncertainty" about taxation and regulation, not President Obama's health-care plan, nor his allegedly flawed leadership. Spending by the private sector—consumers and businesses—is not, at this moment, up to the job of ensuring full employment. So the government needs to provide demand.

The Federal Reserve can facilitate private spending (demand) by keeping interest rates low. The federal government can generate demand by (a) spending (including grants to strapped state and municipal governments); (b) working to reduce the debt overhang constraining homeowners, and/or (c) lowering taxes on the middle class and extending unemployment benefits (the middle class and the poor spend a greater share of their income, and so tax cuts for the middle class are more effective than tax cuts for the rich).

Again, the U.S. economy emerged from the Great Depression because the Government spent like mad. "Future generations" (Baby Boomers, their kids, and their grandchildren) benefited enormously from this debt-financed spending, because they inherited a more prosperous, productive economy, an economy that provided them with educational, economic, and personal opportunities that would not otherwise have been possible. Deficit spending—and the long-run growth that it can facilitate—can be a *gift* to our children and grandchildren.

Let me be completely explicit: an intelligent response to this crisis will lead to *larger* budget deficits in the short term. Budget deficits and government debt are potentially problematic but, at this moment—as in 1939—the benefits of deficit-spending overwhelmingly exceed the costs.

Burdening Our Grandchildren?
Why a Smart Deficit is a Gift to Future Generations

The commonplace assertion that budget deficits are a "burden to our grand-children" is both vague and deceptive, in large part because it fails to acknowledge that deficit spending today can—if done wisely—provide enormous benefits to us, our neighbors, our children, and our grandchildren.

The U.S. government finances its deficits (the difference between revenue and spending) by borrowing. Generally speaking, it borrows by selling bonds—which are essentially IOUs (with interest) from the U.S. Treasury to bondholders (lenders). The government borrows from many sources—individuals, pension funds, banks, foreign governments—and it pays these lenders back with interest.

There is a tendency to think that borrowing is inherently problematic, that it implies that we are "living beyond our means." But this is a dangerously narrow understanding of debt. Individuals borrow money all the time—to finance homes, cars, appliances, and college educations. Businesses borrow money to finance investment in equipment, technology, and research and development; many businesses have lines of credit with their suppliers, and this often works for both parties. Municipalities commonly undertake "bond issues" to finance school construction and other "capital" projects.

Sometimes, of course, borrowing is a bad idea. But borrowing can also allow a family, a business, or a government to make useful and/or productive purchases that otherwise would not be possible. Is borrowing a problem? *It depends on what the borrowing is for, and it depends on the capacity of the borrower to repay the debt.*

Government spending can improve the quality of our lives. Government spending pays for schools, environmental protection, parks and other public spaces, food and drug safety, public colleges and universities, fire and police protection, infrastructure, consumer protection, and health and income security in old age, to name just a few. Beyond the provision of these beneficial services, the government can create (and facilitate the creation of) jobs. When the economy is stagnant, an important benefit of borrowing is that it can lead to job creation.

So, we have a choice. We can limit the growth of the national debt by firing school teachers, cops, firefighters, and mine inspectors; cutting health-care coverage for the poor and elderly; ignoring our long-run energy issues, defunding our public schools and forcing states to raise tuition at our public universities ...*and* destroying millions of jobs. Or we can borrow money to support these services while, at the same time, preserving and creating jobs. The Republicans pretend that cutting the budget is a magic bullet—more jobs, and less debt. But this is utterly wrong.

In 1939, the U.S. national debt was about $40 billion. By 1945, it had grown by a factor of six to $259 billion dollars. The benefits of this borrowing were enormous. First, it allowed the Allies to defeat the Nazis (something that would have been more complicated if Congress were constrained by a balanced budget amendment). Second, this debt-financed increase in government spending facilitated economic growth and employment. The U.S. economy was more productive by far in 1945 than it otherwise would have been. A rich country with a moderate debt burden is, by any reasonable measure, preferable to a moderately rich country with no debt. Deficit spending allowed the United States to avoid six more years of massive waste—that is, unemployment. This was undoubtedly a very wise investment.

This does not imply that budget deficits are always wise. Again, it depends on what the government does with the money. For example, budget deficits soared under President George W. Bush. This stunning increase in debt was a terrible mistake, because the borrowing was used to finance massive tax cuts for the rich, and two expensive, ill-advised wars. (President Bush's policies, by the way, have had a *much* larger effect on the deficit than President Obama's time-limited fiscal stimulus.) In contrast to Bush's folly, borrowing for job creation and mortgage relief during an historic economic downturn is a good idea.

Government debt can be problematic, for sure, but it is *not analogous* to household debt. The U.S. government will not go bankrupt—it has never missed a debt payment and, unless Congress impedes its ability to meet its obligations for political reasons, it never will. That is, the U.S. government's "capacity to repay" is enormous. No one who understands the basics of government finance believes that bankruptcy is an issue for the U.S. government (although deficit hawks often *suggest* that it is, sometimes disingenuously, sometimes out of ignorance). The U.S. government has run budget deficits in all but five years since 1961 (four of them under President Clinton). Sometimes it made sense, other times it did not.

Why are budget deficits problematic? Deficits can cause inflation. They can also put upward pressure on interest rates, and these higher interest rates, by making borrowing more expensive, can restrict the accessibility of capital to businesses and households, which can be a drag on investment and growth. Over the long term, this sort of chronic under-investment can be substantial, as can its effects on our living standards down the road. (For the wonks and/or economics majors among you, economists refer to this as "crowding out," as in government borrowing may *crowd out*, or displace, private borrowing and investment.) It is worth worrying about, for sure.

The "good news" is that, in this depressed economy, interest rates are extraordinarily low. Inflation is also a minor concern; indeed "deflation" is arguably a greater threat. At this moment in time, borrowing is especially easy and cheap because there are lots of potential investors sitting on big piles of cash and, further, in a depressed economy there are relatively few attractive alternatives—especially for risk averse investors.

All of this is to say that the potential benefits of deficit spending during a recession are great—it is by far the most effective way to address the jobs deficit; and borrowing can help us to deliver the goods and services on which many Americans depend, especially during a recession. And at this moment in history, the "costs" of the deficit—its potential effects on inflation and interest rates are all but non-existent.

When the economy recovers sufficiently—when the jobs deficit has been resolved—relatively large budget deficits will probably no longer make sense. But until then, cutting spending is a terrible idea. I repeat: cutting spending during a recession is like blood-letting an anemic patient. The Republican "jobs program" starts with massive dismissals of teachers and other public sector employees. That won't work.

The content of this spending is important, of course. A detailed proposal is beyond the scope of this short paper. This said, it is clear that Congress should pass another economic stimulus package—several hundreds of billions of dollars at least. This package ought to include generous grants to state and municipal governments, investments in green infrastructure, urban jobs programs, extended unemployment benefits, and more generous financial aid for poor and middle class college students.

The Republican Party, the neoliberals, the "efficient market" theorists and other fetishizers of "The Market" are wrong. In contrast, the great John Maynard Keynes was (and is) right: unregulated, let-it-rip capitalism is prone to financial crises; capitalism has no reliable mechanism for resolving a jobs deficit, and the free market generates intolerable levels of inequality. ❑

Sources: Center for American Progress, "Ten Charts that Prove the US is a Low Tax Country," June 10, 2011; Citizens for Tax Justice, "US is one of the least taxed countries," June 30, 2011; Emmanuel Saez, "Striking it Richer: The Evolution of Top Incomes in the US," July 10, 2010 (elsa.berkeley.edu/~saez/); Huffington Post, "Income Inequality is at an all-time high" (report on the work of UC-Berkeley Economist Emmanuel Saez); James Crotty, "The Great Austerity War: What Caused the Deficit Crisis and Who Should Pay to Fix It?" Political Economy Research Institute (PERI), June, 2011; James Fallows, "The Chart that Should Accompany all Discussions of the Debt Ceiling," June 25, 2011; James R. Horney, "Ryan Budget Plan Produces far Less Deficit Cutting than Reported" Center for Budget & Policy Priorities, April 11, 2011; Joseph Stiglitz, "Of the 1%, by the 1%, for the 1%,", May, 2011; Paul Krugman, "No, We Can't? Or Won't?," *New York Times*, July 11, 2011; Paul Krugman, *New York Times*, "The Death of Horatio Alger," January 5, 2004; Robert Pollin, "18 Million Jobs by 2012," *The Nation*, Feburary 18, 2010; Robert Pollin, "Austerity is not a solution: why the deficit hawks are wrong," Political Economy Research Institute, Nov/Dec, 2010 (peri.org); Sabrina Tavernise, "Recession Study Finds Hispanics are Hit the Hardest," *New York Times*, July 26, 2011; Phil Izzo, "Dearth of Demand Seen Behind Weak Hiring," *Wall Street Journal*, July 18, 2011.

Article 2.4

DON'T DRIVE OFF THE FISCAL CLIFF
Congress's newest game of chicken threatens the recovery.

BY HEIDI GARRETT-PELTIER
September/October 2012

The U.S. economy is set to go off the so-called "fiscal cliff" at midnight on December 31, 2012. That's when various tax cuts for people at most income levels will expire. Days later, the federal budget will automatically be cut as the result of an agreement made by both parties last summer, when Congress was in a standoff over the debt ceiling. The deal reached by President Obama and leaders of Congress, called the Budget Control Act of 2011, enabled the federal government to raise its debt ceiling (permitting it to pays its bills) while in turn reducing future budgets. Congress agreed on $1.2 trillion in budget cuts at the time, and tasked a congressional "super committee" with identifying an additional $1.2 trillion in savings. That committee, however, has failed to reach agreement, and now the $1.2 trillion will automatically be cut.

What would go over the cliff this coming January is our hope of economic recovery.

If the cuts happen as planned, nearly $500 billion will be cut from the defense budget and the same amount from non-defense spending over the next decade. That, plus about $200 billion of reduced interest payments on the federal debt, gets us to the $1.2 trillion in savings.

But it's not too late for Congress to change its act. There are four alternatives to driving over the fiscal cliff.

One: Delay debt reduction. Reducing spending during a fragile time of economic recovery is almost certain to make matters much worse. The Congressional Budget Office (CBO) has estimated that this policy of "fiscal restraint" would result in a contraction of the economy by 1.3% during the first half of 2013. Alternatively, the CBO finds that "reduced fiscal restraint," in which none of the automatic cuts take place and no tax cuts expire, would boost GDP growth in 2013 by 3.9 percentage points more than the current course and would save two million jobs.

The debt can wait. While it's true that the government pays interest on the debt and should therefore not let it rise continuously and unsustainably, Congress could delay debt reduction by a few years until the economy is more stable.

Two: Raise revenue. Deficits, and in turn debt, rise when spending outpaces revenues. To reduce the debt without harming economic recovery, we could raise revenue. This includes strategies such as the Obama administration's proposal to eliminate tax breaks for the wealthy. According to the non-partisan center OMB Watch, allowing tax cuts for the top 2% to expire would generate almost a trillion dollars over the next ten years.

Options three and four are two sides of a very contentious coin. One side is to protect the defense budget. The other is to protect non-defense spending. Each side has nearly $500 billion at stake. But they are far from equal.

Three: Slash non-defense spending. This is vice-presidential candidate Paul Ryan's budget plan. The Ryan budget or, as he calls it, "The Path to Prosperity," cuts important domestic programs while protecting military spending, even as the war in Iraq has ended and the war in Afghanistan is supposedly nearing its end. This option has many vocal supporters.

Four: Maintain non-domestic spending while cutting defense spending. Those trying to protect spending for healthcare, education, national parks, research and development, and infrastructure are neither united nor vocal. Yet in terms of economic prosperity, the choice should be clear. Dollar for dollar, non-military domestic programs create many more jobs than military spending. One billion dollars spent on the military (and related industries) supports about 11,200 jobs in the United States. That same amount spent on healthcare supports 17,200 U.S. jobs; spent on education, 26,700 U.S. jobs. Why do these programs create more jobs, dollar-for-dollar, than defense? Because they are more labor-intensive than defense: more of the dollars go to pay salaries rather than to buy materials and equipment. And more of non-defense spending stays in the United States. As teachers and healthcare workers spend their income in their towns and cities, they create more demand for food services, healthcare, and other local industries.

The U.S. economy is still not close to a full recovery from the economic crisis. It would be reckless to drive off the fiscal cliff next January. The more responsible option is to raise taxes on the rich, reduce spending on the military, and shift the money that would have been spent on the military over to domestic spending where we get more bang for the buck. ❑

Article 2.5

WHY DO THEY OPPOSE MORE STIMULUS?
BY ARTHUR MacEWAN
January/February 2011

> Dear Dr. Dollar:
> Why are conservatives, especially wealthy conservatives, against stimulating the economy through the government's deficit spending? Don't businesses' profits and the incomes of the wealthy depend on economic growth?
> —Andy Druding, Richmond, Calif.

As it turns out, business profits are already doing pretty well in spite of—or perhaps because of—the poor economic conditions for most people. Corporate profits have been expanding at a good clip since the beginning of 2009. In the third quarter of 2010, profits of domestic corporations were running at an annual rate of $1.27 trillion—not back up to their peak of $1.40 trillion four years earlier, but well on the way to that high mark. Even after an adjustment for inflation, current profits are in relatively good shape.

So it is not too hard to see why the people whose incomes are tied to profits are not eager to see a dramatic shift of policy. Still, you might think that more economic growth would provide even more profits.

Profits, however, depend on two things: the amount of value that gets created (output) and the share of that value that goes to profits. With a high level of unemployment, workers are in a poor position to demand higher wages—i.e., a larger share of that value. So businesses, and the wealthy who get their income from owning businesses, do not want unemployment to fall too low—low enough to give workers more bargaining power.

The weak position of workers in the current economic situation affects more than wages. While a recession lasts, businesses are able to implement changes more readily than in "normal" times. For example, they can change work rules, get rid of older workers, and bring in new technology more easily, as workers are in a poorer position to resist change. Also, the "shock" imposed on society by bad economic conditions can be used in the political sphere, making it possible for businesses and the wealthy to obtain concessions from government—the tax incentives state governments offer, for example, in the hope of generating some local growth. (However, an economic crisis also opens up possibilities for changes in the other direction. Consider, for example, the progressive changes in the United States that came out of the Great Depression of the 1930s.)

From the perspective of the wealthy, then, perhaps a bit more growth would be better, but not so much as to weaken their positions. Most important, if that growth required the government to spend a lot more by running deficits, the wealthy are not interested. They fear that high deficits now mean more taxes down the line. In part, higher taxes could be needed to pay off the debt the government would incur when it ran those deficits. Perhaps more important, upping government spending today threatens to entrench a long-run higher level of government activity, which would require higher taxes on a permanent basis. The wealthy might be able to push the tax obligations onto lower income groups. Yet, with income inequality as great as it is, it's hard to get much more out of anyone but the wealthy. You can't get blood from a stone.

These concerns about higher taxes generate a strong anti-big-government ideology, and the ideology can trump common sense. There are plenty of people who because they oppose "big government" oppose the spending that would be involved in any program that would provide significant economic stimulus through deficit spending. Of course not all of these people are among the wealthy, but they share the anti-government, anti-tax ideology. After all, they cannot improve their incomes by voting for higher wages, but they can—or think they can—improve their incomes by voting against taxes, which means voting against "big government," which means voting against deficits.

All this said, most of today's large federal budget deficit is not the result of spending designed to stimulate the economy. In fiscal year 2009, the budget deficit was about $1.4 trillion. Yet the February 2009 "stimulus package" accounted for a small share of that deficit. In 2001, the Congressional Budget Office (CBO) estimated the government was on course for a 2009 surplus of $700 billion. Why this $2.1 trillion difference between the CBO estimate and reality?

Slow economic growth in the early 2000s followed by severe downturn in 2008 and 2009 accounted for over 40% of the difference, as tax income declined sharply and some spending automatically increased (e.g., unemployment compensation). About 50% of the difference resulted from legislation enacted in the Bush years— over half of which was war spending, tax breaks for the wealthy, and the bank bailout. The stimulus package of the Obama administration accounted for only about 8% of the difference, a pretty small share.

Businesses and the wealthy who rail against the deficit do have real interests that they are protecting. But they are also using the deficit issue to attack the Obama administration's stimulus efforts, which turn out not to have been all that big. ❏

Chapter 3

TAXATION

Article 3.1

NO FOOLING—CORPORATIONS EVADE TAXES
Forbes Finally Notices what has Been Obvious For Years

BY JOHN MILLER
May/June 2011

> WHAT THE TOP U.S. COMPANIES PAY IN TAXES
> Some of the world's biggest, most profitable corporations enjoy a far lower tax rate than you do—that is, if they pay taxes at all.
>
> The most egregious example is General Electric. Last year the conglomerate generated $10.3 billion in pretax income, but ended up owing nothing to Uncle Sam. In fact, it recorded a tax benefit of $1.1 billion.
>
> Over the last two years, GE Capital [one of the two divisions of General Electric] has displayed an uncanny ability to lose lots of money in the U.S. (posting a $6.5 billion loss in 2009), and make lots of money overseas (a $4.3 billion gain).
>
> It only makes sense that multinationals "put costs in high-tax countries and profits in low-tax countries," says Scott Hodge, president of the Tax Foundation. Those low-tax countries are almost anywhere but the U.S. "When you add in state taxes, the U.S. has the highest tax burden among industrialized countries," says Hodge. In contrast, China's rate is just 25%; Ireland's is 12.5%.
> —Christopher Helman, "What the Top U.S. Companies Pay in Taxes," *Forbes*, April 1, 2011

When *Forbes* magazine, the keeper of the list of the 400 richest Americans, warns that corporations not paying taxes on their profits will raise your hackles, you might wonder about the article's April 1 dateline. If it turns out *not* to be an April Fool's joke, things must be *really* bad.

And indeed they are. As *Forbes* reports, General Electric, the third largest U.S. corporation, turned a profit of $10.3 billion in 2010, paid no corporate income taxes, and got a "tax benefit" of $1.1 billion on taxes owed on past profits. And from 2005 to 2009, according to its own filings, GE paid a consolidated tax rate of just 11.6% on its corporate rates, including state, local, and foreign taxes. That's a far cry from the 35% rate nominally levied on corporate profits above $10 million.

Nor was GE alone among the top ten U.S. corporations with no tax obligations. Bank of America (BofA), the seventh largest U.S. corporation, racked up $4.4 billion in profits in 2010 and also paid no corporate income taxes (or in 2009 for that matter). Like GE, BofA has hauled in a whopping "tax benefit"—$1.9 billion.

For BofA, much like for GE, losses incurred during the financial crisis erased it tax liabilities. BofA, of course, contributed mightily to the crisis. It was one of four banks that controlled 95% of commercial bank derivatives activity, mortgage-based securities that inflated the housing bubble and brought on the crisis.

And when the crisis hit, U.S. taxpayers bailed them out, not once but several times. All told BofA received $45 billion of government money from the Troubled Asset Relief Program (TARP) as well as other government guarantees. And while BofA paid no taxes on their over $4 billion of profits, they nonetheless managed to pay out $3.3 billion in bonuses to corporate executives. All of that has made BofA a prime target for US Uncut protests (see p. 6) against corporate tax dodging that has cost the federal government revenues well beyond the $39 billion saved by the punishing spending cuts in the recent 2011 budget deal.

These two corporate behemoths and other many other major corporations paid no corporate income taxes last year, even though 2010 U.S. corporate profits had returned their level in 2005 in the midst the profits-heavy Bush expansion before the crisis hit.

An Old Story

But why is *Forbes* suddenly noticing corporate tax evasion? After all, corporations not paying taxes on their profits is an old story. Let's take a look at the track record of major corporations paying corporate income before the crisis hit and the losses that supposedly explain their not paying taxes.

The Government Accounting Office conducted a detailed study of the burden of the corporate income tax from 1998 to 2005. The results were stunning. Over half (55%) of large U.S. corporations reported no tax liability for at least one of those eight years. And in 2005 alone 25% of those corporations paid no corporate income taxes, even though corporate profits had more than doubled from 2001 to 2005.

In another careful study, the Treasury Department found that from 2000 to 2005, the share of corporate operating surplus that that U.S. corporations pay in taxes—a proxy for the average tax rate—was 16.7% thanks to various corporate loopholes, especially three key mechanisms:

- Accelerated Depreciation: allows corporations to write off machinery and equipment or other assets more quickly than they actually deteriorate.

- Stock Options: by giving their executives the option to buy the company's stock at a favorable price, corporations can take a tax deduction for the difference between what the employees pay for the stock and what it's worth.

- Debt Financing: offers a lower effective tax rate for corporate investment than equity (or stock) financing because the interest payments on debt (usually incurred by issuing bonds) get added to corporate costs and reduce reported profits.

Corporate income taxes are levied against reported corporate profits, and each of these mechanisms allows corporations to inflate their reported costs and thereby reduce their taxable profits.

And then there are overseas profits. U.S.-based corporations don't pay U.S. corporate taxes on their foreign income until it is "repatriated," or sent back to the parent corporation from abroad. That allows multinational corporations to defer payment of U.S. corporate income taxes on their overseas profits indefinitely or repatriate their profits from foreign subsidiaries when their losses from domestic operations can offset those profits and wipe out any tax liability, as GE did in 2010.

Hardly Overtaxed

Nonetheless, Scott Hodge, the president of the right-wing Tax Foundation, steadfastly maintains that U.S. corporations are overtaxed, and that that is what driving U.S. corporations to park their profits abroad (and lower their U.S. taxes). Looking at nominal corporate tax rates, Hodge would seem to have a case. Among the 19 OECD countries, only the statutory corporate tax rates in Japan surpass the (average combined federal and state) 39.3% rate on U.S. corporate profits. And the U.S. rate is well above the OECD average of 27.6%.

But these sorts of comparisons misrepresent where U.S. corporate taxes stand with respect to tax rates actually paid by corporations in other advanced countries. Why? The tax analyst's answer is that the U.S. corporate income tax has a "narrow base," or in plain English, is riddled with loopholes. As a result U.S. effective corporate tax rates—the proportion of corporate profits actually paid out in taxes—are not only far lower than the nominal rate but below the effective rates in several other countries. The Congressional Budget Office, for instance, found that U.S. effective corporate tax rates were near the OECD average for equity-financed investments, and below the OECD average for debt-financed investments. And for the years from 2000 to 2005, the Treasury Department found the average corporate tax rate among OECD countries was 21.6%, well above the U.S. 16.7% rate.

Current U.S. corporate tax rates are also extremely low by historical standards. In 1953, government revenue from the U.S. corporate income taxes were the equal of 5.6% of GDP; the figure was 4.0% of GDP in 1969, 2.2% of GDP from 2000 to 2005, and is currently running at about 2.0% of GDP.

By all these measures U.S. corporations are hardly over-taxed. And some major corporations are barely taxed, if taxed at all.

Closing corporate loopholes so that corporate income tax revenues in the United States match the 3.4% of GDP collected on average by OECD corporate income taxes would add close to $200 billion to federal government revenues—more than five times the $39 billion of devastating spending cuts just made in the federal budget in 2011. Returning the corporate income tax revenues to the 4.0% of GDP level of four decades ago would add close to $300 billion a year to government revenues.

The cost of not shutting down those corporate loopholes would be to let major corporations go untaxed, to rob the federal government of revenues that could, with enough political will, reverse devastating budget cuts, and to leave the rest of us to pay more and more of the taxes necessary to support a government that does less and less for us. ❑

Sources: "Corporate Tax Reform: Issues for Congress," by Jane G. Gravelle and Thomas L. Hungerford, CRS Report for Congress, October 31, 2007; "Treasury Conference On Business Taxation and Global Competitiveness," U.S. Department of the Treasury, Background Paper, July 23, 2007; "Six Tests for Corporate Tax Reform," by Chuck Marr and Brian Highsmith, Center on Budget and Policy Priorities, February 28, 2011; "Tax Holiday For Overseas Corporate Profits Would Increase Deficits, Fail To Boost The Economy, And Ultimately Shift More Investment And Jobs Overseas," by Chuck Marr and Brian Highsmith, Center on Budget and Policy Priorities, April 8, 2011; and, "Comparison of the Reported Tax Liabilities of Foreign and U.S.-Controlled Corporations, 1998-2005," Government Accounting Office, July 2008.

Article 3.2

TRANSACTION TAX: SAND IN THE WHEELS, NOT IN THE FACE

Why a transaction tax is a really good idea.

BY JOHN MILLER
March/April 2010

> WHY TAXING STOCK TRADES IS A REALLY BAD IDEA
> [S]urely it is "socially useful" to let free people transact freely, without regulators and legislators micromanaging them. ... It's Economics 101 that the free actions of market participants cause supply and demand to reach equilibrium. And isn't that what investors—indeed even speculators—do? Can they do it as well when facing the dead-weight costs of a transaction tax?
> If not, then trading volume in our stock markets will fall. Beyond the tax, everyone—investors and speculator, great and small—who buys or sells stocks will pay more to transact in markets that are less liquid. In such a world, markets would necessarily be more risky, and the cost of capital for business would necessarily rise. The consequence of that is that innovation, growth, and jobs would necessarily fall. That would be the full and true cost of the trading tax.
> —Donald L. Luskin and Chris Hynes, "Why Taxing Stock Trades Is a Really Bad Idea," *Wall Street Journal,* January 5, 2010

"Some financial activities which proliferated over the last 10 years were socially useless," Britain's Finance Service Authority Chairman Adiar Turner told a black-tie gathering of financial executives in London in September 2009. That is why he had proposed a transaction tax for the United Kingdom and why British Prime Minister Gordon Brown would propose an international transaction tax at the November G-20 summit.

The gathered bankers "saw red," as one report described their reaction. Investment bankers Donald L. Luskin and Chris Hynes are still irate.

In some ways their reaction is surprising. A financial transaction tax is nothing other than a sales tax on trading stocks and other securities. Transaction taxes are already in place in about 30 countries, and a transaction tax applied to the sale of stock in the United States from 1914 to 1964.

In addition, the transaction tax rates on a single trade are typically quite low. For instance, the "Let Wall Street Pay for the Restoration of Main Street Act of 2009," proposed by U.S. Representative Peter DeFazio (D-Ore.), would assess a one quarter of one percent (.25%) tax on the value of stock transactions, and two one hundredths of one percent (.02%) tax on the sale on a variety of derivative assets—including credit default swaps, which played such a large role in the mortgage crisis. To target speculators, the bill exempts retirement accounts, mutual funds, education and health savings accounts, and the first $100,000 of transactions annually.

In other ways, Luskin's and Hynes's reaction is not surprising at all. At its heart, a transaction tax is a radical measure. Its premise is that faster-acting financial markets driven by speculation don't bring relief to the economy—instead, they loot the economy. Its purpose, as Nobel Prize-winning economist James Tobin put it when he proposed his original transaction tax on international money markets during the 1970s, is to "throw sand in the wheels" of our financial markets.

Also, while its tax rate is low, the burden of a transaction tax adds up as securities are repeatedly traded, as is the practice on Wall Street today. For instance, even after accounting for its exemptions and allowing for a sizable decline in trading, the DeFazio bill would still raise $63.5 billion annually, according to the estimates of Dean Baker, co-director of the Center for Economic Policy Research.

Luskin and Hynes have two main objections to the transaction tax. The first is that a transaction tax would affect every single person who owns and invests in stocks, not just speculators. Customers would not have to pay a tax to buy or sell mutual funds, but, as Luskin and Hynes emphasize, the mutual funds themselves would have to pay a tax every time they trade stocks. So everyone holding mutual funds would still end up paying the tax.

What Luskin and Hynes don't say is this: Mutual funds that actively trade stocks would pay three times the transaction taxes of an average fund, as the Investment Company Institute, the fund industry trade group, reports. And stock index funds, which hold a sample of all stocks but seldom trade them, are taxed the least. Those funds have historically outperformed other mutual funds. So a transaction tax would work to push mutual fund customers to invest their savings more wisely, providing some with higher rates of return with a transaction tax than their previous funds provided without it. And that would mean fewer broker fees and lower profits for the fund industry.

But what really sticks in Luskin's and Hynes's craw is the assertion that financial trading is not socially useful. That claim flies in face of the long-held contention, buttressed by much of finance theory, that the equilibrium outcomes of financial markets are efficient. And if financial markets are efficient, there is no need for a tax that will reduce trading.

But much of what Luskin and Hynes have to say is not right. First, as anyone who *paid attention* in Economics 101 would know, reaching an equilibrium is not in and of itself desirable. To endorse the outcomes of today's speculative financial markets as desirable because they reach an equilibrium is the equivalent of describing a gambler in a poker game raking in a big pot as desirable because it clears the table. And the gamblers in our financial markets did rake in some awfully big pots betting that subprime borrowers would default on their loans. The last few years show us just how undesirable that equilibrium turned out to be.

Second, speculation dwarfs financing investment in U.S. stock markets. During the 1970s, for every dollar of new investment in plants and equipment, $1.30 in stocks were traded on the U.S. exchanges, reports Robert Pollin, co-director of the Political Economy Research Institute. But from 1998 to 2007, $27 in stocks were traded on the U.S. exchanges for every dollar of corporate investment in plant equipment. Such a rapid stock turnover has diverted the attention of managers of enterprises from long-term planning. Whatever damage that churning caused on Main Street, it paid off handsomely on Wall Street. From 1973 to 2007, the size of the financial (and insurance) sector relative to the economy doubled, financial sector profits went from one-quarter to two-fifths of domestic profits, and compensation in the finance industry went from just about average to 180% of the private industry average.

By counteracting these trends, a transactions tax can actually enhance, not diminish, the efficiency of financial markets. If it forces the financial sector to fulfill its function of transferring savings to investment with less short-term churning, then the tax will have freed up resources for more productive uses.

A transaction tax would surely be a step in the right direction toward reducing the bloat of the finance industry, righting the balance of speculation over enterprise, and restoring the focus on long-term planning and job-creation in the economy.

None of that will happen unless every last grain of the decades' worth of sand the bullies on Wall Street have kicked in our faces gets thrown into the wheels of finance. That is a tall order. But as DeFazio's and Turner's example shows, some of today's policymakers are up to the task. ❏

Sources: "The Benefits of a Financial Transaction Tax," by Dean Baker, Center For Economic and Policy Research, December 2008; ""Public Investment, Industrial Policy, and U.S. Economic Renewal," by Robert Pollin and Dean Baker, Political Economy Research Institute, December 2009; "Turner Plan on 'Socially Useless' Trades Make Bankers See Red," by Caroline Binham, Bloomberg.com; "Taxing Wall Street Today Wins Support for Keynes Idea (Update 1)," by Yaiman Onaran, Bloomberg.com; "The Potential Revenue from Financial Transactions Taxes, by Dean Baker, Robert Pollin, Travis McArthur, and Matt Sherman, Political Economy Research Institute, Working paper no. 212, December 2009; "Why Taxing Stock Trades Is a Really Bad Idea," by Donald L. Luskin and Chris Hynes, *Wall Street Journal*, January 5, 2010; "Lawmakers Weigh A Wall Street Tax," by John McKinnon, *Wall Street Journal*, December 19, 2009; Tobin Tax, freerisk.org/wiki/index.php/Tobin_tax; text of HR 4191—"Let Wall Street Pay for the Restoration of Main Street Act of 2009," www.govtrack.us.

Article 3.3

TAXING THE RICH, FROM RIGHT TO LEFT
Romney, Obama, Sarkozy, Hollande

BY JOHN MILLER
May/June 2012

> "The Buffett Alternative: The Rich don't pay lower average tax rates," *Wall Street Journal*, Review & Outlook, September 20, 2011
>
> "The Bottom 0.1%: The Buffett rule yields a pittance," *Wall Street Journal*, Review & Outlook, March 21, 2012
>
> "Sarkozy's Last Stand: France's choice now is more of the same or jump off the Socialist cliff," *Wall Street Journal*, Review & Outlook, April 22, 2012
>
> "Socialist France," *Wall Street Journal*, Review & Outlook, May 7, 2012

The editors of the *Wall Street Journal* were seeing red when President Obama began touting the Buffet Rule as the key to restoring tax fairness to the U.S. tax code. But things went from bad to worse when François Hollande, the Socialist party candidate, topped the preliminary ballot for French President, the editors were reduced to bemoaning the "unenviable" choice facing the French electorate in the runoff election. And then got worse still two weeks later in the runoff election, when, as the *Journal* editors put it, "the French chose to to leap off the Socialist cliff without a parachute."

The Buffett Rule backed by Obama comes off as a slap on the wrist when compared to Hollande's plan to raise France's top income tax brackets. And Obama tax policies would do less to tax the rich than the tax policies of Hollande's opponent, the French neoconservative incumbent President Nicolas Sarkozy, would have if he had been reelected.

This is all bad news for the *Journal* editors, who consider pro-rich tax cuts the cure for any troubled economy, but let's take a look just how much good news it is for the rest of us.

The Buffett Rule and Mitt's Tax Holiday

The Buffett Rule takes its name from billionaire investor Warren Buffett, who quite rightly insists that a fair tax code would demand that his income be taxed at a higher rate than that of his secretary. That's not the case with the U.S. income tax. The very highest-paid workers can pay a tax rate as high as 35% on their last dollars of wages, while investors pay no more than a 15% tax rate on any income from their capital gains or dividends, no matter now great their income. To ensure that millionaires and billionaires aren't taxed at a lower rate than regular wage and salary workers, the Buffett Rule would impose a 30% minimum tax on anyone with an income of more than $1 million.

That might sound fair, but the *Journal* editors insist that the whole premise of the tax, that millionaires currently pay lower tax rates than middle-class employees, is "a fairy tale." And they believe they've got the numbers to prove it: the average income tax rate paid by millionaires in 2008 was more than twice the rate paid by taxpayers with income in the $50,000 to $100,000 range.

But the *Journal* editors' numbers are hardly convincing. To begin with, they look at just income tax rates and not all federal taxes, in that way ignoring Social Security and Medicare taxes, among other federal taxes. When the Congressional Research Service (CRS) looked at all federal taxes, they found that the difference in the average tax rate of millionaires (24%) and the average rate for moderate income taxpayers with income under $100,000 (19%) is far smaller than what the editors' numbers suggest. In addition, the editor's numbers are average tax rates that obscure the variation in tax rates within income groups. And that too makes a difference. For instance, the CRS found that "roughly a quarter of all millionaires face a tax rate that is lower than the tax rate faced by 10.4 million moderate income taxpayers."

The tax plans of Republican presidential candidate Mill Romney would not correct this gross inequity—it would make it worse. Romney would continue the pro-rich Bush tax cuts, repeal the estate tax, and then lower the federal income tax rates, including dropping the top bracket from 35% to 28%. Altogether, his proposal would reduce the tax rate of the richest 1% of taxpayers, with an average income of $1.4 million, by three times as much as the tax rate of a middle-income taxpayer, with an average income of $42,000. Those cuts would also likely slice as much as $3.4 million off Romney's own tax bill in 2013.

For the *Journal* editors, not only is the Buffett Rule bad, but its portions are small. According to the Congress's Joint Economic Committee, the Buffett Rule would raise no more than $47 billion in new tax revenues over the next decade, assuming the Bush tax cuts for the rich are allowed to expire. But the combined effect of the Buffett Rule and allowing the Bush tax cuts for taxpayers with income above $250,000 to expire, including letting the top income tax bracket rise to 39.6%, as Obama has proposed, would raise more than $1 trillion additional tax revenues over the next decade. A study by the nonpartisan Tax Policy Center found that those two tax changes would take an additional 5.3% of income of the top 1%, pushing their effective federal tax rate (or how much of their income they paid in all federal taxes) up to 36.8%. That would be just about what the richest 1% paid out in federal taxes in 1979, before three decades of pro-rich tax cuts. They can well afford it. From 1979 to 2007, the after-tax income (corrected for inflation) of the top 1% nearly tripled, increasing 281%, while the income of those in the middle of the distribution of income increased just 35% over those years.

Taxing the Rich, French-Style

The top income-tax bracket in France is already 41%, higher than even the 39.6% rate Obama would impose. In addition, French investors pay a tax of 32.5% on their capital gains as opposed to the 15% rate in the United States. On the other hand, the Sarkozy government enacted a "tax shield" to protect rich taxpayers. This cap stipulates that no taxpayer will pay more than half their income in national taxes (the sum of what they pay in income taxes and other taxes). The tax shield has led to the unseemly practice of the French government writing out large refund check for income taxes withheld to some of its wealthy citizens at the same time it lays off public employees and its budget deficit soars.

Sarkozy's tax policies were a mixed bag. Early on in his term, his tax cuts, especially the tax shield, overwhelmingly benefited France's richest 10%, although he also eliminated taxes on overtime pay as a political response to the 35-hour workweek backed by the Socialist Party. After that, Sarkozy went along with imposing an additional 3% levy on taxpayers with a incomes greater than $650,000, and in the recent presidential campaign he pledged not to lower taxes for the rich. Earlier this year he promised, if reelected, to take the lead in pushing for a financial transaction tax (on the trades of stocks and other securities) that he argued would have those who caused the financial crisis "repay for the damage they have caused." That's a measure President Obama has never endorsed publicly. Finally, the conservative Sarkozy has endorsed these policies in a country with a tax code that has a wealth tax and a substantial estate tax and where the share of income of the richest 1% is but one half that in the United States.

In his debate with Sarkozy, Socialist Party presidential candidate François Hollande promised that under his administration, "the richest [w]ould be sending checks to the treasury" and not the other way around. Hollande intends to push up the top French income tax bracket to from 41% to 75% for income over one million euros (or about $1.3 million).

On other economic issues, Hollande would insist that the European Union adopt a "growth pact," which would include a financial transaction tax and government bonds jointly issued by the Eurozone countries to finance infrastructure projects. On top of that, the Hollande campaign championed financial reforms from banning stock options and management bonuses to separating investment and retail banks, two measures rejected by the Obama administration. We will now see just how much of his economic program Hollande can get enacted in France or across the Eurozone.

No Socialists Here

It is hardly surprising that Mitt Romney's campaign positions are far to the right of the mainstream of French political debate. Nor is it surprising, even though Republicans contend otherwise, that the Obama campaign's policies on financial reform and taxation are far from the socialist positions of Hollande. But when it comes to taxing the rich, the Obama campaign's policies are more conservative than the policies endorsed by France's center-right ex-president Sarkozy.

If the Obama campaign did no more than add a financial transaction tax, endorsed by Hollande and Sarkozy, to the Buffet Rule and the repeal the Bush tax cuts for the well-to-do, which it already advocates, those measures, if enacted, would counteract a good bit of today's gaping inequality and financial instability. And that surely would send the *Journal* editors scurrying off to their medicine cabinets in search of a bottle of Maalox, assuming there is something left in the bottle now that they have had to stomach the news of a "Socialist France." ❏

Sources: Thomas L. Hungerford, "An Analysis of the 'Buffet Rule'," , Congressional Research Service, Report for Congress, March 28, 2012; John McKinnon, "Top 1% Would See $90,000 Tax Rise, Report Says," *Wall Street Journal*, March 22, 2012; "Believe in America: Mitt Romney's Plan for Jobs and Economic Growth" (mittromney.com); "The President's Record on Taxes" (barackobama.com); "CTJ Analysis Shows Romney's Plan Would Cut His Own Taxes Almost in Half," Citizens for Tax Justice, January 19, 2012; "GOP Presidential Candidates' Tax Plans Favor Richest 1 Percent," Citizens for Tax Justice, January 6, 2012; "France: Sarkozy v Hollande on the economy," BBC News, May 2, 2012; Gabriele Parussini, "French Front-Runner Pledges 75% Tax Bracket," *Wall Street Journal*, February 29, 2012; "Hollande vows to push EU to ease debt policy," Associated Press, *Boston Globe*, April 26, 2012; Gabriele Parussini and William Horobin, "No Coup de Grace Emerges in Debate for French Leader," *Wall Street Journal*, May 3, 2012; and "Divided We Stand: Why Inequality Keeps Rising," Directorate for Employment, Labour and Social Affairs, OECD, December 2011.

Article 3.4

WHAT'S WRONG WITH A FLAT TAX?
BY ARTHUR MacEWAN
September/October 2012

> Dear Dr. Dollar:
> Today a minister asked me why a flat tax, where "everybody pays their fair share," is not the best idea. I did not have a short, convincing explanation. Can you help? —Arthur Milholland, Silver Springs, MD

Although flat tax proposals differ, they have one basic thing in common: they would all reduce the tax rates for people with high incomes. Thus they would either shift the tax burden to people with lower incomes or lead to a reduction in government services or both.

Currently, the federal personal income tax is quite progressive on paper and somewhat progressive in fact. A "progressive" income tax system is one where people with higher incomes pay a larger percentage of their income as taxes than do people with lower incomes. (A "regressive" system is one where people with lower incomes pay a higher share of their income as taxes; a "proportional" system is one where everyone pays the same proportion of their income as taxes. A flat tax and a proportional tax are the same.)

The justification for a progressive tax system is fairness: people with higher incomes have a greater ability to pay taxes and therefore should be subject to a higher tax rate. For example (to take an extreme case), a family with an income of $2 million can pay $200,000 in taxes more easily (i.e., with less impact on their circumstances) than a family with an income of $20,000 can pay $2,000 in taxes. Also, the principle of fairness suggests that high-income families should pay higher rates to support a system that provides so well for them. These concepts of fairness have been long-established in the U.S. personal income-tax system.

Even today, with rates for high-income people lowered from earlier years, the system still has a significant element of progressivity. For example, a family with taxable income of $20,000 would supposedly pay $2,150 (10.75%), while a family with taxable income of $1 million would supposedly pay $320,000 (32%). Of course many people, especially those with high-incomes, find various "loopholes," and do not end up paying as much in taxes as they otherwise would. Many loopholes are in the deductions that allow people to keep their taxable income—and therefore their taxes—down. At the same time, many people with low incomes have their taxes greatly reduced—sometimes resulting in payments *from* the government rather than tax payments *to* the government.

The Tax Policy Center has estimated that in 2010 people in the lowest 40% of the income distribution on average got money back from the government (because of the Earned Income Tax Credit and the Child Tax Credit), while people in the highest-income 20% on average paid taxes at a rate of 13.6%. People at the very top, the highest-income 1%, paid on average 18.6%.

Conservative ideologues like to jump on the fact that many low-income people pay no federal income tax at all. Yet federal income taxes are only part of the tax story. Low-income people still pay Social Security and Medicare taxes, sales taxes at the state level, and various other taxes. Overall, the U.S. tax system is hardly progressive at all, and may even be regressive.

Advocates of a flat tax claim it would be better to get rid of all the complications in the federal income tax—the adjustments, the credits, the deductions, etc.—and just charge everyone the same rate. Also, they argue that a flat tax would boost the economy because the current high rates on people with high incomes harm the incentive to invest and to work. Yet there is no way around the simple arithmetic: to lower the top rate and to obtain the same amount of revenue from a flat tax as from the current system, people below the top would have to have their tax rates increased. (While advocates of a flat tax generally reject the principles of fairness on which the progressivity of the U.S. tax code has long been based, it would be possible to introduce an element of progressivity into a flat tax by exempting all income below a certain level. Still, except for those people near the bottom, tax rates would have to be raised for most people—though not for those at the top.)

Furthermore, the claim that with a flat tax all the adjustments, credits, deductions, etc. would be eliminated is not credible. Indeed, since a flat tax would increase the after-tax income of those at the top, it would increase the amount of money they would have to buy influence to get their favorite "complications" reinstated (as if they didn't have enough influence already!). As to the argument that reducing the tax rate on people with high incomes would boost the economy, well, we have seen how well that has worked since the Bush tax cuts for the wealthy were put in place in 2001.

So a flat tax would be one more break for the rich, increasing their income on the backs of the great majority of the populace. Not fair at all. That's what's wrong with a flat tax. ❑

Article 3.5

THE "OBAMACARE" TAX HIKE AND REDISTRIBUTION
BY JOHN MILLER
May/June 2010

> OBAMACARE'S WORST TAX
> Opponents [of ObamaCare] should go down swinging, and that means exposing such policy debacles as President Obama's 11th-hour decision to apply the 2.9% Medicare payroll tax to "unearned income."
> That's what savings and investment income are called in Washington, and this destructive tax wasn't in either the House or Senate bills, though it may now become law with almost no scrutiny.
> For the first time, the combined employer-worker Medicare rate would be extended beyond wages to interest, dividends, capital gains, annuities, royalties and rents for individuals with adjusted gross income above $200,000 and joint filers over $250,000.
> Earning even a single dollar more than $200,000 in adjusted gross income will slap the tax on every dollar of a taxpayer's investment income, creating a huge marginal-rate spike that will most hurt middle-class earners, as opposed to the superrich.
> —*Wall Street Journal* editorial, March 17, 2010

There are plenty of legitimate complaints about "Obamacare," but its tax hike on unearned income is surely not one of them.

The new tax does take a bite out of the income of the rich. It adds 0.9 percentage points to the current hospital-insurance tax on most wage-income above $200,000. It also levies a 3.8% tax on investment income (e.g., dividends and capital gains). Only the richest 5% of taxpayers, with 2009 incomes above $231,179, will pay the new tax. And the richest 1%, with incomes in excess of $624,396 in 2009, will pay 85% of the tax hike.

That is a good thing, doing a bit to reduce the great income inequalities that have developed in recent decades. But the new tax hardly constitutes soaking the rich. Even after the tax, the rich will hand over a smaller portion of their income in federal income taxes than they did before three decades of pro-rich tax cutting. According to the Tax Policy Center, the new tax would push up the tax burden of the richest one percent by 1.3 percentage points, to 33.6% of their income, still well below their 37.0% effective tax rate in 1979. In any case, the rich can surely afford it. The incomes of the top 1% roughly doubled from 1979 to 2009 (after correcting for inflation).

Beyond that, the new tax was a compromise. It replaced the 5.4% tax on any income above $1 million in the House healthcare bill. That tax would have been paid exclusively by the richest 1%. So the *WSJ* editors should be happy that its friends got off as well as they did. Also the new tax postponed the start date for the excise tax on high-cost healthcare plans in the Senate bill, but didn't eliminate it. When it goes into effect in 2018, the tax on "Cadillac" healthcare plans will fall mostly on better-off households, but nonetheless will collect one-third of its taxes from individuals who currently have incomes between $50,000 and $100,000.

What really has the *WSJ* editors in a lather is levying hospital-insurance taxes on non-wage, or "unearned," income. They claim that middle-income taxpayers, not the super-rich, will ultimately bear the burden of the tax. Why? Because by taxing savings and investment income, the new tax will put a stopper in "trickle-down economic growth" (not that we have seen much trickling down over recent decades).

But economic evidence suggests that they are just plain wrong. First, unearned income is not the same thing as savings and investment. Take stock-trading, the source of most capital gains. From 1998 to 2007, $27 in stocks was traded on the U.S. exchanges for very dollar corporations invested in plant and equipment, according to a recent study by economists Robert Pollin and Dean Baker. The bulk of the gains of financial investors, therefore, comes from trading existing assets, not financing investment in new assets. Second, there is no solid evidence that lower taxes on unearned income do much to spur economic growth. Economist Joel Selmrod, director of the Office of Tax Policy Research at the University of Michigan, reports: " I know of no evidence that establishes a connection between prosperity and the rate we tax capital gains." Finally, the *WSJ* editors fail to take into account that the new tax hike will go to expand health insurance coverage for families with incomes below four times the poverty level.

Health-care reform surely could have done more to redistribute income and economic power, by squeezing out private insurers' massive overhead costs and profits, and relying on the House tax on income over $1 million. But even as is, Obamacare should do more than any legislation in many years to help generate the bottom-up economic growth that could replace the "trickle-down" economic growth that has rewarded so few with so much. ❑

Sources: David Leonhardt, "In Health Bill, Obama Attacks Wealth Inequality," *New York Times*, March 23, 2010; Robert Pollin and Dean Baker, "Public Investment, Industrial Policy, and U.S. Economic Renewal," Political Economy Research Institute, December 2009; Tax Policy Center, "The Medicare Tax as Proposed in H.R. 3590 (Senate Health Bill) and H.R 48723 (Reconciliation Act of 2010)," March 19, 2010.

Article 3.6

TAXES AND ECONOMIC GROWTH
BY ARTHUR MacEWAN
July/August 2011

> Dear Dr. Dollar:
> It seems to be an article of faith amongst the "serious people" that low taxes on dividends and capital gains will stimulate the economy. While most economists (I understand) pretty much agree that any reduction in taxes will have some positive effect on the economy by stimulating demand, is there any empirical evidence that these particular tax cuts help the economy by encouraging productive investment (as opposed to increasing demand)?
> —Stuart E. Baker, Tallahassee, Fla.

In 1993, when Clinton and the Democrats in Congress increased taxes, Republicans screamed that this action would stifle economic growth. The remaining seven years of the Clinton administration saw the economy grow at the relatively high rate of 4% per year.

After the 2001 recession, the Bush tax cuts were enacted as "The Economic Growth and Tax Relief Reconciliation Act of 2001." Then, between 2001 and 2007, the economy expanded at only 2.7% per year, the slowest post-recession recovery on record. So the general experience of the last two decades is hardly a brief for the positive impact of tax cuts on economic growth.

The Clinton tax increase mainly affected society's highest income groups. The Bush tax cuts were focused on the wealthy and included specific reductions in tax rates on capital gains and dividends. So these two cases provide some empirical evidence—albeit crude empirical evidence—that tax cuts on these categories of income do not generate more productive investment and more rapid economic growth, and that tax increases on these categories of income do not curtail investment and growth. (Moreover, no one should expect much impact on demand, one way or the other, from changes in taxes on high-income groups because their expenditures are not very sensitive to changes in their incomes.)

There is also more finely focused evidence that lowering taxes on capital gains and dividends does not have much, if any, positive impact on economic growth. For example, in a 2005 "Tax Facts" piece from the Tax Policy Center, economists Troy Kravitz and Leonard Burman point out that "Capital gains [tax] rates display no contemporaneous correlation with real GDP growth during the last 50 years."

One reason that preferential tax treatment for capital gains does not have much, if any, positive impact on productive investment is that this treatment creates strong incentives for the wealthy to invest in non-productive tax shelters. Burman, who is the author of *The Labyrinth of Capital Gains Tax Policy*, comments: "…the creative energy devoted to cooking up tax shelters could otherwise be channeled into something productive."

Also, when tax reductions for the rich result in an increase in the federal deficit, as is generally the case, and thus more government borrowing, the result could be higher interest rates. And the higher interest rates would tend to negate any positive impact of the tax reduction on investment.

A useful summary of the issues, including references to relevant studies, is the November 2005 report by Joel Friedman of the Center on Budget and Policy Priorities, "Dividend and Capital Gains Tax Cuts Unlikely to Yield Touted Economic Gains."

Those who support the reduction of taxes on the wealthy, capital gains taxes, and taxes on dividends do tout studies that tend to support their position. And there is no denying the fact that people's behavior is affected by tax policy, including the investment behavior of those with high levels of income. Yet the evidence we have does not support the argument that tax adjustments on capital gains and dividends are major factors affecting the course of the economy.

Many of these issues were examined by Joel Slemrod, professor of business economics and public policy, director of the Office of Tax Policy Research at the University of Michigan, and a leading expert on tax issues, in a 2003 interview in *Challenge* magazine. Slemrod summed his view thus: "there is no evidence that links aggregate economic performance to capital gains tax rates." ❑

Sources: Troy Kravitz and Leonard Burman, "Capital Gains Tax Rates, Stock Markets, and Growth," *Tax Notes*, November 7, 2005 (taxpolicycenter.org); Leonard Burman, "Under the Sheltering Lie," Tax Policy Center, December 20, 2005 (taxpolicycenter.org); Joel Friedman, "Dividend and Capital Gains Tax Cuts Unlikely to Yield Touted Economic Gains," Center on Budget and Policy Priorities, November 2005 (cbpp.org); "The Truth about Taxes and Economic Growth: Interview with Joel Semrod," *Challenge*, vol. 46, no. 1, January/February 2003, pp. 5–14 (challengemagazine.com).

Chapter 4

MONEY, BANKING, AND FINANCE

Article 4.1

ABOLISHING THE FED IS NO SOLUTION TO A REAL PROBLEM

BY ARTHUR MacEWAN
July/August 2012

> Dear Dr. Dollar:
> Is the Federal Reserve, the Fed, as important to the operation of the economy as it seems? How does it work? If it is so important, how can anyone take seriously politicians such as Ron Paul, who calls for the Fed's abolition?
> —*Tom Prebis, Cleveland, Ohio*

Yes, the Federal Reserve, the central banks of the United States, is a powerful institution, important to the operation of the economy. By regulating the supply of money and influencing (if not fully determining) interest rates, the Fed has a major impact on the overall level of production, employment, and inflation. Also, the Fed has a large role (along with some other agencies) in regulating the operations of banks.

Yet the Fed is structured in a very undemocratic way. Although it derives its authority from Congress, its actions do not have to be approved by Congress, the president or any other segment of the government. Its funding is not set by Congress, and the members of its Board of Governors (the controlling group), though appointed by the president and approved by Congress, have terms that span multiple presidential and congressional terms. Also, while the Fed regulates the banks, bankers have a special role in the operation of the Fed. Some seats on the boards of directors of the twelve regional branches are reserved for bankers, giving them formal capacity to influence the Fed's policies, including its regulation of the banks.

Not surprisingly, the Fed has exercised its regulation of the banks with "a light hand." And its overall regulation of the economy—through affecting the money supply and interest rates—has often sacrificed employment to maintain the profitability of business in general and the banks in particular.

The Banks' Man at the Fed

To get some useful insight on the undemocratic and pro-business bias of the Fed, consider:

Jaimie Dimon, the head of JPMorgan Chase, is a member of the Board of Directors of the Federal Reserve Bank of New York. Cheek by jowl with Wall Street, the N.Y. Fed plays a major role in the dealings between the Fed and the large private banks. As the financial meltdown became apparent in 2008, the N.Y. Fed was fully involved in the actions that the Fed and the Treasury took in their efforts to manage the crisis.

Dimon's bank is one of the country's largest, with $19 billion in after-tax profits in 2011. In 2008, the bank received $25 billion in the government's bank bailout. Perhaps the bailout saved the economy from a more severe economic crisis, but it also saved the bankers—Dimon and the others—along with their absurd salaries. Other means of saving the system—such as temporary nationalization of the big banks (to say nothing of a permanent nationalization)—were never on the Fed's agenda.

Dimon has become one of the most vociferous and aggressive opponents of bank regulation. In 2012, he has frequently been in the news because his bank experienced a huge loss—at least $3 billion and perhaps as much as $9 billion—in a complex and risky operation, exactly the kind of banking activity that regulation is supposed to prevent, and exactly the kind of activity that could generate another financial crisis. Dimon has not moderated his opposition to regulation.

Does anyone see anything wrong here? Does the metaphor "fox guarding the henhouse" seem appropriate?

It is only a slight simplification to say that the Fed is run by and for the country's banks. If one believes that the interests of the banks are the same as the interests of the rest of us, no problem. This is the line that Dimon peddles, claiming that the banks play a crucial role in allocating funds to the most productive activity, supporting economic growth and jobs. More regulation, he claims, would prevent banks from doing this good work. In the wake of the financial crisis, it is impressive that anyone can spew such nonsense with a straight face.

Regulating the Economy

The Fed plays its role of affecting the money supply and interest rates by, in part, loaning money to the banks and then regulating the extent to which the banks can use this money to make loans to the businesses and public. More loans means more money in circulation; more money in circulation tends to reduce interest rates (i.e., the price of money), which tends to induce economic expansion. Also, in regulating the banks' activities, the Fed is supposed to maintain economic stability—preventing the banks from undertaking excessively risky activities, which, by endangering the banks themselves, would undermine the operation of the whole economy.

In the period leading up to the financial crisis that emerged in 2007-2008, the Fed certainly operated "with a light hand" in regulating the banks. Indeed, Fed Chairman Ben Bernanke took a "what, me worry?" approach, denying the existence of the housing bubble and turning a blind eye to the signs of impending crisis.

Having failed to use its power to prevent the financial crisis, the Fed has in subsequent years attempted to push economic growth by acting to increase the money supply and to keep interest rates low. Its success in this direction has been limited partly because it has not pushed as hard as it could. Right-wing congressmen and others of their ilk have accused the Fed of encouraging inflation, and perhaps Bernanke and others on the Fed's Board of Governors share this inflation fear. In earlier periods, the Fed has often given attention to maintaining low inflation at the expense of higher unemployment.

The Fed's lack of success in promoting economic growth in the current period also results from the fact that private non-financial firms have been reluctant to make new investments, even with low interest rates. So instead of making new loans for productive, job-generating investment, banks have used the low-cost money from the Fed for their own speculative activity—the sort of activity that led to JPMorgan Chase's multi-billion dollar loss, but which can also make lots of money for the banks.

The Appeal of "End the Fed"

Given the Fed's history of frequently sacrificing employment in the name of preventing inflation, its support of banks and the role of bankers in affecting its operations, its failure to prevent the recent financial crisis, its role in bailing out the banks and the bankers, and its failure to act strongly enough in the current period, there is a good deal of animosity towards the country's central bank. Ron Paul and others have been able to use this popular animosity to promote a broader agenda of reducing government regulation of the economy. Their call to "end the Fed" is one more effort to push the idea that the economy works best when the government works least. One would think that this is a pretty hard line to swallow in light of recent experience, when the "light hand" of government regulation was a key element in generating our current economic malaise. Yet it seems to have appeal.

In advocating an end to the Fed, Paul has called for a return to the gold standard as a means to regulate the money supply without government involvement. Ironically, at the center of Paul's right-wing attack on the Fed has been the claim that it has debased our currency and is generating inflation; the gold standard would supposedly prevent this debasement. The argument is ironic because reality has often been the opposite of Paul's claim—at many times in its history Fed policies have kept inflation in check but generated high unemployment, which tends to keep wages down.

In any case, the problem with the Fed is not the existence of a government authority that regulates the country's money. Before the Fed started operating in 1914, economic crises had been at least as frequent and severe as in later years. The gold standard (which the U.S. abandoned in steps, especially in the 1930s and ultimately in 1971) certainly did not provide stability and general economic well-being. The problem is the *nature* of the regulatory authority, run as it is in the interests of the banks and bankers, in particular, and of business, in general. The right's effort to "end the Fed," however, would likely throw us into an era of even greater economic instability, having us jump out of the frying pan and into the fire.

What to Do?

So what should be done about the Fed? Unfortunately, the Fed is part of the general economic and political problems of the country, and we should not expect to have a central bank that serves people's real needs until we have a more democratic society, a society in which money does not dominate politics and in which economic policy is not organized around the idea that maintaining profits is always the first priority.

Still, doing something about the Fed could be one step in doing something about those general problems. To begin a process of change, Dimon and other bankers should be removed from their positions of authority within the Fed. The removal of bankers from their positions of special influence would need to be followed by larger changes in the way members of the boards of directors of the regional Federal Reserve banks are chosen, and ultimately also the way members of the Board of Governors of the Fed are selected. Also, the Fed could be given a stronger mandate to act in ways that would reduce unemployment. Most generally, the goal should be to subject the Fed to democratic control.

At the end of the day, changing the Fed—changing how the U.S. economy is controlled—is a part of the larger struggle to change power in the United States so that it is in the hands of most people instead of the very few. ❑

Article 4.2

HOW HAVE BANKS MANAGED TO REPAY THE BAILOUT?

BY ARTHUR MacEWAN
May/June 2012

Dear Dr. Dollar:
Many of the banks that were bailed out by the Bush and Obama administrations—to the tune of some trillions of dollars (no one seems to know exactly how much)—have, according to news reports, already paid back the huge sums of money they were loaned to avoid bankruptcy. How is this possible if, as the news reports also tell us, the banks have been extremely reluctant to loan money in these recessionary times? Since banks only make money by making loans, how were they able to pay off their huge debts to the U.S. Treasury in so short a period of time?
—*Clifford Anderson, Sacramento, Calif.*

Actually, banks make money in lots of ways, and for the big banks, making loans is not the main way that they make money.

Which raises the question: What is a bank? Consider the infamous Wall Street firm of Goldman Sachs, generally viewed as a bank and a recipient of substantial bailout funds from the federal government. In 2010, Goldman Sachs had revenues of $39.2 billion, but a tiny fraction of this was interest income from loans. The largest share of its revenues, $21.8 billion, came from "Institutional Client Services," fees for handling financial transactions for institutional clients (other firms, investment funds, and governments). Activity involving "Investment and Lending" provided Goldman with $7.5 billion, but this does not mean making new loans; it means mainly buying and selling existing loans—for example, those packages of mortgages, called "collateralized debt obligations," which were so important in the financial meltdown of 2008.

Another example is provided by JPMorgan Chase, which differs from Goldman Sachs in that its operations include a large amount of what we usually view as banking—that is, commercial banking operations of holding checking and savings deposits and making loans to individuals and businesses. Still, in 2010 slightly more than half of the firm's $102.7 billion revenue was non-interest revenue. (And much of the interest revenue, we may assume, was not from making new loans.) The largest component of JPMorgan Chase's 2010 non-interest revenue, $13.5 billion, is listed in its annual report as "Asset management, administration and commissions."

In 2010, Goldman reported $8.3 billion in after-tax profits and JPMorgan Chase reported $17.4 billion. So they had a good deal of money with which to reward their stockholders, pay something back to the U.S. Treasury, and provide bonuses to executives—though bonuses would come as expenses, not deductions from profits. (It appears that these firms and large banks generally did not do so well in 2011, but final figures are not yet available).

There is a good deal of controversy over how much money was actually provided to the banks and other financial firms. So it is difficult to figure out how much has been paid back. In a December 6, 2011, letter to Congress, Ben Bernanke, chairman of the Federal Reserve Bank, wrote:

> … one article asserted that the Federal Reserve lent or guaranteed more than $7.7 trillion during the financial crisis. Others have estimated the amounts to be $16 trillion or even $24 trillion. All of these numbers are wildly inaccurate. As disclosed on the Federal Reserve's balance sheet, published weekly and audited annually by independent auditors, total credit outstanding under the liquidity programs was never more than about $1.5 trillion; that was the peak reached in December 2008.

There is not necessarily a conflict between Bernanke's $1.5 trillion and the larger estimates. If the Fed provided $1 trillion in ten other months—money which was paid back each month— and $1.5 trillion in December 2008, the total provision of funds would be $11.5 trillion, but the peak, as Bernanke says, would still be $1.5 trillion.

Also, in what is called "quantitative easing," the Fed bought a large amount of long-term securities form the banks, which put money into the banks' hands—another way of keeping them afloat, but not through providing loans to the banks.

How does one count all this? It all depends on how you want to spin it.

However, if Bernanke's claim is correct, this means that, while a lot more than $1.5 billion was provided to the banks, the great majority of it was short term and was paid back—so the peak never rose above that $1.5 trillion.

The bottom line? The Fed provided several trillion dollars to the banks at very low interest rates. These funds allowed many banks, most of the big ones in particular, to stay in operation, make lots of money by pursing their investment strategies (but not much by making new loans), and pay back a large share of what they borrowed from the Fed.

Did this save us from an even worse financial crisis? Probably yes. Were there other ways to do it that would have bailed out the banks but not the bankers who led us into this crisis? Other ways that would have put conditions on the banks, preventing them from enriching their executives and leading us towards another crisis? Probably yes again. ❏

Article 4.3

THE JOBS ACT AND GREEN SLIME
In place of a real jobs bill, an invitation to fraud.

BY WILLIAM K. BLACK
May/June 2012

We learned recently about the secret adulteration of our hamburgers with "pink slime." Agribusiness companies created pink slime from ultra-fatty beef tissue that was more likely to harbor salmonella and e. coli. They processed it with ammonia (Mr. Clean) in a partially successful effort to reduce the risk of infecting the consumer. Pink slime, unbeknownst to the public, comprised up to 15% of our hamburgers.

The financial sector is far worse. Pink slime represented a relatively small portion of each burger and generally did not make the consumer sick. In the financial sector, "green slime"—slime with the color of money—came to dominate entire sectors, and it always caused severe damage. "Liar's loans," made without the lender verifying the borrower's actual income, were 90% fraudulent. Collateralized debt obligations (CDOs), securities giving their owners claim to a part of debtors' interest payments, were typically composed overwhelmingly of fraudulent liar's loans. It was lenders who overwhelmingly put the lies in liar's loans, issuing loans that were nothing more than "green slime" and then turning around and selling them as Grade A Prime cuts.

The production of "green slime" has thrived—indeed, can only exist—in the shadows of an unregulated financial system. The United States' deregulated and fraud-friendly "shadow banking" system produced over a trillion dollars in green slime and set off a global depression. Only four years later, the Jumpstart Our Business Startups Act (JOBS Act) seeks to create a shadow stock (equity) system where the green slime can multiply once more.

The JOBS Act purports to create jobs by giving entrepreneurs easier access to start-up capital. But the new law does so by eliminating protections for investors. It extends, from two years to five, the amount of time that a new public company has before it is subject to key regulations and disclosure requirements. But such regulations were put in place to prevent fraud and protect investors. So in place of a real jobs bill, we have an invitation to fraud. The JOBS Act reduces transparency, which makes fraud harder to spot, and directly encourages fraud by exempting smaller companies from requirements to ensure that their internal controls work and reducing the requirement for audited financial statements. It allows frauds to target the most vulnerable potential investors by allowing stock issuers to raise money through "pre-prospectus" presentations. These glorified commercials would deliberately target the least financially sophisticated investors and allow the sale of securities to be made without providing even the most unsophisticated investors of modest wealth with the information essential to make a prudent investment decision. Your grandmother and your kids will be leading targets of the frauds who are certain to exploit the anti-regulatory provisions of the JOBS Act.

For four years of severe crisis and mass unemployment, Congress has failed to do anything constructive about creating jobs. Now, the Obama administration and members of Congress are trumpeting the JOBS Act as a way to promote small business and spur job creation. The bill, however, is a sham. For any "jobs" bill to pass, it has to be a sham, because the Republican members of Congress are universally opposed to any real bill to spur job creation. They have locked themselves into absolute opposition to any further stimulus spending or direct job creation by the federal government, and are celebrating vast government job destruction at the state and local level.

Cynical incumbents of both parties realized that there was one way to build a bipartisan consensus for something that could be labeled a "jobs bill." Congressional Republicans are universally in favor of deregulation. Their fondest goal in the financial sphere is to gut the Sarbanes-Oxley Act, the 2002 financial regulation law that, in the wake of Enron other similar fraud scandals, overwhelmingly passed both houses of Congress and was signed into law by George W. Bush. If enough Democrats joined the Republicans on deregulation, and if the Democrats were willing to call the resulting atrocity a "jobs" bill, then the bill was certain to pass with strong majorities in both houses.

To its undying shame (if it were capable of such), the Obama administration pushed this cynical, sham deal through its "competitiveness" council. This is a nonpartisan group composed overwhelmingly of business executives who share one common desire—to gut regulation faster and further than other countries, to "win" the "race to the bottom." The token labor representative on the council, AFL-CIO President Richard Trumka, denounced the JOBS Act for what it is: "The bill …," he argued, "will do nothing to create good jobs and stabilize the U.S. economy. Instead, it will deregulate Wall Street—voiding investor protections put in place after Enron and the 2008 financial crisis to protect the retirement savings of America's workers from fraud and other risks." The anti-fraud community—the nation's top criminologists studying financial fraud, the Securities and Exchange Commission, the Commodities Futures Trade Commission, the state securities supervisors, and accountants—likewise, all opposed the JOBS Act. That is why the administration and the congressional leaders refused to hold real hearings on the bill.

President Obama's signing ceremony speech on behalf of the Act is eerily reminiscent of his predecessors' statements when they signed the deregulation laws that have created one crisis after another. In particular, he claimed that modern times require us to deregulate: "Right now, you can only turn to a limited group of investors—including banks and wealthy individuals—to get funding. Laws that are nearly eight decades old make it impossible for others to invest. But a lot has changed in 80 years, and it's time our laws did as well." This rhetoric channels the same claims by supporters of the Clinton-era financial deregulation. The titles of both of the Clinton-era deregulation laws include this modernization motif: the Commodities Futures Modernization Act (which deliberately created a regulatory black hole for credit default swaps (CDS) that Enron and AIG promptly exploited) and the Financial Services Modernization Act of 1999 (which repealed the 1933 Glass-Steagall Act's prohibition on commercial banks' participation in risky stock speculation).

The claim that, because we live in modern times, we no longer need financial regulation to prevent fraud is absurd on its face. If anyone made that claim in the context of "street" crime—we no longer need police because we are modern—we would know that they were delusional. There is nothing "modern" about deregulating the financial sector and allowing elite frauds to commit their crimes with impunity. We just ran this experiment in the shadow banking system and produced an epidemic of green slime that brought the global financial system to the brink of catastrophe. It was saved only by government intervention. Now, the Obama administration and Congress are creating a similar fraud-friendly (or "criminogenic") environment by allowing those issuing equities to operate in the shadows.

For millennia, the normal rules typically did not apply to elites—clan leaders and nobles. They often used that impunity to loot the public in order to enrich themselves and their kin. Allowing elites to act in a rules-free environment is actually an antiquated, discredited idea that always leads to disaster. The modern, effective approach that America, at its best, champions is the exact opposite—that no person is "above the law." ❑

Sources: CNN Money, "JOBS Act Opens Fundraising Doors for Small Firms," April 6, 2012 (cnn.com); "Small Biz Jobs Act Is a Bipartisan Bridge Too Far," Bloomberg News, March 18, 2012 (bloomberg.com); "Statement by AFL-CIO President Richard Trumka on So-called 'JOBS Act," March 22, 2012 (aflcio.org); "Remarks by the President at JOBS Act Bill Signing," April 5, 2012 (whitehouse.gov).

Article 4.4

PRIVATE EQUITY MOGULS AND THE COMMON GOOD
Can Wall Street corporate raiders cure creaking capitalism?

BY JOHN MILLER
July/August 2012

> [In May], the Obama administration unveiled an attack ad against Mitt Romney's old private equity firm, Bain Capital.... But the larger argument is about private equity itself, and about the changes private equity firms and other financiers have instigated across society. Over the past several decades, these firms have scoured America looking for underperforming companies. Then they acquire them and try to force them to get better.
>
> Most of the time they succeed. Research from around the world clearly confirms that companies that have been acquired by private equity firms are more productive than comparable firms.... [And] the overall effect on employment is modest.... Private equity firms are not lovable, but they forced a renaissance that revived American capitalism.
>
> —"How Change Happens," by David Brooks, *New York Times*, May 21, 2012

The Obama campaign may have launched an attack against Romney's record at Bain Capital, but Vice President Biden and President Obama have been careful not to challenge the legitimacy of the private equity (PE) business or to take on Brooks' larger argument that the PE business has been good for the U.S. economy, not just its owners.

But is the private equity business legitimate? Do private equity moguls create wealth, or do they merely transfer wealth to the richest of the richest 1% by sucking dry the companies they take over? And has creating wealth for themselves and their investor revived American capitalism as Brooks maintains?

Before we can assess the record of these PE firms, we need to look more closely at how they go about making their money.

Inside Private Equity

Private equity is the new name for what used to be called "leveraged buyout" firms. PE firms are private partnerships that raise money from large investors, including pension funds, other investment funds, and wealthy individuals.

PE firms then use that money to purchase other companies, typically with the intention of selling them off within three to five years. That's the "buyout" part of a leverage buyout. But PE firms also borrow money, usually lots of it, from investment banks to pay for the companies they buy up. (The investment banks in turn package the loans into commercial mortgage-backed securities and sell them to other institutions.) PE firms' extensive reliance on debt is the "leveraged" part of the buyout.

But taking out so much debt comes with a twist. PE firms make the companies they take over responsible for repaying the loans. That way, the PE firm and the investors in its funds risk only the money they put up as a down payment.

As the defenders of private equity tell the story, PE firms acquire underperforming firms and make them more efficient by jettisoning a company's bad investments, cutting costs, and pushing the company into more productive investments. PE moguls, including Romney, like to think of themselves as engaged in an act of "creative destruction," the phrase famed Austrian-born Harvard economist Joseph Schumpeter used for breaking the eggs necessary to make the omelet of innovation.

The result, when it works, is a more valuable company. The PE firm then sells the company back to the public, paying off its debt and making a profit. In addition to the profits from selling off a company, the PE firm partners collect a 2% to 3% management fee paid to the investors in the fund, as well as 20% of any returns to the limited investors that exceeded an agreed upon standard, usually about 7% or 8% a year.

This sounds plausible. But in fact, the story of Wall Street takeover artists whipping self-indulgent Main Street managers into shape to the benefit of all of us has some awfully big holes in it.

Holes in the PE Story

To begin with, it is not at all clear that PE firms take over "underperforming corporations." For instance, average employment growth was actually stronger in businesses acquired by private equity in the five-year period prior to a buyout than in similar businesses, according to the very study that Brooks uses to argue that the effects on these takeovers on employment is modest. Similarly, economists Bo Becker and Joshua Pollet found that more profitable public firms are more likely to be taken over than less profitable public firms.

Nor is it clear that a PE takeover boosts the productivity of the companies PE firms acquire in a sustained way. Several studies confirm that labor productivity of companies after they have been taken over by PE firms is higher than in other similar companies. Also these companies under PE management are much more likely to close divisions of their business with lower productivity than were similar companies not taken over. But as economists Eileen Appelbaum and Rosemary Batt rightly maintain in their thoroughgoing primer on PE firms, it is not possible in these studies to distinguish productivity increases due to greater investments in employee skills and new technology from those due to management's intensification of work for fear of their company being downsized or closed.

Beyond that, these findings pertain to the time period when the target firms are managed by the PE firm, and have not assessed if those productivity gains are sustained after the firms are sold off.

There are real reasons to doubt that is the case. With a heavy debt burden and pressure from their PE owners to boost profits in the near term, managers have every incentive to downsize jobs and to forego investments in new technology and employee skills. Two well-known studies of U.S. leveraged buyouts during the 1980s, one conducted by economists at the Brookings Institution and another by economists at the National Science Foundation, found that research and development expenditures in post-takeover corporations declined at the same time as research and development expenditures in other large corporations increased. That pattern surely seems to be at odds with a management strategy that would boost productivity for the long haul.

But the issue that most of us care about is whether PE firms create or destroy jobs. While PE firms surely create some jobs and destroy others, the net effect of PE takeovers in job destruction is hardly modest, as Brooks claims in his column.

Brooks bases this claim on the widely cited large-scale study conducted by Steven J. Davis and four other economists. Their study, "Private Equity and Employment," surveyed private-equity transactions between 1980 and 2005. They conclude that, "employment shrinks by less than 1 percent at target firms relative to controls [comparable firms not taken over] in the first two years after private equity buyouts."

But a closer look at the study suggests that the effect of PE takeovers on employment is far less benign than what Brooks and even Davis and his co-authors maintain.

For instance, their study also reports a "clear pattern of slower growth at [private equity] targets post buyout"—a difference of 3.2% of employment in the first two years post-buyout and 6.4% over five years. In the words of *BusinessWeek* reporter Peter Coy, that means "having your company acquired by a private equity firm is like living through a national recession."

So how do Davis and company nonetheless reach the conclusion that employment growth at private equity-owned firms is only slightly slower than at other similar companies? They include in their jobs total not only the net effect of employees hired and fired by the private equity owned company, but also add in any employees in businesses that the company acquired while the PE firm owned it.

Counting jobs created by PE investment in new ventures is reasonable enough. But the authors of the paper also add in the jobs in already-established companies the PE firm acquires. Those jobs might be new to the PE firm, but, as economists Appelbaum and Batt emphasize, they are not new jobs for the economy, and should not be included in any accurate tally of the jobs created by PE takeovers.

Despite their dubious employment record, PE partners benefit from the "carried interest" tax loophole, which will cost the federal government $13.5 billion in tax revenues over the next ten years, according to Obama administration estimates. This provision allows private equity capital managers (and hedge fund and other financial managers as well) to have their fees and share of profits treated as capital gains and therefore taxed at the 15% marginal tax rate, versus the 35% top tax bracket for wage and salary income.

But unlike the profits of other investors, carried interest is profit paid to PE partners for putting other people, not their own money, at risk. In addition, much of the earnings of PE firms, the majority of their earnings according to some studies, come from their management fees, paid to them by investors regardless of performance. And to its credit, the Obama administration has proposed repealing the carried interest tax loophole.

PE vs. the Public Interest

The truth is that the record of private equity managers is long on cost cutting, amassing debt, and destroying jobs as they enrich themselves, and short on creating jobs, fostering innovation for over the long haul, and paying taxes on the millions they accumulate.

If being good for the economy and in that way serving the common interest is what makes a business legitimate, then not just Romney's Bain Capital but the PE business as a whole has failed the test. ❑

Sources: Eileen Appelbaum and Rosemary Batt, "A Primer on Private Equity at Work Management, Employment, and Sustainability," Center for Economic and Policy Research, February 2012; Orlando Segura, Jr., "Private Equity Exposed," *Dollars & Sense*, July/August 2008; "Private Equity: Fact, Fiction and What Lies in Between," Knowledge@Wharton, February 08, 2012; Peter Coy, "Private Equity: Hero or Villain?" *Bloomberg BusinessWeek*, January 11, 2012; Steven J. Davis et al., "Private Equity and Employment," National Bureau of Economic Research, September 2011; "Private equity under scrutiny: Bain or blessing?" *The Economist* January 28, 2012; John Gilligan and Mike Wright, Private Equity Demystified: An Explanatory Guide, 2nd edition, ICAEW, April 2010; Bo Becker and Joshua Pollet, "The Decision to Go Private," working paper for the Goizueta Business School, Emory University, June 2008; James Crotty and Don Goldstein, "Do U.S. Financial Markets Allocate Credit Efficiently? The Case of Corporate Restructuring in the 1980s," Working Group on Monetary and Financial Restructuring, Economic Policy Institute, December 1992.

Article 4.5

IS CHINA'S CURRENCY MANIPULATION HURTING THE U.S.?

BY ARTHUR MacEWAN
November/December 2010

Dear Dr. Dollar:
Is it true that China has been harming the U.S. economy by keeping its currency "undervalued"? Shouldn't the U.S. government do something about this situation? —*Jenny Boyd, Edmond, W.Va.*

The Chinese government, operating through the Chinese central bank, does keep its currency unit—the yuan—cheap relative to the dollar. This means that goods imported *from* China cost less (in terms of dollars) than they would otherwise, while U.S. exports *to* China cost more (in terms of yuan). So we in the United States buy a lot of Chinese-made goods and the Chinese don't buy much from us. In the 2007 to 2009 period, the United States purchased $253 billion more in goods annually from China than it sold to China.

This looks bad for U.S workers. For example, when money gets spent in the United States, much of it is spent on Chinese-made goods, and fewer jobs are then created in the United States. So the Chinese government's currency policy is at least partly to blame for our employment woes. Reacting to this situation, many people are calling for the U.S. government to do something to get the Chinese government to change its policy.

But things are not so simple.

First of all, there is an additional reason for the low cost of Chinese goods—low Chinese wages. The Chinese government's policy of repressing labor probably accounts for the low cost of Chinese goods at least as much as does its currency policy. Moreover, there is a lot more going on in the global economy. Both currency problems and job losses involve much more than Chinese government actions—though China provides a convenient target for ire.

And the currency story itself is complex. In order to keep the value of its currency low relative to the dollar, the Chinese government increases the supply of yuan, uses these yuan to buy dollars, then uses the dollars to buy U.S. securities, largely government bonds but also private securities. In early 2009, China held $764 billion in U.S. Treasury securities, making it the largest foreign holder of U.S. government debt. By buying U.S. government bonds, the Chinese have been financing the federal deficit. More generally, by supplying funds to the United States, the Chinese government has been keeping interest rates low in this country.

If the Chinese were to act differently, allowing the value of their currency to rise relative to the dollar, both the cost of capital and the prices of the many goods imported from China would rise. The rising cost of capital would probably not be a serious problem, as the Federal Reserve could take counteraction to keep interest rates low. So, an increase in the value of the yuan would net the United States some jobs, but also raise some prices for U.S. consumers.

It is pretty clear that right now what the United States needs is jobs. Moreover, low-cost Chinese goods have contributed to the declining role of manufacturing in the United States, a phenomenon that both weakens important segments of organized labor and threatens to inhibit technological progress, which has often been centered in manufacturing or based on applications in manufacturing (e.g., robotics).

So why doesn't the U.S. government place more pressure on China to raise the value of the yuan? Part of the reason may lie in concern about losing Chinese financing of the U.S. federal deficit. For several years the two governments have been co-dependent: The U.S. government gets financing for its deficits, and the Chinese government gains by maintaining an undervalued currency. Not an easy relationship to change.

Probably more important, however, many large and politically powerful U.S.-based firms depend directly on the low-cost goods imported from China. Wal-mart and Target, as any shopper knows, are filled with Chinese-made goods. Then there are the less visible products from China, including a power device that goes into the Microsoft Xbox, computer keyboards for Dell, and many other goods for many other U.S. corporations. If the yuan's value rose and these firms had to pay more dollars to buy these items, they could probably not pass all the increase on to consumers and their profits would suffer.

Still, in spite of the interests of these firms, the U.S. government may take some action, either by pressing harder for China to let the value of the yuan rise relative to the dollar or by placing some restrictions on imports from China. But don't expect too big a change. ❑

Article 4.6

LIBOR LIABILITY
A scandal unfolds that has already affected millions of people.

BY MAX FRAAD WOLFF
July/August 2012

The summer of 2012 is heating up for leading financial firms. HSBC is poised to settle money-laundering charges. JPMorgan is struggling to put billions of bad trade losses behind it. Wells Fargo is settling on mortgage discrimination charges. And now, a growing scandal surrounding leading banks' alleged manipulation of key reference interest rates has claimed large fines, senior executives' careers, and the attention of both regulators and the public.

The London InterBank Offered Rates, known as "Libor," are the interest rates at which banks borrow funds from each other. Each day, the British Bankers' Association (BBA) compiles and reports 150 Libor rates (for ten different currencies and fifteen different "maturities," or borrowing terms) with the business-data provider Thomson Reuters. Libor rates are the most widely cited and influential rates for setting adjustable interest rates on trillions of dollars in loans and derivative contracts.

Since 1986, the BBA has arranged to have between eight and sixteen leading banks report the interest rates at which they can borrow in different currencies. Different committees comprised of multiple leading banks set the rates. The names under investigation read like a roll call of banks that received trillions in assistance from governments during the financial crisis.

Libor rates are set in a self-regulatory process arranged, executed, and policed by private entities (the member banks, the BBA, and Thompson Reuters). Thus, Libor reports are a service by and for financial firms. However, they have impact across the global economy: Libor rates are seen as a measure of bank health and financial-market health, and they affect values and interest rates of hundreds of trillions of dollars worth of financial products and loans—including credit cards, student loans, adjustable-rate mortgage, and small-business loans. When Libor rates rise, individuals, governments, and firms pay more to borrow. When rates fall, they pay less.

Libor rates are created by collecting and averaging individual bank rates from multiple institutions, so each individual bank has only a marginal influence on reported rates. However, investigators have found allegations of traders working to coordinate misreporting and fix interest rates. Emails and calls between traders suggest that some worked to guide reported rates up or down across several years. Although regulators in the United States, the UK, and beyond have long been aware of irregularities in Libor rate reporting, authorities have been slow to take action, and the public is still waiting for details. Reports that regulators encouraged underreporting Libor rates to give an appearance of calm and stability in interbank lending markets during the crisis do not boost public confidence in financial markets.

As of now, authorities in the U.S. and British governments as well as across Asia and Europe are investigating the scandal. Several jurisdictions will bring charges and receive settlements in the many millions of dollars. Barclays has already paid over $450 million and replaced its three most senior executives, and other involved banks are scrambling to reach settlements and avoid serious penalties.

But the Libor scandal is a developing story, with much more still to be told. It appears that separately and together, many of the world's leading banks provided inaccurate and misleading information, possibly in illegal concert, and reported incorrect rates. Sometimes this was done to affect the prices of financial products and make ill-gotten gains. On other occasions, particularly in the depths of the financial crisis 2008-2009, false rates were reported to hide the high rates and low trust among banks.

Since rates were both under- and over-reported, it's difficult to determine the net effect of misreporting. Because Libor literally sets interest rate benchmarks, we can't be sure what the rates would have been without the tampering. But it's clear that regulators, clients, states, cities, and citizens were misled, affecting millions of people and trillions of dollars.

As clients sue and regulators investigate, investor confidence will continue to suffer. The scandal couldn't have come at a worse time for the global economy. Whatever your views on finance and your interest level in the Libor scandal, if you borrow or invest money, this saga has been a part of your life for at least four years. Libor rate-fixing will be added to the swirl of public anger about mortgage securities, ratings agencies, bad trades, and predatory lending. Accumulating incidents suggest our flawed regulatory framework and dependence on large financial institutions remain painful vulnerabilities in the global economic system. ❑

Chapter 5

SOCIAL POLICY

Article 5.1

UNIVERSAL HEALTH CARE: CAN WE AFFORD ANYTHING LESS?

Why only a single-payer system can solve America's health-care mess.

BY GERALD FRIEDMAN
July/August 2011

America's broken health-care system suffers from what appear to be two separate problems. From the right, a chorus warns of the dangers of rising costs; we on the left focus on the growing number of people going without health care because they lack adequate insurance. This division of labor allows the right to dismiss attempts to extend coverage while crying crocodile tears for the 40 million uninsured. But the division between problem of cost and the problem of coverage is misguided. It is founded on the assumption, common among neoclassical economists, that the current market system is efficient. Instead, however, the current system is inherently inefficient; it is the very source of the rising cost pressures. In fact, the only way we can control health-care costs and avoid fiscal and economic catastrophe is to establish a single-payer system with universal coverage.

The rising cost of health care threatens the U.S. economy. For decades, the cost of health insurance has been rising at over twice the general rate of inflation; the share of American income going to pay for health care has more than doubled since 1970 from 7% to 17%. By driving up costs for employees, retirees, the needy, the young, and the old, rising health-care costs have become a major problem for governments at every level. Health costs are squeezing public spending needed for education and infrastructure. Rising costs threaten all Americans by squeezing the income available for other activities. Indeed, if current trends continued, the entire economy would be absorbed by health care by the 2050s.

Conservatives argue that providing universal coverage would bring this fiscal Armageddon on even sooner by increasing the number of people receiving care. Following this logic, their policy has been to restrict access to health care by raising insurance deductibles, copayments, and cost sharing and by reducing access to insurance. Even before the Great Recession, growing numbers of American adults were uninsured or underinsured. Between 2003 and 2007, the share of non-elderly adults without adequate health insurance rose from 35% to 42%, reaching 75 million. This number has grown substantially since then, with the recession reducing employment and with the continued decline in employer-provided health insurance. Content to believe that our current health-care system is efficient, conservatives assume that costs would have risen more had these millions not lost access, and likewise believe that extending health-insurance coverage to tens of millions using a plan like the Affordable Care Act would drive up costs even further. Attacks on employee health insurance and on Medicare and Medicaid come from this same logic—the idea that the only way to control health-care costs is to reduce the number of people with access to health care. If we do not find a way to control costs by increasing access, there will be more proposals like that of Rep. Paul Ryan (R-Wisc.) and the Republicans in the House of Representatives to slash Medicaid and abolish Medicare.

The Problem of Cost in a Private, For-Profit Health Insurance System

If health insurance were like other commodities, like shoes or bow ties, then reducing access might lower costs by reducing demands on suppliers for time and materials. But health care is different because so much of the cost of providing it is in the administration of the payment system rather than in the actual work of doctors, nurses, and other providers, and because coordination and cooperation among different providers is essential for effective and efficient health care. It is not cost pressures on providers that are driving up health-care costs; instead, costs are rising because of what economists call transaction costs, the rising cost of administering and coordinating a system that is designed to reduce access.

The health-insurance and health-care markets are different from most other markets because private companies selling insurance do not want to sell to everyone, but only to those unlikely to need care (and, therefore, most likely to drop coverage if prices rise). As much as 70% of the "losses" suffered by health-insurance providers—that is, the money they pay out in claims—goes to as few as 10% of their subscribers. This creates a powerful incentive for companies to screen subscribers, to identify those likely to submit claims, and to harass them so that they will drop their coverage and go elsewhere. The collection of insurance-related information has become a major source of waste in the American economy because it is not organized to improve patient care but to harass and to drive away needy subscribers and their health-care providers. Because driving away the sick is so profitable for health insurers, they are doing it more and more, creating the enormous bureaucratic waste that characterizes the process of billing and insurance handling. Rising by over 10% a year for the past 25 years, health insurers' administrative costs are among the fastest-growing in the U.S. health-care sector. Doctors in private practice now spend as much as 25% of their revenue on administration, nearly $70,000 per physician for billing and insurance costs.

For-profit health insurance also creates waste by discouraging people from receiving preventive care and by driving the sick into more expensive care settings. Almost a third of Americans with "adequate" health insurance go without care every year due to costs, and the proportion going without care rises to over half of those with "inadequate" insurance and over two-thirds for those without insurance. Nearly half of the uninsured have no regular source of care, and a third did not fill a prescription in the past year because of cost. All of this unutilized care might appear to save the system money. But it doesn't. Reducing access does not reduce health-care expenditures when it makes people sicker and pushes them into hospitals and emergency rooms, which are the most expensive settings for health care and are often the least efficient because care provided in these settings rarely has continuity or follow-up.

The great waste in our current private insurance system is an opportunity for policy because it makes it possible to economize on spending by replacing our current system with one providing universal access. I have estimated that in Massachusetts, a state with a relatively efficient health-insurance system, it would be possible to lower the cost of providing health care by nearly 16% even after providing coverage to everyone in the state currently without insurance (see Table 1). This could be done largely by reducing the cost of administering the private insurance system, with most of the savings coming within providers' offices by reducing the costs of billing and processing insurance claims. This is a conservative estimate made for a state with a relatively efficient health-insurance system. In a report prepared for the state of Vermont, William Hsiao of the Harvard School of Public Health and MIT economist Jonathan Gruber estimate that shifting to a single-payer system could lead to savings of around 25% through reduced administrative cost and improved delivery of care. (They have also noted that administrative savings would be even larger if the entire country shifted to a single-payer system because this would save the cost of billing people with private, out-of-state insurance plans.) In Massachusetts, my conservative estimates suggests that as much as $10 billion a year could be saved by shifting to a single-payer system.

TABLE 1: SOURCES OF SAVINGS AND ADDED COSTS FOR A HYPTHETICAL MASSACHUSETTS SINGLE-PAYER HEALTH SYSTEM

Change in health-care expenditures	Size of change as share of total health-care expenditures
Savings from single-payer system	
Administration costs within health-insurance system	-2.0%
Administrative costs within providers' offices	-10.1%
Reduction in provider prices through reducing market leverage for privileged providers	-5.0%
Savings:	-17.1%
Increased costs from single-payer	
Expansion in coverage to the uninsured	+1.35%
Increased utilization because of elimination of copayments, balanced by improvements in preventive care	+/- 0.0%
Total increased costs:	+1.35%
Net change in health-care expenditures:	-15.75%

Source: Calculations by the author from data in OECD Health Data 2010 (oecd.org).

Single-Payer Systems Control Costs by Providing Better Care

Adoption of a single-payer health-insurance program with universal coverage could also save money and improve care by allowing better coordination of care among different providers and by providing a continuity of care that is not possible with competing insurance plans. A comparison of health care in the United States with health care in other countries shows how large these cost savings might be. When Canada first adopted its current health-care financing system in 1968, the health-care share of the national gross domestic product in the United States (7.1%) was nearly the same as in Canada (6.9%), and only a little higher than in other advanced economies. Since then, however, health care has become dramatically more expensive in the United States. In the United States, per capita health-care spending since 1971 has risen by over $6,900 compared with an increase of less than $3,600 in Canada and barely $3,200 elsewhere (see Table 2). Physician Steffie Woolhandler and others have shown how much of this discrepancy between the experience of the United States and Canada can be associated with the lower administrative costs of Canada's single-payer system; she has found that administrative costs are nearly twice as high in the United States as in Canada—31% of costs versus 17%.

The United States is unique among advanced economies both for its reliance on private health insurance and for rapid inflation in health-care costs. Health-care costs have risen faster in the United States than in any other advanced economy: twice as fast as in Canada, France, Germany, Sweden, or the United Kingdom. We might accept higher and rapidly rising costs had Americans experienced better health outcomes. But using life expectancy at birth as a measure of general health,

TABLE 2: GREATER INCREASE IN COST FOR U.S. HEALTH-CARE SYSTEM, 1971-2007

	U.S. vs. Canada		U.S. vs. 5-country average	
	Dollars	Share of GDP	Dollars	Share of GDP
Extra increase 1971-2007	$3,356	5.40%	$3,690	4.72%
Extra adjusted for smaller life expectancy gain	$4,006	5.98%	$4,480	5.73%
	As share of national health expenditures			
Extra increase 1971-2007	45%		49%	
Extra adjusted for smaller life expectancy gain	53%		59%	

Note: The first line shows how much faster health-care spending rose per person and as a share of gross domestic product in the United States compared with Canada and with the average of five countries (Canada, France, Germany, Sweden, and the United Kingdom). The second row adjusts this increase for the slower rate of growth in life expectancy in the United States than in these other countries. The third and fourth rows estimate the degree of waste in our health-care system as the proportion of total expenditures accounted for by the extra increases in health-care expenditures in the United States.

Source: Calculations by the author from data in OECD Health Data 2010 (oecd.org).

we have gone from a relatively healthy country to a relatively unhealthy one. Our gain in life expectancy since 1971 (5.4 years for women) is impressive except when put beside other advanced economies (where the average increase is 7.3 years).

The relatively slow increase in life expectancy in the United States highlights the gross inefficiency of our private health-care system. Had the United States increased life expectancy at the same dollar cost as in other countries, we would have saved nearly $4,500 per person. Or, put another way, had we increased life expectancy at the same rate as other countries, our spending increase since 1971 would have bought an extra 15 years of life expectancy, 10 years more than we have. The failure of American life expectancy to rise as fast as life expectancy elsewhere can be directly tied to the inequitable provision of health care through our private, for-profit health-insurance system. Increases in life expectancy since 1990 have been largely restricted to relatively affluent Americans with better health insurance. Since

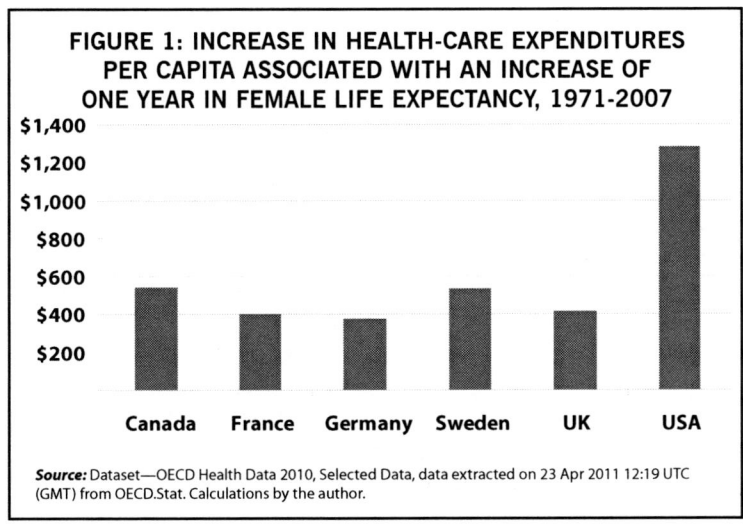

FIGURE 1: INCREASE IN HEALTH-CARE EXPENDITURES PER CAPITA ASSOCIATED WITH AN INCREASE OF ONE YEAR IN FEMALE LIFE EXPECTANCY, 1971-2007

Source: Dataset—OECD Health Data 2010, Selected Data, data extracted on 23 Apr 2011 12:19 UTC (GMT) from OECD.Stat. Calculations by the author.

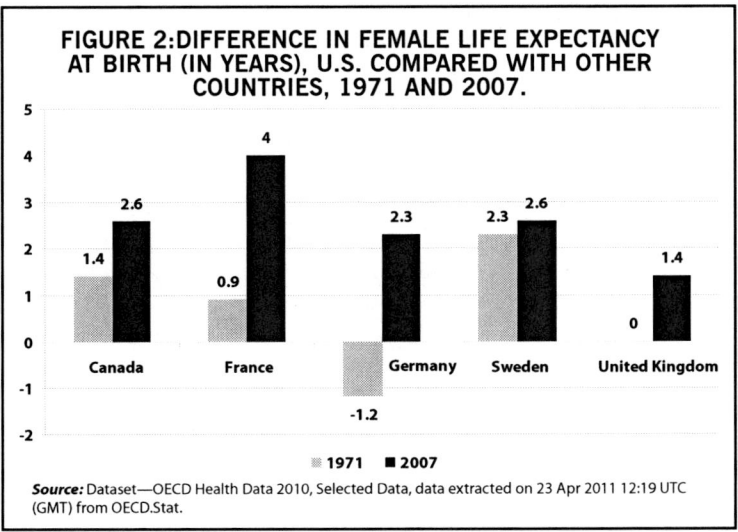

FIGURE 2: DIFFERENCE IN FEMALE LIFE EXPECTANCY AT BIRTH (IN YEARS), U.S. COMPARED WITH OTHER COUNTRIES, 1971 AND 2007.

Source: Dataset—OECD Health Data 2010, Selected Data, data extracted on 23 Apr 2011 12:19 UTC (GMT) from OECD.Stat.

1990, men in the top 50% of the income distribution have had a six-year increase in life expectancy at age 65 compared with an increase of only one year for men earning below the median.

Rising health-care costs reflect in part the greater costs of caring for an aging population with more chronic conditions. As such, the United States looks especially bad because our population is aging less quickly than that of other countries because of high rates of immigration, relatively higher fertility, and the slower increase in life expectancy in the United States. Countries also buy higher life expectancy by spending on health care; rising health expenditures have funded improvements in treatment that have contributed to rising life expectancy throughout the world. Female life expectancy at birth has increased by nearly nine years in Germany since 1971, by over eight years in France, by seven years in Canada and the United Kingdom, and by six years in Sweden. By contrast, the United States, where female life expectancy increased by a little over five years, has done relatively poorly despite increasing health-care expenditures that dwarf those of other countries. In other countries, increasing expenditures by about $500 per person is associated with an extra year of life expectancy. With our privatized health-insurance system, we need spending increases over twice as large to gain an extra year of life (see Figure 1, previous page).

The international comparison also provides another perspective on any supposed trade-off between containing costs and expanding coverage. In countries other than the United States, almost all of the increase in health-care spending as a share of national income is due to better quality health care as measured by improvements in life expectancy (see Figure 2, previous page). The problem of rising health-care costs is almost unique to the United States, the only advanced industrialized country without universal coverage and without any effective national health plan.

In short, the question is not whether we can afford a single-payer health-insurance system that would provide adequate health care for all Americans. The real question is: can we afford anything else? ❑

Sources: Cathy Shoen, "How Many Are Underinsured? Trends Among U.S. Adults, 2003 and 2007," *Health Affairs*, June 10, 2008; "Insured but Poorly Protected: How Many Are Underinsured? U. S. Adults Trends, 2003 to 2007," Commonwealth Fund, June 10, 2008 (commonwealthfund.org); David Cutler and Dan Ly, "The (Paper) Work of Medicine: Understanding International Medical Costs," *Journal of Economic Perspectives*, Spring 2011; Stephen M. Davidson, *Still Broken: Understanding the U.S. Health Care System*, Stanford Business Books, 2010; P. Franks and C. M. Clancy, "Health insurance and mortality. Evidence from a national cohort," *The Journal of the American Medical Association*, August 11, 1993; Allan Garber and Jonathan Skinner, "Is American Health Care Uniquely Inefficient?" *Journal of Economic Perspectives*, Fall 2008; Jonathan Gruber, "The Role of Consumer Co-payments for Health Care: Lessons from the RAND Health Insurance Experiment and Beyond," Kaiser Family Foundation, October 2006 (kff.org); David Himmelstein and Steffie Woolhandler, "Administrative Waste in the U.S. Health Care System in 2003," *International Journal of Health Services*, 2004; "The Uninsured: A Primer: Supplemental Data Tables," Kaiser Family Foundation, December 2010; Karen Davis and Cathy Shoen, "Slowing the Growth of U.S. Health Care Expenditures: What are the Options?" Commonwealth Fund, January 2007 (commonwealthfund.org); "Accounting for the

Cost of Health Care in the United States," McKinsey Global Institute, January 2007 (mckinsey.com); "Investigation of Health Care Cost Trends and Cost Drivers," Office of Massachusetts Attorney General Martha Coakley, January 29, 2010 (mass.gov); Trends in Mortality Differentials and Life Expectancy for Male Social Security-Covered Workers, by Average Relative Earnings by Hilary Waldron, Social Security Administration, October 2007; Richard G. Wilkinson, *The Spirit Level*, Bloomsbury Press, 2010; William Hsiao and Steven Kappel, "Act 128: Health System Reform Design. Achieving Affordable Universal Health Care in Vermont," January 21, 2011 (leg.state.vt.us); Steffie Woolhandler and Terry Campbell, "Cost of Health Care Administration in the United States and Canada," *New England Journal of Medicine*, 2003.

Article 5.2

DIFFERENT ANTI-POVERTY REGIME, SAME SINGLE-MOTHER POVERTY

BY RANDY ALBELDA
January/February 2012

Four years into a period of deep recession and persistent economic crisis, only now has the p-word—poverty—finally surfaced. The Census Bureau's September 13 announcement that the U.S. poverty rate had increased to 15.1% in 2010, up from 14.3% in 2009, put the issue of poverty onto page one, albeit briefly. In fact, poverty and how to address it have not been prominent items on the national agenda since the "welfare reform" debates of the 1980s and early 1990s.

"Welfare queens" may have disappeared from politicians' rhetoric, but poor people, disproportionately single mothers and their children, are still around. Single-mother families have been and continue to be particularly vulnerable to being poor. The September report showed the poverty rate for single mothers and their children rose as well: from 32.5% in 2009 to 34.2% in 2010.

It is remarkably hard to be the primary caregiver *and* garner enough income to support a family. This reality was built into the design of the first generation of federal anti-poverty programs in the United States. Developed beginning in the New Deal era, these programs were aimed at families with no able-bodied male breadwinner and hence no jobs or wages—single mothers, people with disabilities, and elders. Putting single mothers to work was thought to be undesirable. Or, white single mothers—there was much less reluctance in the case of black single mothers, who were largely excluded from the various anti-poverty programs until the 1960s.

The most important of the anti-poverty programs for single mothers was the cash assistance program, Aid to Dependent Children (later renamed Aid to Families with Dependent Children, or AFDC), established in 1935—also commonly referred to as "welfare." Other programs developed in the succeeding decades included Food Stamps, Medicaid, and housing assistance.

Then, in 1996, with the support of President Clinton, Congress abolished AFDC, replacing it with a block grant called TANF (Temporary Assistance to Needy Families), and passed a spate of other changes to related programs. The new anti-poverty regime implied a new social compact with the non-disabled, non-elder poor, supported by both conservatives and liberals: to require employment in exchange for—and ultimately be weaned off of—government support. In other words, the new mandate for poor adults, especially single mothers, was to get a job—any job.

And, in fact, in the ensuing years the number of poor families with wages from work increased. Moreover, welfare rolls dropped. And, in the first four years following welfare "reform," the official poverty rate for single-mother families fell too. (It has been increasing since 2000, although not quite back to its 1996 level.) But despite their higher wage income, many single-mother families are no better able to provide for their basic needs today than before the mid-1990s. Even the lower poverty rate may not reflect the real material well-being of many single moms and their children, given that their mix of resources has shifted to include more of the kinds of income counted by poverty measures and less of the uncounted kinds.

While TANF and the other legislative changes promote employment in theory, they did not reshape anti-poverty programs to genuinely support employment. Key programs are insufficiently funded, leaving many without access to child care and other vital work supports; income eligibility requirements and benefit levels designed for those with no earnings work poorly for low-wage earners; and the sheer amount of time it takes to apply for and keep benefits is at odds with holding down a job.

Ironically, there has been little or no talk of revisiting these policies despite the massive job losses of the Great Recession. With job creation at a standstill, in 2010 the unemployment rate for single mothers was 14.6% (more than one out of every seven). For this and other reasons it is time to "modernize" anti-poverty programs by assuring they do what policy makers and others want them to do—encourage employment while reducing poverty. And they must also serve as an important safety net when work is not available or possible. But changes to government policies are not enough. If employment is to be the route out of poverty, then wages and employer benefits must support workers at basic minimum levels.

Ending "Welfare" And Promoting Employment

Among the changes to U.S. anti-poverty programs in the 1990s, the most sweeping and highly politicized involved AFDC, the cash assistance program for poor parents. The 1996 legislative overhaul gave states tremendous leeway over eligibility rules in the new TANF program. For the first time there was a time limit: states are not allowed to allocate federal TANF money to any adult who has received TANF for 60 months—regardless of how long it took to accrue 60 months of aid. And the new law required recipients whose youngest child is over one year old to do some form of paid or unpaid work—most forms of education and job training don't count—after 24 months of receiving benefits.

To accommodate the push for employment, Congress expanded the Earned Income Tax Credit, which provides refundable tax credits for low-income wage earners; expanded the Child Care Development Block Grant, which gives states money to help provide child care to working parents with low incomes, including parents leaving TANF; and established the State Children's Health Insurance Program (S-CHIP), in part out of a recognition that single mothers entering the workforce were losing Medicaid coverage yet often working for employers who provided unaffordable health insurance coverage or none at all. Even housing assistance programs started promoting employment: the Department of Housing and Urban Development encouraged local housing authorities to redesign housing assistance so as to induce residents to increase their earnings.

The strategy of promoting employment was remarkably successful at getting single mothers into the labor force. In 1995, 63.5% of all single mothers were employed; by 2009, 67.8% were. This rate exceeds that of married mothers, at 66.3%. So with all that employment, why are poverty rates still so high for single-mother families? The answer lies in the nature of low-wage work and the mismatch between poverty reduction policies and employment.

Single Mothers and Low-Wage Jobs Don't Mix

There are two fundamental mismatches single mothers face in this new welfare regime. The first has to do with the awkward pairing of poor mothers and low-wage jobs. In 2009 over one-third of single mothers were in jobs that are low paying (defined as below two-thirds of the median hourly wage, which was $9.06). In addition to the low pay, these jobs typically lack benefits such as paid sick or vacation days and health insurance. Many low-wage jobs that mothers find in retail and hospitality have very irregular work hours, providing the employers with lots of flexibility but workers with almost none. These features of low-wage work wreak havoc for single moms. An irregular work schedule makes child care nearly impossible to arrange. A late school bus, a sick child, or a sick child-care provider can throw a wrench in the best-laid plans for getting to and staying at work. Without paid time off, a missed day of work is a missed day of pay. And too many missed days can easily cost you your job.

Medicaid, the government health insurance program for the poor, does not make up for the lack of employer-sponsored health insurance common in low-wage jobs. Medicaid income eligibility thresholds vary state by state, but are typically so low that many low-wage workers don't qualify. Only 63% of low-wage single mothers have any health insurance coverage at all, compared to 82% of all workers. The new Patient Protection and Affordable Care Act (a.k.a. Obamacare) may help, depending on the cost of purchasing insurance, but for now many low-wage mothers go without health care coverage.

Finally, there is the ultimate reality that there are only 24 hours in a day. Low wages mean working many hours to earn enough to cover basic needs. Yet working more hours means less time with kids. This can be costly in several ways. Hiring babysitters can be expensive. Relying heavily on good-natured relatives who provide care but may not engage and motivate young children also has costs, as does leaving younger children in the care of older brothers and sisters, who in turn can miss out on important after-school learning. Long work hours coupled with a tight budget might mean little time to help do homework, meet with teachers, or participate in in- and out-of-school activities that enrich children's lives.

A New Mismatch

The first generation of anti-poverty programs were designed on the assumption that recipients would not be working outside the home. Unfortunately, their successor programs such as TANF and SNAP, despite their explicit aim of encouraging employment, still do not work well for working people.

What does it mean that these programs are not designed for those with employment? There are two important features. First, income thresholds for eligibility tend to be very low—that is, only those with extremely low earnings qualify. For example, only two states have income thresholds above the poverty line for TANF eligibility. To get any SNAP benefits, a single mother needs to have income below 130% of the poverty line. Working full-time at $10 an hour (that's about $1,600 a month in take-home pay) would make a single mother with one child ineligible for

Poverty Remeasured

According to the Census Bureau, 46.2 million Americans were poor in 2010. But what exactly does "poor" mean? The academic and policy debates over how to measure poverty fill volumes. Some questions relate to the establishment of the poverty threshold. On what basis should the poverty line be drawn? Is poverty relative or absolute—in other words, if the average standard of living in a society rises, should its poverty threshold rise as well? Other questions concern measuring income. What kinds of income should be counted? Before or after taxes and government benefits? Who is included in the poverty assessment? (For example, those in institutional settings such as prisons are excluded from the official U.S. poverty measure—not a minor point when you consider that nearly 2.3 million adults were incarcerated in the United States as of the end of 2009.)

Established in 1963 by multiplying an emergency food budget by three, and adjusted solely for inflation in the years since, the official U.S. poverty thresholds are notoriously low. A family of four bringing in over $22,314—*including* any TANF cash assistance, unemployment or workers' comp, Social Security or veterans' benefits, and child support—is not officially poor. In many parts of the United States, $22K would not be enough to keep one person, let alone four people, off the street and minimally clothed and fed.

An interagency federal effort to develop a more realistic poverty level has just released its new measure, known as the Supplemental Poverty Measure. The SPM makes many adjustments to the traditional calculation:

It counts the Earned Income Tax Credit and non-cash benefits such as food stamps and housing assistance as income.

It subtracts from income out-of-pocket medical costs, certain work-related expenses (e.g., child care), and taxes paid.

Its thresholds are adjusted for cost-of-living differences by region and are relative rather than absolute—basic expenses that are the building blocks of the threshold are pegged at the 33rd percentile of U.S. households.

The SPM poverty rate for 2009 was 15.7%, somewhat higher than the 14.5% official rate. More dramatic differences between the two poverty rates appeared in some subgroups, especially the elderly: 9.9% by the traditional measure versus 16.1% by the SPM, largely due to their high out-of-pocket medical expenses.

—Amy Gluckman

Sources: "Measure by Measure," *The Economist*, January 20, 2011; Ellen Frank, "Measures of Poverty," *Dollars & Sense*, January 2006; Center for Women's Welfare, Univ. of Wash. School of Social Work, "How Does the Self-Sufficiency Standard Compare to the New Supplemental Poverty Measure?"; U.S. Census Bureau, "How the Census Bureau Measures Poverty" and "Poverty Thresholds by Size of Family and Number of Children: 2010."

both programs in all states. Moreover, even if you are eligible, these benefits phase out sharply. With TANF (in most states), SNAP, and housing assistance, for every additional dollar you earn, you lose about 33 cents in each form of support. This means work just does not pay.

Second, applying for and maintaining benefits under these programs often takes a great deal of time. Each program has particular eligibility requirements; each requires different sets of documents to verify eligibility. While some states have tried to move to a "one-stop" system, most require separate applications for each program and, often, one or more office visits. Recertification (i.e., maintaining eligibility) can require assembling further documentation and meeting again with caseworkers. If you have ever applied for one of these programs, maybe you have experienced how time-consuming—and frustrating—the process can be.

In short, the programs were designed for applicants and recipients with plenty of time on their hands. But with employment requirements, this is not the right assumption. Missing time at work to provide more paperwork for the welfare office is just not worth it; there is considerable evidence that many eligible people do not use TANF or SNAP for that reason. Even the benefit levels assume an unlimited amount of time. Until recently, the maximum dollar amount of monthly SNAP benefits was based on a very low-cost food budget that assumed hours of home cooking.

Unlike cash assistance or food assistance, child care subsidies are obviously aimed at "working" mothers. But this program, too, often has onerous reporting requirements. Moreover, in most states the subsidy phases out very quickly especially after recipients' earnings reach the federal poverty line. This means that a worker who gets a small raise at work can suddenly face a steep increase in her child-care bill. (Of course, this is only a problem for the lucky parents who actually receive a child-care subsidy; as mentioned earlier, the lack of funding means that most eligible parents do not.)

The Earned Income Tax Credit is a notable exception. The refundable tax credit was established explicitly to help working parents with low incomes. It is relatively easy to claim (fill out a two page tax form along with the standard income tax forms), and of all the anti-poverty programs it reaches the highest up the income ladder. It even phases out differently: the credit increases as earnings rise, flattens out, and then decreases at higher levels of earnings. Most recipients get the credit in an annual lump sum and so use it very differently from other anti-poverty supports. Families often use the "windfall" to pay off a large bill or to pay for things long put off, like a visit to the dentist or a major car repair. While helpful and relatively easy to get, then, the Earned Income Tax Credit does not typically help with day-to-day expenses as the other anti-poverty programs do.

Has Employment-Promotion "Worked"?

The most striking change in the anti-poverty picture since welfare reform was enacted is that the welfare rolls have plummeted. In 1996, the last full year under the old system, there were 4.43 million families on AFDC nationwide; in 2010, amid the worst labor market in decades, the TANF caseload was only 1.86 million. In fact, when unemployment soared in 2008, only 15 states saw their TANF caseloads increase. The rest continued to experience reductions. Plus, when the TANF rolls fell sharply in the late 1990s, so did Medicaid and Food Stamps enrollments. These programs have since seen increases in usage, especially since the recession, but it's clear that when families lose cash assistance they frequently lose access to other supports as well.

Welfare reform has worked very well, then, if receiving welfare is a bad thing. Indeed, advocates of the new regime tout the rapid and steep decline in welfare use as their main indicator of its success. In and of itself, however, fewer families using anti-poverty programs does not mean less poverty, more personal responsibility, or greater self-sufficiency. During the economic expansion of the late 1990s, the official poverty rate for single mothers and their children fell from 35.8% in 1996 to 28.5% in 2000. It has risen nearly every year since, reaching 34.2% in 2010. But if a successful anti-poverty effort is measured at all by the economic well-being of the targeted families, then that slight drop in the poverty rate is swamped by the 60% decrease in the number of families using welfare over the same period. Far fewer poor families are being served. In 1996, 45.7% of all poor children received some form of income-based cash assistance; in 2009, only 18.7% did. The Great Recession pushed 800,000 additional U.S. families into poverty between 2007 and 2009, yet the TANF rolls rose by only 110,000 over this period.

Data from two federal government reports on TANF, depicted in the chart below, nicely illustrate the dilemmas of the new welfare regime. The chart shows the total average amounts of earnings and the value of major government supports ("means-tested income") for the bottom 40% of single-mother families (by total income) between 1996 and 2005. It is clear that since welfare reform, these families are relying much more on earnings. But despite the additional work effort, they find

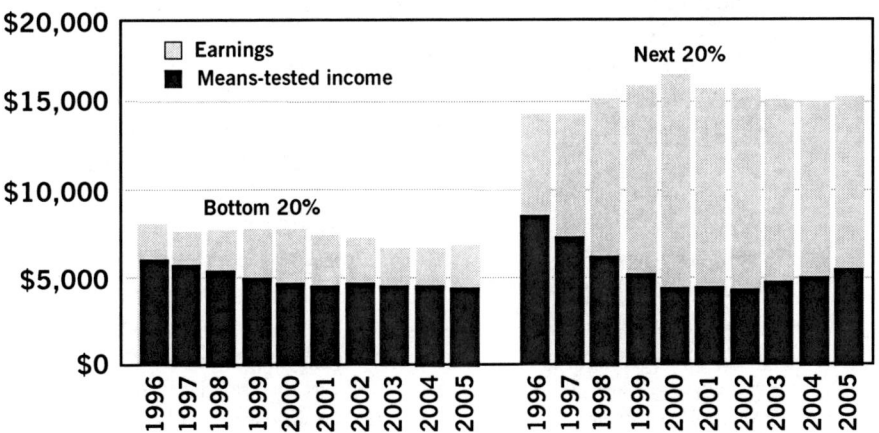

EARNINGS AND MEANS-TESTED INCOME FOR THE BOTTOM TWO QUINTILES OF SINGLE-MOTHER FAMILIES, 1996-2005 (IN 2005 DOLLARS)

Notes: Those with negative income not included. Means-tested income is the total of Supplemental Security Income, Public Assistance, certain Veteran's Benefits, Food Stamps, School Lunch, and housing benefits.

Source: U.S. Department of Health and Human Services, the Office of Assistant Secretary for Planning and Evaluation, Table 4:3 of TANF 6th Annual Report to Congress (November 2004) and Table 4:2 of TANF 8th Annual Report to Congress (June 2009), using tabulations from the U.S. Census Bureau, 1996-2005.

themselves essentially no better off. The bottom 20% saw their package of earnings and government benefits *fall*: their average earnings have not increased much while government supports have dropped off, leaving them with fewer resources on average in 2006 than in 1996. For the second quintile, earnings have increased substantially but benefits have fallen nearly as much, leaving this group only slightly better off over the period. And that is without taking into account the expenses associated with employment (e.g. child care, transportation, work clothes) and with the loss of public supports (such as increased co-payments for child care or health insurance). These women are working a lot more—in the second quintile about double—but are barely better off at all! So much for "making work pay."

More hours of work also means fewer hours with children. If the time a mother spends with her children is worth anything, then substituting earnings for benefits represents a loss of resources to her family.

What Might Be Done?

Employment, even with government supports, is unlikely to provide a substantial share of single-mother families with adequate incomes. Three factors—women's lower pay, the time and money it takes to raise children, and the primary reliance on only one adult to both earn and care for children—combine to make it nearly impossible for a sizeable number of single mothers to move to stable and sufficient levels of resources.

Addressing the time- and money-squeeze that single mothers faced in the old anti-poverty regime and still face in the new one will take thoroughgoing changes in the relations among work, family, and income.

- *Make work pay by shoring up wages and employer benefits.* To ensure that the private sector does its part, raise the minimum wage. A full-time, year-round minimum wage job pays just over the poverty income threshold for a family of two. Conservatives and the small business lobby will trot out the bogeyman of job destruction, but studies on minimum-wage increases show a zero or even positive effect on employment. In addition, mandate paid sick days for all workers and require benefit parity for part-time, temporary, and subcontracted workers. This would close a loophole that a growing number of employers use to dodge fringe benefits.

- *Reform anti-poverty programs to really support employment.* To truly support low-wage employment, anti-poverty programs should increase income eligibility limits so that a worker can receive the supports even while earning and then phase out the programs more gradually so low-wage workers keep getting them until they earn enough not to need them. Also, streamline application processes and make them more user-friendly. Many states have done this for unemployment insurance, car registration, and driver's license renewal. Why not do the same for SNAP, TANF and Medicaid?

- *Support paid and unpaid care work.* A society that expects all able-bodied adults to work—regardless of the age of their children—should also be a society that shares the costs of going to work, by offering programs to care for children and others who need care. This means universal child care and afterschool programs. It also means paid parental leave and paid time off to care for an ill relative. The federal Family and Medical Leave Act gives most workers the right to take unpaid leaves, but many can't afford to. California and New Jersey have extended their temporary disability insurance benefits to cover those facing a wide range of family needs—perhaps a helpful model.

New anti-poverty regime, but same poverty problems. Most single mothers *cannot* work their way out of poverty—definitely not without the right kinds of supplemental support. There are many possible policy steps that could be taken to help them and other low-wage workers get the most out of an inhospitable labor market. But ultimately, better designed assistance to poor and low-income families, old fashioned cash assistance, and minimal employment standards must be part of the formula. ❑

Sources: Randy Albelda and Chris Tilly, *Glass Ceilings and Bottomless Pits: Women's Work, Women's Poverty*, South End Press, 1997; U.S. Census Bureau, *Historical Tables on Poverty*; Kaiser Family Foundation, "Income Eligibility Limits for Working Adults at Application as a Percent of the Federal Poverty Level by Scope of Benefit Package," statehealthfacts.org, January 2011; U.S. Dept. of Health and Human Services, *TANF 6th and 8th Annual Report to Congress,* November 2004 and July 2009; U.S. Dept. of Health and Human Services, *Estimates of Child Care Eligibility and Receipt for Fiscal Year 2006*, April 2010; Thomas Gabe, *Trends in Welfare, Work, and the Economic Well-being of Female Headed Families with Children: 1987-2005*, Congressional Research Service Report RL30797, 2007; Randy Albelda and Heather Boushey, *Bridging the Gaps: A Picture of How Work Supports Work in Ten States,* Center for Social Policy, Univ. of Mass. Boston and Center for Economic and Policy Research, 2007; Author's calculations from the U.S. Census Bureau's Current Population Survey, various years.

Article 5.3

THE BIG LIE ABOUT THE "ENTITLEMENT STATE"

BY ALEJANDRO REUSS
November/December 2012

> In 1960, government transfers to individuals totaled $24 billion. By 2010, that total was 100 times as large. Even after adjusting for inflation, entitlement transfers to individuals have grown by more than 700 percent over the last 50 years. ...
>
> There are sensible conclusions to be drawn from these facts. You could say that the entitlement state is growing at an unsustainable rate and will bankrupt the country.
>
> —David Brooks, "Thurston Howell Romney," *New York Times*, September 17, 2012

Is the view that "entitlements"—government programs like Social Security, Medicare, and Medicaid—"will bankrupt the country" a "sensible conclusion"? No. It's scare-mongering of the "OH MYGOD WE'RE ALL GOING TO DIE!" variety, completely unjustified by a sober look at data on government transfer payments between 1960 and 2010.

New York Times columnist David Brooks starts the passage on entitlements in his September 17 column by noting that total government transfer payments have increased by an alarming-sounding 100 times over the last half-century. In the next sentence, he acknowledges that this figure is not adjusted for inflation. (Nor for population growth.) As it turns out, the "100 times" mostly reflects the increase in the general price level (more than seven-fold between 1960 and 2010) and the growth of the U.S. resident population (not quite doubled), not the growth in transfer programs specifically. Correcting for these factors, Brooks admits, the increase is just "700 percent." One can only guess that he switched to percentage terms because he's trying to sound scary, and "700 percent" sounds far scarier than "seven times." (Brooks actually describes this figure simply as "after adjusting for inflation," but it appears that he actually adjusted for both inflation and population growth.)

That's as far as Brooks gets, so he misses another crucial adjustment. The average income in the United States is far greater today than it was in 1960. Real GDP per capita grew by more than two-and-a-half times between 1960 and 2010. Now, looking at real entitlements spending per capita relative to real GDP per capita (or just real entitlements spending relative to real GDP), the growth over the last 50 years is down to less than three-fold. It makes perfect sense that cash benefits programs like Social Security—which send people checks and allow them to spend the money as they see fit—should grow with increasing incomes. These programs are meant to help people maintain something resembling the customary standards of living of today, after all, not those of the Eisenhower era.

With a few sensible adjustments, then, Brooks' alarming initial figure of "100 times" vanishes almost into thin air. That still leaves, however, an increase of a little less than three times. What accounts for that?

To begin with, over 70% of the increase in social benefits at all levels of government, over the half century between 1960 and 2010, is accounted for by three programs: Social Security, Medicare, and Medicaid. Two of these, Medicare and Medicaid, did not even exist in 1960. (Social Security, meanwhile, did not cover anywhere near the percentage of the labor force it covers today.) It is rather disingenuous to bemoan the "unsustainable growth" of certain government programs, over a certain period, when they did not even exist at the beginning of that period.

More generally, the growth in the Big Three social-benefits programs is the combined result of several different effects. Party, it reflects changes in the demographic composition of the population. Social Security and Medicare primarily benefit the elder population. This age group has grown as a percentage of the overall U.S. population because people are, on average, living longer and because the demographic "bump" of the baby-boom generation is beginning to reach retirement age. Partly, the increase reflects the growth in medical costs, which has been faster than the increase in the general price level. Finally, it reflects the expansion of benefits associated with these programs (Social Security retirement benefits, for example, are tied to lifetime earnings, so as earnings go up so do benefits).

Even aside from the numbers, Brooks is fundamentally wrong that transfer programs can "bankrupt the country." Transfer programs, like their name suggests, transfer income from one part of the population to another. Social Security, for example, is primarily an intergenerational transfer program. It taxes current workers to fund benefits for current retirees. (Most people pay taxes that fund other people's benefits, during one part of their lives, and then receive benefits paid for by other people's taxes, during another part.) The "losses" for those who are paying the taxes, at any given time, are not losses to society as a whole. They are balanced by the gains to those who are receiving the benefits.

In another sense, the benefits to everyone covered by these programs greatly exceed just the cash amount of the transfers. Social Security provides not only a retirement annuity (insurance against destitution during old age), but also disability benefits (insurance against being unable to work) and survivors' benefits (insurance for family members against the death of a financial provider). Medicare and Medicaid, meanwhile, pay for medical services and prescription medicines. These programs, in short, offer meaningful protection against many of life's possible calamities.

When we think of costs (of a government program or of something else) to "society as a whole," we need to think about the use of real resources—a part of society's total labor time, buildings, tools, etc.—that could have been used for some other purpose. The real costs of the Big Three transfer programs, in this sense, fall into two categories.

First, there are costs involved in administering the programs. The work hours and other resources (office buildings, desks, chairs, computers, electricity, pencils, paper clips, etc.) used to keep program records, send out benefits checks, and so on, could have been used for something else. So those represent real costs to society. In the case of the major transfer programs, however, the administrative costs are very small relative to the total benefits paid. The costs of administering Social Security, for example, are less than one percent.

Second, there are real costs for the goods and services for which government transfers pay. Medicare and Medicaid, for example, pay medical practices, hospitals, medical-supply companies, and pharmaceutical manufacturers to deliver medical care and medicines to program beneficiaries. Total transfer program costs, therefore, have increased along with rising medical costs. Part of the reason for rising medical costs has been that people now receive medical services they once could not. Magnetic resonance imaging (MRI) scans, for example, were not widely available two decades age. Now they are. Another is the rising real incomes of (some) medical professionals and the burgeoning profits of pharmaceutical manufacturers. Perhaps the most important, however, is that the U.S. health-care delivery system has enormous administrative costs, far above those of other high-income countries.

Advocates of single-payer (public) health insurance point out that such a system could 1) rein in pharmaceutical costs by using the government's purchasing power to negotiate lower prices and 2) dramatically reduce administrative costs by eliminating the crazy quilt of different private-insurance billing systems. (See Gerald Friedman, "Funding a National Single-Payer System," March/April 2012; Gerald Friedman, "Universal Health Care: Can We Afford Anything Less?" July/August 2011). Maybe David Brooks should start a clamor about that.

Two obvious ways to pay for growing transfer programs, from a public-finance standpoint, are: First, keep government revenue the same, but change its uses. For example, the United States could fight fewer wars, have a smaller military, and buy less military hardware. Or it could liberalize laws on recreational drug use, and reduce spending on police, courts, and prisons. (Or both!) It could use some of the savings to fund the Big Three and other social programs. Second, increase government revenue. Contrary to current mythology, the U.S. population is not being taxed to the very limits of its endurance. Of thirty high-income OECD countries, the United States ranks dead last in total tax revenue (for all levels of government) as a percentage of GDP, at less than 25%. The figure is 30% or more for 24 of the 30 countries, and over 40% for eight.

Brooks acts as if budget issues are one-sided: a matter only of how much a particular program or combination of programs costs. This one-sided view is especially evident in U.S. political discourse on deficits, which politicians and commentators often frame as a problem of excessive spending. A budget deficit, however, is the difference between expenditures and revenue—it is an inherently two-sided issue—so looking at the expenditures side alone doesn't help us understand the causes of deficits or the possible policy responses.

Could the U.S. government just raise more revenue, as a percentage of GDP, to pay for transfers that have grown as a share of GDP? Well, somehow a couple of dozen other countries seem to manage. So probably yes. ❑

Sources: Bureau of Economic Analysis, National Income and Product Accounts, Table 3.1.Government Current Receipts and Expenditures (bea.gov); Bureau of Labor Statistics, Consumer Price Index - All Urban Consumers (Series ID: CUSR0000SA0) (bls.gov); Bureau of Economic Analysis, National Income and Product Accounts, Table 1.1.3. Real Gross Domestic Product, Quantity Indexes (bea.gov); U.S. Census Bureau, Population Estimates (census.gov); Social Security Administration, Actuarial Publications, Administrative Expenditures (ssa.gov); OECD Tax Database, Table A. Total tax revenue as percentage of GDP (oecd.org/tax).

Article 5.4

GO AHEAD AND LIFT THE CAP
Assessing a Campaign Flyer on Social Security

BY JOHN MILLER
March/April 2008

> **Barack Obama.** A plan with a trillion dollar tax increase on America's hard-working families. Lifting the cap on Social Security taxes to send more of Nevada families' hard-earned dollars to Washington. Senator Obama said, "I think that lifting the cap [on Social Security taxes] is probably going to be the best option."
>
> **Hillary Clinton.** A blueprint to rebuild the road to middle-class prosperity. Provide tax relief for the middle class and address Social Security without putting burdens on hard-working families or seniors. Strengthen Social Security and the economy by returning to balanced budgets.
>
> *—Official campaign flyer distributed by Nevadans for Hillary, January 2008*

Back in January [2008], even before things got really nasty in the Democratic primary, Barack Obama and Hillary Clinton were already going after each other about taxes and Social Security.

The Clinton campaign sent a flyer to Nevada voters before that state's January 19 Democratic caucuses, accusing Obama of planning to impose "a trillion dollar tax increase on America's hard-working families" by lifting the cap on income subject to Social Security taxes. Clinton, the flyer claimed, does "not want to fix the problems of Social Security on the backs of middle-class families and seniors."

The truth was something different. First, Obama did not exactly propose removing the cap, which was $97,500 in 2007. (In other words, employers and employees each pay a flat percentage of the first $97,500 of each employee's salary, but no tax on the income above that.) He did discuss adjusting it as "the best way to approach this [reforming Social Security]," preferable to either cutting benefits or increasing the retirement age, later adding that he would consider keeping the exemption from $97,500 to around $200,000, lifting it only for any income above $200,000.

More important, lifting the cap would in no way increase the tax burden on middle-income families. Just under 6% of U.S. wage earners make more than $97,500 in wages, so even removing the cap altogether would raise taxes only for that small group.

Now, there is a legitimate progressive objection to Obama's discussion of fixing Social Security by adjusting the cap: any talk of reforming Social Security inevitably plays into the hands of those out to privatize it by trumping up a phony crisis. But that hardly seems to be the point of the Clinton campaign flyer.

Too bad it wasn't. Clinton gets it: in the past she herself has warned that acting as if Social Security is in crisis is "a Republican trap." Yet last October, an Associated Press reporter overhead her telling an Iowa voter that she would consider lifting the cap on payroll taxes as long as wages between $97,500 and $200,000 remained exempt—precisely the proposal she derides in the Nevada flyer.

Inside Social Security

Let's remind ourselves that Social Security, which cut poverty rates among the elderly from 35% in 1960 to 9.4% in 2006, is no Robin Hood plan that robs the rich to pay for the retirement of the working class. Rather, it is a mildly redistributive public retirement program financed by contributions from the wages of working people. In fact, Social Security taxes fall far more heavily on the poor and working class than on the well-to-do. Payroll taxes are a fixed 12.4% (actually 6.2% on employees and 6.2% on employers); they are levied only on wage income, not on property income; and the cap on wages subject to the tax (the subject of the debate between Clinton and Obama) means that while most workers pay the tax on every dollar of their income, the highest earners pay it only on a part.

Even FDR acknowledged that relying on payroll contributions to finance Social Security was regressive, although he famously argued that with those contributions in place, "no damn politician can ever scrap my Social Security program."

George W. Bush's 2005 push to privatize Social Security only underscored FDR's point. Bush made more than 40 trips around the United States to stump for his plan, but fewer people supported Social Security privatization afterwards than before he started. Ironically enough, the only aspect of Social Security reform that has generated widespread support is lifting the cap: in a February 2005 Washington Post poll, 81% of respondents agreed that Americans should pay Social Security taxes on wages over the cap.

This is no radical or hare-brained idea. It has the endorsement of the AARP, the largest seniors' lobby. And there is a clear precedent. A similar cap used to apply to the payroll tax that funds Medicare, but a 1993 law removed that cap and now every dollar of wage income is taxed to pay for Medicare. It certainly does not warrant the derision heaped on it by the Clinton campaign or the unwillingness of the Obama campaign to embrace it. In fact, lifting the cap would rewrite this one rule to favor working people more—just what the Obama campaign claims to support.

Lifting the cap on Social Security taxes would raise a significant amount of revenue: $1.3 trillion dollars over ten years according to the libertarian Cato Institute, and $124 billon a year according to the left-of-center Citizens for Tax Justice. Long term, lifting the payroll tax cap would just about cover the shortfall Social Security will face if economic growth slows to a snail's pace in the decades ahead, as forecast by the Social Security Administration (SSA). (See "The Social Security Administration's Cracked Crystal Ball" and "Social Security Isn't Broken," in this volume, for critiques of the SSA's forecasts.) According to Stephen Goss, the SSA's chief actuary, lifting the cap while giving commensurate benefit hikes to high-income taxpayers once they retire would cover 93% of the SSA's projected shortfall in Social Security revenues over the next 75 years. Removing the cap without raising

EFFECT OF REMOVING THE EARNINGS CAP ON SOCIAL SECURITY TAXES BY INCOME CATEGORY

RESULTING SOCIAL SECURITY TAX INCREASE AND TOTAL SOCIAL SECURITY TAX AS SHARES OF TOTAL INCOME IN 2007

Income Group	Increase in Social Social Security Tax	Revised Total Security Tax Paid
$0 – 10K	—	6.8%
$10K – 20K	—	6.2%
$20K – 30K	—	7.8%
$30K – 40K	—	8.7%
$40K – 50K	—	9.0%
$50K – 75K	—	9.4%
$75K – 100K	+0.0%	9.7%
$100K – 150K	+0.5%	9.6%
$150K – 200K	+1.5%	9.1%
$200K – 300K	+2.7%	8.3%
$300K – 400K	+4.1%	7.7%
$400K – 500K	+4.5%	7.4%
$500K – 750K	+4.7%	6.9%
$750K – 1M	+4.7%	6.4%
$1M – 2M	+4.4%	5.5%
$2M – 5M	+4.0%	4.5%
$5M – 10M	+3.8%	4.0%
$10M – 20M	+3.2%	3.3%
over $20M	+2.7%	2.7%

Source: "An Analysis of Eliminating the Cap on Earnings Subject to the Social Security Tax & Related Issues," (Citizens for Tax Justice, November 30, 2006).

those benefits would actually produce a surplus in the system over the same period—even if the economy creeps along as the SSA predicts it will.

Finally, the combination of the cap and the unprecedented inequality of the last two decades has shrunk the Social Security tax base. Some 90% of wages fell below the cap in 1983. Today, with the increased concentration of income among the highest-paid, that figure is down to 84%—even as the number of workers with earnings above the cap has dropped. The cap would have to rise to $140,000 just to once again cover 90% of all wages; the additional revenues resulting from just this change would close about one-third of the long-term Social Security deficit projected by the SSA.

Hardly Soaking the Rich

Making high earners pay the Social Security tax on all of their wage income, as low- and middle-income earners already have to, might not strike you as class warfare—but the high flyers sure think it is. Just listen to the financial establishment squeal. Investment Management chairman Robert Pozen, architect of the benefit-cutting proposal endorsed by the Bush administration (and deceptively labeled "progressive indexing"), warns that lifting the cap would represent "one of the greatest tax increases of all time" and "is so crazy it's beyond belief." The editors of the *Wall Street Journal* agreed. And the conservative Heritage Foundation ginned up numbers purporting to show that lifting the cap would impose a "massive 12.4 percentage point tax hike" that would return federal tax rates to levels not seen since the 1970s.

Just how wet would the rich get if the cap on Social Security taxes was lifted? The data suggest they would get damp, but hardly soaked.

For starters, lifting the cap affects just 5.9% of wage-earners. This group benefited massively from three rounds of Bush tax cuts, as evidenced by the fact that the effective federal tax rate (i.e., the share of income actually paid in federal taxes, once all deductions and exemptions have been taken) on the richest 5% of taxpayers fell from 31.1% in 2000 to 28.9% in 2005, according to the Congressional Budget Office.

So, lifting the wage cap on Social Security taxes would not do much more than reverse those tax giveaways to the wealthy. And the wealthiest taxpayers, those with incomes over $1 million, would still be paying a smaller portion of their income in payroll taxes than all other taxpayers. (See table, previous page.) For the top 5% of taxpayers, lifting the cap would push their effective federal tax rate up to 31.5%, a bit above where it was when Bush took office but still below the 31.8% level they paid back in 1979, before nearly three decades of pro-rich tax cutting. The top 1% would pay an effective federal tax rate of 33.8% —again, higher than it was in 2000 but still well below its 1979 level of 37.0%.

That is hardly soaking the rich. In any case they can afford it. The best-off 5% of households had an average income of $520,200 in 2005, some 81% higher than in 1979 after correcting for inflation. The richest 1%, with an average income of $1,558,500 in 2005, saw their after-tax income rise a whopping 176% over the same period.

Lifting the cap on payroll taxes would not only resolve any alleged crisis in Social Security, but also help to right the economic wrongs of the last few decades. And it is popular to boot. Isn't that an idea any progressive politician should seriously consider? ❑

Sources: M. Sullivan, "Budget Magic and the Social Security Tax Cap," *Tax Notes*, March 14, 2005; "Social Security: Raising or Eliminating the Taxable Earnings Base," Congressional Rsch Svc, May 2, 2005; R. Dederman et al., "Keep the Social Security Wage Cap; Nearly a Million Jobs Hang in the Balance," Center for Data Analysis Report #05-04 (Heritage Foundation, April 22, 2005); Robert C. Pozen, "A 'Progressive' Solution to Social Security," *Wall Street Journal*, March 15, 2005; "Social Security Progressives," *Wall Street Journal*, March 15, 2005; Greg Ip, "Wage Gap Figures in Social Security's Ills," *Wall Street Journal*, April 11, 2005; "Social Security Memorandum to Stephen C. Goss," February 7, 2005; "An Analysis of Eliminating the Cap on Earnings Subject to the Social Security Tax & Related Issues," (Citizens for Tax Justice, November 30, 2006); "Obama: Clinton Also Considering $1 Trillion Social Security Tax Hike on Wealth," (Associated Press, January 16, 2008); "Barack Obama on Social Security," *On the Issues*; "Effective Federal Tax Rates, 1979 to 2005," Congressional Budget Office, December 2007.

Article 5.5

HARD WORK AT AN ADVANCED AGE

BY AMY GLUCKMAN
September/October 2010

Among the many proposals that the Social-Security-is-in-crisis crowd is touting is an increase in the retirement age. The Social Security "full retirement age" was 65 from the program's inception until 1983, when Congress legislated a gradual increase, based on year of birth, to 67. The 1983 amendments did not change the age of earliest eligibility for Social Security retirement benefits, which remains 62. However, those who opt to start receiving benefits before they reach the full retirement age for their cohort face a lifetime cut in their monthly payment.

At first glance, it seems reasonable to push the retirement age upward in line with average life expectancy, which rose rapidly in the United States during the 20th century. But that rise in life expectancy owes a great deal to sharp drops in infant and child mortality. For those who survive to adulthood and especially to old age,

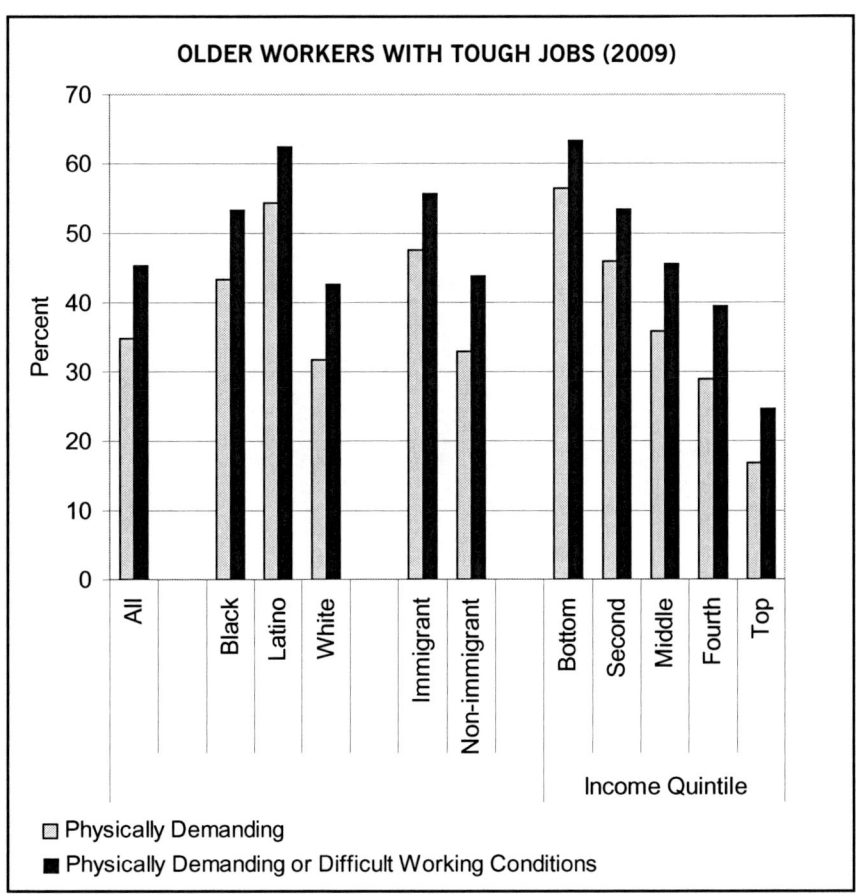

the change is far less dramatic. People who turned 65 in 1940, the first year monthly Social Security retirement benefits were paid out, could expect to live to nearly 79; those who turned 65 in 1990 had a life expectancy only about four years longer.

What would it mean to ratchet up the full retirement age further? The answer is: It depends. Some 60- and 70-somethings can readily continue working and postpone receiving Social Security benefits; a few have sufficient personal savings and/or private pensions that they will never need to rely on Social Security at all. But for the millions of older custodians, cooks, cashiers, construction workers, and others who do physically demanding work, having to put in even a few more years on the job before they can receive their full Social Security benefits is a different story.

A surprising number of older workers have these kinds of jobs, as a study by Hye Jin Rho of the Center for Economic and Policy Research shows. Following the classifications used in the U.S. Labor Department's Occupational Information Network database, the study defines "physically demanding" jobs as those that require significant time standing or walking, repetitive motions, or handling and moving objects. "Difficult working conditions" include outdoor work, use of hazardous equipment, and exposure to contaminants. Of the 18.8 million U.S. workers who are 58 or older, over 45% have physically demanding jobs and/or difficult working conditions. The rate is even higher for the 5.2 million workers 66 and up (48.2%).

Certain groups of older workers perform these tough jobs at disproportionate rates (see figure). Not surprisingly, the workers who can least afford to take an early-retirement penalty in their monthly Social Security check are often those who are most likely to reach their mid-60s saying, "Time to quit!" ❑

Sources: Hye Jin Rho, "Hard Work? Patterns in Physically Demanding Labor Among Older Workers," Center for Economic and Policy Research, August 2010; U.S. Social Security Administration, "Life Expectancy for Social Security"; Laura Shrestha, "Life Expectancy in the United States," Congressional Research Service, August 2006.

Article 5.6

PUTTING THE SCREWS TO GENERATION SCREWED
Wall Street Journal *editors oppose expanded Pell grants.*

BY JOHN MILLER
September/October 2012

> - Pell Grants are now so broad that more than half of all undergrads benefit.
>
> - Better-off students often receive the large Pell Grants and apply them to more expensive schools.
>
> - Pell Grants and other student aid are contributing to the ever-higher tuition spiral. Write 100 times on the chalkboard: Student aid raises tuition.
>
> - Overall graduation rates were lower for students who received Pell Grants than for those who didn't.
>
> - The best thing Mr. Obama could do for students, and taxpayers, is to get Pell Grants away from being a broad entitlement and back to their core mission of helping the poorest students.
>
> —Claims from "Pell Grants Flunk Out: The subsidy program has strayed far from its origins," *Wall Street Journal*, June 18, 2012.

More than $1 trillion of U.S. student debt. Better than nine of ten college graduates with student debt. Over one quarter of the repayments on those loans past due.

"A Generation Hobbled by the Soaring Cost of College" is how the *New York Times* put it in their recent exposé on college debt. And if you mix in the worst economy since the Great Depression, one that has hit those without a college degree especially hard and has left the employment prospects of even college graduates much diminished, this generation is not just hobbled but screwed. Apparently, however, not screwed enough for the editors of the *Wall Street Journal*. The editors rail against the ongoing expansion of Pell Grants, the chief form of federal aid to low- and middle-income students that can reduce the debt burden students incur.

The prospect of Pell Grants becoming an ever-more-universal entitlement must really have the *Wall Street Journal* editors spooked.

Below is a closer look at the predicament of students and former students burdened by debt and exactly why expanding Pell Grants should be supported, not opposed.

Generation Screwed

The cost of college tuition and fees has skyrocketed and student debt along with it. Since 1978, the cost of college tuition and fees has increased eleven-fold, rising faster than even the cost of medical care, and many times faster than family incomes. Since 1999, student loan debt has increased fivefold. It has eclipsed credit-card debt and is now second only to mortgage debt.

With bankruptcy not an option, borrowers can be stuck repaying their student loans long after leaving college. The federal government is now garnishing the Social Security benefits of an increasing number of retirees with student debt. The Treasury Department reports that in the first seven months of this year, the federal government withheld money from roughly 115,000 retirees' Social Security checks because they had fallen behind on federal student loans. That's nearly double the 60,000 cases in all of 2007. There were just six cases in 2000.

A college degree is now the minimum credential needed for entrance into much of today's economy. "In the mid 1970s, less than 30% of jobs in America required any education beyond high school," reports Jamie P. Merisotis, president and chief executive officer of Lumina Foundation, a private foundation dedicated to expanding higher-education opportunity. "Today, the majority of U.S. jobs require a postsecondary degree or credential." A recent study conducted by the Georgetown Center on Education and the Workforce projects that 63% of job openings in 2018 will require at least some college education.

On top of that, the penalty for not obtaining a college degree has increased dramatically over the last three decades. Beginning with the loss of manufacturing jobs beginning in the late 1970s, the gap between the earnings of college graduates and those with just high school education has steadily widened. The Georgetown study calculated that in 1980 college graduates' lifetime earnings were 44% higher than those of high-school graduates. In 2010 college graduates' lifetime earnings were nearly twice (97% more than) those of high school graduates.

At the same time, the employment prospects of even college graduates are far from bright. First off, having graduated from college is no guarantee of full-time employment. The Economic Policy Institute Briefing Paper on "The Class of 2012" found that the unemployment rate for young college graduates (ages 21 to 24) averaged 9.4% from April 2011 to March 2012. Another 19.1% of of this group was underemployed--unable to find full-time work--during that time period. Second, pay for college grads is down. On average, wages for full-time workers with four-year college degrees fell by 5.4% (adjusted for inflation) between 2000 and 2011. Finally, many graduates do not find the kinds of jobs they wanted. More than a third (37.8%) of college graduates under 25, reports a recent study by economist Andrew Sum of Northeastern University's Center for Labor Market Studies, were working at jobs that did not require a college degree.

For workers without a college degree the numbers are even worse. In May 2012 about one quarter (24%) of new high school graduates from 17 to 20 years old were unemployed, and about half (54% for April 2011 to March 212) were underemployed, unable to get a full time job. Finally, average hourly wages for young high-school graduates plummeted from 2000 to 2011, falling 11.1% after adjusting for inflation.

Pell-Mell

The *WSJ* editors stand four square against providing relief for those hobbled by student debt, especially by expanding Pell Grants to an ever-wider swath of college students. But there is plenty wrong with the editors' long list of complaints about Pell Grants.

To start with, contrary to the editors' complaints, Pell Grants are well targeted. The evidence from a report by the conservative John William Pope Center, which is the source of many of the editors' claims, shows as much. In academic year 2009-2010, a year when the median household income was $51,190, some 94.2% of Pell grant recipients had a family income less than $50,000, and the majority (58.9%) had a family income of less than $20,000.

Nor is it surprising that the graduation rates for Pell Grant recipients are lower than other students. Proportionally, nearly twice as many Pell recipients have parents with only a high school diploma and nearly twice as many come from non-English-speaking homes as other undergraduates. Even the Pope Center recognizes that these are risk factors for dropping out.

The size of Pell Grants is another reason why it is hardly surprising that the graduation rates of Pell recipients are lower than those of other undergraduates. Award amounts for Pell recipients have remained relatively flat in real terms, but covered less and less of college costs. The $5,550 maximum Pell Grant in 2011 covered just one-third of the average cost of attending a public four-year college, just one half the level it covered in 1980-81, according to the Institute for College Access and Success. [Add something like: If Pell Grants covered more of college costs, students from lower-income families would be less likely to drop out due to economic hardship--like being unable to make tuition due to tight family budgets.

In addition, better-off students do not often receive large Pell Grants, as the editors contend. The College Board reports that in academic year 2010-2011 just 1.6% of recipients from families with an income above $60,000 received the maximum Pell Grant of $5,550, well below the 33.8% of the recipients from families with incomes between $15,000 and $20,000 who got the maximum grant. While a bit more than one-fifth of those high-income recipients did apply their Pell Grants to schools that cost $30,000 or more, that amounts to less than one half of one percent of all Pell Grants going to help these high-income recipients attend "more expensive" colleges.

Finally, writing 100 times on the chalkboard "student aid raises tuition," as the editors have suggested, might convince some readers that Pell Grants are driving up tuition. But the evidence is far from conclusive. The Pope Center report states that, "most studies show at least some effect of aid on tuition," which implies that other studies show that student aid has had zero effect on tuition. Indeed they do. For instance, David L. Warren, president of the National Association of Independent Colleges and Universities, reports, "Studies conducted during three successive administrations—Bill Clinton, George W. Bush, and Barack Obama—have found no link between student aid and tuition increases."

One must also ask how Pell Grants with a maximum grant that now covers just one third of the cost of attending a public four-year college, could have fueled the rise in college tuition. What's more, the College Board reports that the average inflation-adjusted net tuition and fees (published tuition and fees minus grants from all sources and federal tax benefits) at private, nonprofit colleges and universities actually dropped from 2006-07 to 2011-12, even as total Pell Grant expenditures more than doubled after correcting for inflation.

A Universal Entitlement

The Obama administration has undertaken some positive steps to expand access to Pell Grants and toward providing debt relief for students. In 2010, the President signed legislation that converted all federally guaranteed student loans (loans issued by private banks to students, with the federal government promising to pay back the loan if the debtor failed to do so) to direct loans administered by the government. This change eliminated fees paid to the private banks that had acted as intermediaries, saving nearly $68 billion over the next 11 years, $36 billion of which is to be used to expand Pell Grants. This year, the Obama Consumer Financial Protection Bureau issued a report recommending that Congress enact legislation letting borrowers discharge their private student loans (those not backed by the federal government) through bankruptcy.

But much more needs to be done. Private student loans account for just 10% of student loans. A good first step toward genuine debt relief would be for Congress to pass the Student Loan Forgiveness Act of 2012, introduced by Representative Hansen Clarke, a Michigan Democrat, which would allow "existing borrowers" to be forgiven up to $45,000 in student debt after the borrower has made ten years of income-based payments (no more than 10% of income).

Pell Grants need to be not only a entitlement, but expanded to a near universal entitlement A recent report from the Pell Institute's newsletter, Postsecondary Education Opportunity, throws into to sharp relief the need to do yet more. Only 10.7% of students from families in the bottom fourth by family income, below $33,050, had attained a bachelor's degree by 24 years of age; among students from families in the second fourth by family income, with incomes between $33,050 and $61,600, only 15%. At the same time, 79.1% of students from the top fourth by family income, above $98,875, had a bachelor's degree by age 24.

As more and more families rely on Pell Grants to reduce the cost of a college education for their children, the more likely it is that Pell Grants will continue to withstand the budget cuts likely to come in the upcoming years. And more fulsome and the more universal Pell Grants will help make merit, not economic means, the determinant of who gets a college degree. ❏

Sources: Anthony Carnevale, Tamara Jayasundera, and Ban Cheah, "The College Advantage: Weathering the Economic Storm," Center on Education and the Workforce, Georgetown University, August 15, 2012; Jenna Ashley Robinson and Duke Cheston, "Pell Grants: Where Does All the Money Go?" John W. Pope Center for Higher Education Policy, June 2012; Rep. Hansen Clarke, The Student Loan Forgiveness Act of 2012; "Public Policy Analysis of Opportunity for Postsecondary Education," Postsecondary Education Opportunity newsletter, January 2012; Heidi Shierholz, Natalie Sabadish, and Hilary Wething, "The Class Of 2012:

Labor market for young graduates remains grim," Economic Policy Institute Briefing Paper, May 3, 2012; Meta Brown, Andrew Haughwout, Donghoon Lee, Maricar Mabutas, and Wilbert van der Klaauw, "Federal Student Financial Aid: Grading Student Loans," Federal Reserve Bank of New York, March 05, 2012; Charley Stone, Carl Van Horn, Cliff Zukin, and John J. Heldrich, "Chasing the American Dream: Recent College Graduates and the Great Recession," Center for Workforce Development, May 2012.

Chapter 6

THE ENVIRONMENT

Article 6.1

THE PHANTOM MENACE
Environmental regulations are not "job-killers" after all.

BY HEIDI GARRETT-PELTIER
July/August 2011

Polluting industries, along with the legislators who are in their pockets, consistently claim that environmental regulation will be a "job killer." They counter efforts to control pollution and to protect the environment by claiming that any such measures would increase costs and destroy jobs. But these are empty threats. In fact, the bulk of the evidence shows that environmental regulations do not hinder economic growth or employment and may actually stimulate both.

One recent example of this, the Northeast Regional Greenhouse Gas Initiative (RGGI), is an emissions-allowance program that caps and reduces emissions in ten northeast and mid-Atlantic states. Under RGGI, allowances are auctioned to power companies and the majority of the revenues are used to offset increases in consumer energy bills and to invest in energy efficiency and renewable energy. A report released in February of this year shows that RGGI has created an economic return of $3 to $4 for every $1 invested, and has created jobs throughout the region. Yet this successful program has come under attack by right-wing ideologues, including the Koch brothers-funded "Americans for Prosperity"; as a result, the state of New Hampshire recently pulled out of the program.

The allegation that environmental regulation is a job-killer is based on a mischaracterization of costs, both by firms and by economists. Firms often frame spending on environmental controls or energy-efficient machinery as a pure cost—wasted spending that reduces profitability. But such expenses should instead be seen as investments that enhance productivity and in turn promote economic development. Not only can these investments lead to lower costs for energy use and waste disposal, they may also direct innovations in the production process itself that could increase the firm's long-run profits. This is the Porter Hypothesis, named after Harvard Business School professor Michael Porter. According to studies conducted by Porter, properly and flexibly designed environmental regulation can trigger innovation that partly or completely offsets the costs of complying with the regulation.

The positive aspects of environmental regulation are overlooked not only by firms, but also by economists who model the costs of compliance without including its widespread benefits. These include reduced mortality, fewer sick days for workers and school children, reduced health-care costs, increased biodiversity, and mitigation of climate change. But most mainstream models leave these benefits out of their calculations. The Environmental Protection Agency, which recently released a study of the impacts of the Clean Air Act from 1990 to 2020, compared the effects of a "cost-only" model with those of a more complete model. In the version which only incorporated the costs of compliance, both GDP and overall economic welfare were expected to decline by 2020 due to Clean Air Act regulations. However, once the costs of compliance were coupled with the benefits, the model showed that both GDP and economic welfare would increase over time, and that by 2020 the economic benefits would outweigh the costs. Likewise, the Office of Management and Budget found that to date the benefits of the law have far exceeded the cost, with an economic return of between $4 and $8 for every $1 invested in compliance.

Environmental regulations do affect jobs. But contrary to claims by polluting industries and congressional Republicans, efforts to protect our environment can actually create jobs. In order to reduce harmful pollution from power plants, for example, an electric company would have to equip plants with scrubbers and other technologies. These technologies would need to be manufactured and installed, creating jobs for people in the manufacturing and construction industries.

The official unemployment rate in the United States is still quite high, hovering around 9%. In this economic climate, politicians are more sensitive than ever to claims that environmental regulation could be a job-killer. By framing investments as wasted costs and relying on incomplete economic models, polluting industries have consistently tried to fight environmental standards. It's time to change the terms of the debate. We need to move beyond fear-mongering about the costs and start capturing the benefits. ❑

Article 6.2

WAY BEYOND GREENWASHING
Have corporations captured "Big Conservation"?

BY JONATHAN LATHAM
March/April 2012

Imagine an international mega-deal. The global organic food industry agrees to support international agribusiness in clearing as much tropical rainforest as they want for farming. In return, agribusiness agrees to farm the now-deforested land using organic methods, and the organic industry encourages its supporters to buy the resulting timber and food under the newly devised "Rainforest Plus" label. There would surely be an international outcry.

Virtually unnoticed, however, even by their own membership, the world's biggest wildlife conservation groups have agreed to exactly such a scenario, only in reverse. Led by the World Wide Fund for Nature (WWF, still known as the World Wildlife Fund in the United States), many of the biggest conservation nonprofits including Conservation International and the Nature Conservancy have already agreed to a series of global bargains with international agribusiness. In exchange for vague promises of habitat protection, sustainability, and social justice, these conservation groups are offering to greenwash industrial commodity agriculture.

The big conservation nonprofits don't see it that way, of course. According to WWF's "Vice President for Market Transformation" Jason Clay, the new conservation strategy arose from two fundamental realizations.

The first was that agriculture and food production are the key drivers of almost every environmental concern. From issues as diverse as habitat destruction to over-use of water, from climate change to ocean dead zones, agriculture and food production are globally the primary culprits. To take one example, 80-90% of all fresh water extracted by humans is for agriculture, according to the UN Food and Agriculture Organization's "State of the World's Land and Water" report.

This point was emphasized once again in an analysis published in the scientific journal *Nature* in October 2011. The lead author of this study was Professor Jonathan Foley. Not only is Foley the director of the University of Minnesota-based Institute on the Environment, but he is also a science board member of the Nature Conservancy.

The second crucial realization for WWF was that forest destroyers typically are not peasants with machetes but national and international agribusinesses with bulldozers. It is the latter who deforest tens of thousands of acres at a time. Land clearance on this scale is an ecological disaster, but Claire Robinson of Earth Open Source points out it is also "incredibly socially destructive," as peasants are driven off their land and communities are destroyed. According to the UN Permanent Forum on Indigenous Issues, 60 million people worldwide risk losing their land and means of subsistence from palm plantations.

By about 2004, WWF had come to recognize the true impacts of industrial agriculture. Instead of informing their membership and initiating protests and boycotts, however, they embarked on a partnership strategy they call "market transformation."

Market Transformation

With WWF leading the way, the conservation nonprofits have negotiated approval schemes for "Responsible" and "Sustainable" farmed commodity crops. According to WWF's Clay, the plan is to have agribusinesses sign up to reduce the 4-6 most serious negative impacts of each commodity crop by 70-80%. And if enough growers and suppliers sign up, then the Indonesian rainforests or the Brazilian Cerrado will be saved.

The ambition of market transformation is on a grand scale. There are schemes for palm oil (the Roundtable on Sustainable Palm Oil; RSPO), soybeans (the Round Table on Responsible Soy; RTRS), biofuels (the Roundtable on Sustainable Biofuels), Sugar (Bonsucro) and also for cotton, shrimp, cocoa and farmed salmon. These are markets each worth many billions of dollars annually and the intention is for these new "Responsible" and "Sustainable" certified products to dominate them.

The reward for producers and supermarkets will be that, reinforced on every shopping trip, "Responsible" and "Sustainable" logos and marketing can be expected to have major effects on public perception of the global food supply chain. And the ultimate goal is that, if these schemes are successful, human rights, critical habitats, and global sustainability will receive a huge and globally significant boost.

The role of WWF and other nonprofits in these schemes is to offer their knowledge to negotiate standards, to provide credibility, and to lubricate entry of certified products into international markets. On its UK website, for example, WWF offers its members the chance to "Save the Cerrado" by emailing supermarkets to buy "Responsible Soy." What WWF argues will be a major leap forward in environmental and social responsibility has already started. "Sustainable" and "Responsible" products are already entering global supply chains.

Reputational Risk

For conservation nonprofits these plans entail risk, one of which is simple guilt by association. The Round Table on Responsible Soy (RTRS) scheme is typical of these certification schemes. Its membership includes WWF, Conservation International, Fauna and Flora International, the Nature Conservancy, and other prominent nonprofits. Corporate members include repeatedly vilified members of the industrial food chain. As of January 2012, there are 102 members, including Monsanto, Cargill, ADM, Nestle, BP, and UK supermarket ASDA.

That is not the only risk. Membership in the scheme, which includes signatures on press-releases and sometimes on labels, indicates approval for activities that are widely opposed. The RTRS, for example, certifies soybeans grown in large-scale chemical-intensive monocultures. They are usually genetically modified organisms (GMOs). They are mostly fed to animals. And they originate in countries with hungry populations. When, according to an ABC News poll, 52% of Americans think GMOs are unsafe and 93% think GMOs ought to be labeled, for example, this is a risk most organizations dependent on their reputations probably would not consider.

The remedy for such reputational risk is high standards, rigorous certification, and watertight traceability procedures. Only credibility at every step can deflect the seemingly obvious suspicion that the conservation nonprofits have been hoodwinked or have somehow "sold out."

So, which one is it? Are "Responsible" and "Sustainable" certifications indicative of a genuine strategic success by WWF and its fellows, or are the schemes nothing more than business as usual with industrial-scale greenwashing and a social-justice varnish?

Low and Ambiguous Standards

The first place to look is the standards themselves. The language from the RTRS standards (see sidebar), to stick with the case of soy, illustrates the tone of the RTRS principles and guidance.

There are two ways to read these standards. The generous interpretation is to recognize that the sentiments expressed are higher than what is actually practiced in many countries where soybeans are grown, in that the standards broadly follow common practice in Europe or North America. Nevertheless, they are far lower than organic or fair-trade standards; for example, they don't require crop rotation, or prohibit pesticides. Even a generous reading also needs to acknowledge the crucial point that adherence to similar requirements in Europe and North America has contaminated wells, depleted aquifers, degraded rivers, eroded the soil, polluted the oceans, driven species to extinction, and depopulated the countryside—to mention only a few well-documented downsides.

There is also a less generous interpretation of the standards. Much of the content is either in the form of statements, or it is merely advice. Thus section 4.2 reads: "Pollution is minimized and production waste is managed responsibly." Imperatives, such as: "must," "may never," "will," etc., are mostly lacking from the document. Worse, key terms such as "pollution," "minimized," "responsible," and "timely" (see sidebar) are left undefined. This chronic vagueness means that both certifiers and producers possess effectively infinite latitude to implement or judge the standards. They could never be enforced, in or out of court.

The Round Table on Responsible Soy Standards

RTRS standards (version 1, June 2010) cover five "principles." Principle 1: Legal Compliance and Good Business Practices. Principle 2: Responsible Labour Conditions. Principle 3: Responsible Community Relations. Principle 4: Environmental Responsibility. Principle 5: Good Agricultural Practice.

Language typical of the standards includes, under Principle 2 (Responsible Labour Conditions), section 2.1.1 states: "No forced, compulsory, bonded, trafficked, or otherwise involuntary labor is used at any stage of production," while section 2.4.4 states, "Workers are not hindered from interacting with external parties outside working hours."

Under Principle 3 (Responsible Community Relations), section 3.3.3 states: "Any complaints and grievances received are dealt with in a timely manner."

Under Principle 4 (Environmental Responsibility), section 4.2 states: "Pollution is minimized and production waste is managed responsibly," and section 4.4 states: "Expansion of soy cultivation is responsible."

Under Principle 5 (Good Agricultural Practice), Section 5.9 states: "Appropriate measures are implemented to prevent the drift of agrochemicals to neighboring areas."

Dubious Verification and Enforcement

Unfortunately, the flaws of RTRS certification do not end there. They include the use of an internal verification system. The RTRS uses professional certifiers, but only those who are members of RTRS. This means that the conservation nonprofits are relying on third parties for compliance information. It also means that only RTRS members can judge whether a principle was adhered to. Even if they consider it was not, there is nothing they can do, since the RTRS has no legal status or sanctions.

The "culture" of deforestation is also important to the standards. Rainforest clearance is often questionably legal, or actively illegal, and usually requires removing existing occupants from the land. It is a world of private armies and bribery. This operating environment makes very relevant the irony under which RTRS members, under Principle 1, volunteer to obey the law. The concept of volunteering to obey the law invites more than a few questions. If an organization is not already obeying the law, what makes WWF suppose that a voluntary code of conduct will persuade it? And does obeying the law meaningfully contribute to a marketing campaign based on responsibility?

Of equal concern is the absence of a clear certification trail. Under the "Mass Balance" system offered by RTRS, soybeans (or derived products) can be sold as "Responsible" that were never grown under the system. Mass Balance means vendors can transfer the certification quantity purchased, to non-RTRS soybeans. Such an opportunity raises the inherent difficulties of traceability and verification to new levels.

How Will Certification Save Wild Habitats?

A key stated goal of WWF is to halt deforestation through the use of maps identifying priority habitat areas that are off-limits to RTRS members. There are crucial questions over these maps, however. First, even though soybeans are already being traded, the maps have yet to be drawn up. Secondly, the maps are to be drawn up by RTRS members themselves. Thirdly, RTRS maps can be periodically redrawn. Fourthly, RTRS members need not certify all of their production acreage. This means they can certify part of their acreage as "Responsible," but still sell (as "Irresponsible"?) soybeans from formerly virgin habitat. This means WWF's target for year 2020 of 25% coverage globally and 75% in WWF's "priority areas" would still allow 25% of the Brazilian soybean harvest to come from newly deforested land. And of course, the scheme cannot prevent non-members, or even non-certified subsidiaries, from specializing in deforestation.

These are certification schemes, therefore, with low standards, no methods of enforcement, and enormous loopholes. Pete Riley of UK GM Freeze dubs their instigator the "World Wide Fund for naïveté" and believes "the chances of Responsible soy saving the Cerrado are zero." Claire Robinson of Earth Open Source agrees: "The RTRS standard will not protect the forests and other sensitive ecosystems. Additionally, it greenwashes soy that's genetically modified to survive being sprayed with quantities of herbicide that endanger human health and the environment." There is even a website (www.toxicsoy.org) dedicated to exposing the greenwashing of GMO soy.

Many other groups apparently share that view. More than 250 large and small sustainable farming, social justice, and rainforest preservation groups from all over the world signed a "Letter of Critical Opposition to the RTRS" in 2009. Signatories included the Global Forest Coalition, Friends of the Earth, Food First, the British Soil Association and the World Development Movement.

Other commodity certifications involving WWF have also received strong criticism. The Mangrove Action Project in 2008 published a "Public Declaration Against the Process of Certification of Industrial Shrimp Aquaculture" while the World Rainforest Movement issued "Declaration against the Roundtable on Sustainable Palm Oil (RSPO)," signed by 256 organizations in October 2008.

What Really Drives Commodity Certification?

Commodity certification is in many ways a strange departure for conservation nonprofits. In the first place the big conservation nonprofits are more normally active in acquiring and researching wild habitats. Secondly, these are membership organizations, yet it is hard to envisage these schemes energizing the membership. How many members of the Nature Conservancy will be pleased to find that their organization has been working with Monsanto to promote GM crops as "Responsible"? Indeed, one can argue that these programs are being actively concealed from their members, donors, and the public. From their advertising, their websites, and their educational materials, one would presume that poachers, population growth and ignorance are the chief threats to wildlife in developing countries. It is not true, however, and as WWF's Jason Clay and the very existence of these certification schemes make clear, senior management knows it well.

In public, the conservation nonprofits justify market transformation as cooperative; they wish to work with others, not against them. However, they have chosen to work preferentially with powerful and wealthy corporations. Why not cooperate instead with small farmers' movements, indigenous groups, and already successful standards, such as fair-trade, organic and non-GMO? These are causes that could use the help of big international organizations. Why not, with WWF help, embed into organic standards a rainforest conservation element? Why not cooperate with your membership to create engaged consumer power against habitat destruction, monoculture, and industrial farming? Instead, the new "Responsible" and "Sustainable" standards threaten organic, fair-trade, and local food systems—which are some of the environmental movement's biggest successes.

One clue to the enthusiasm for "market transformation" may be that financial rewards are available. According to Nina Holland of Corporate Europe Observatory, certification is "now a core business" for WWF. Indeed, WWF and the Dutch nonprofit Solidaridad are currently receiving millions of euros from the Dutch government (under its Sustainable Trade Action Plan) to support these schemes. According to the plan, 67 million euros have already been committed, and similar amounts are promised.

The Threat From the Food Movement

Commodity-certification schemes like RTRS can be seen as an inability of global conservation leadership to work constructively with the ordinary people who live in and around wild areas of the globe; or they can be seen as a disregard for fair-trade and organic labels; or as a lost opportunity to inform and energize members and potential members as to the true causes of habitat destruction; or even as a cynical moneymaking scheme. These are all plausible explanations of the enthusiasm for certification schemes and probably each plays a part. None, however, explains why conservation nonprofits would sign up to schemes whose standards and credibility are so low. Especially when, as never before, agribusiness is under pressure to change its destructive social and environmental practices.

The context of these schemes is that we live at an historic moment. Positive alternatives to industrial agriculture, such as fair trade, organic agriculture, agro-ecology, and the System of Rice Intensification, have shown they can feed the planet, without destroying it, even with a greater population. Consequently, there is now a substantial international consensus of informed opinion that industrial agriculture is a principal cause of the current environmental crisis and the chief obstacle to hunger eradication.

This consensus is one of several roots of the international food movement. As a powerful synergism of sustainability, social-justice, sustainability, food-quality, and environmental concerns, the food movement is a clear threat to the long-term existence of the industrial food system. Incidentally, this is why big multinationals have been buying up ethical brands.

Under these circumstances, evading the blame for the environmental devastation of the Amazon, Asia, and elsewhere, undermining organic and other genuine certification schemes, and splitting the environmental movement must be a dream come true for members of the industrial food system. A true cynic might surmise that the food industry could hardly have engineered it better had they planned it themselves.

Who Runs Big Conservation?

To guard against such possibilities, nonprofits are required to have boards of directors whose primary legal function is to guard the mission of the organization and to protect its good name. In practice, for conservation nonprofits this means overseeing potential financial conflicts and preventing the organization from lending its name to greenwashing.

So, who are the individuals guarding the mission of global conservation nonprofits? U.S.-WWF boasts (literally) that its new vice-chair was the last CEO of Coca-Cola, Inc. (a member of Bonsucro) and that another board member is Charles O. Holliday Jr., the current chairman of the board of Bank of America, who was formerly CEO of DuPont (owner of Pioneer Hi-Bred International, a major player in the GMO industry). The current chair of the executive board at Conservation International is Robert Walton, better known as chair of the board of Wal-Mart (which now sells "sustainably sourced" food and owns the supermarket chain ASDA). The boards of WWF and Conservation International do have more than a sprinkling of members with conservation-related careers. But they are heavily outnumbered by business representatives. On the board of Conservation International, for example, are GAP, Intel, Northrop Grumman, JP Morgan, Starbucks, and UPS, among others.

The Nature Conservancy's board of directors has only two members (out of 22) who list an active affiliation to a conservation organization in their board CV (Prof. Gretchen Daly and Cristian Samper, head of the U.S. Museum of Natural History). Only one other member even mentions among his qualifications an interest in the subject of conservation. The remaining members are like Shona Brown, who is an employee of Google and a board member of Pepsico, or Meg Whitman, the current president and CEO of Hewlett-Packard, or Muneer A. Satter, a managing director of Goldman Sachs.

So, was market transformation developed with the support of these boards or against their wishes? The latter is hardly likely. The key question then becomes: Did these boards in fact instigate market transformation? Did it come from the very top?

Never Ending

Leaving aside whether conservation was ever their true intention, it seems highly unlikely that WWF and its fellow conservation groups will leverage a positive transformation of the food system by bestowing "Sustainable" and "Responsible" standards on agribusiness. Instead, it appears much more likely that, by undermining existing standards and offering worthless standards of their own, habitat destruction and human misery will only increase.

Market transformation, as envisaged by WWF, nevertheless might have worked. However, WWF neglected to consider that successful certification schemes start from the ground up. Organic and fair-trade began with a large base of committed farmers determined to fashion a better food system. Producers willingly signed up to high standards and clear requirements because they believed in them. Indeed, many already were practicing high standards without certification. But when big players in the food industry have tried to climb on board, game the system and manipulate standards, problems have resulted, even with credible standards like fair-trade and organic. At some point big players will probably undermine these standards. They seem already to be well on the way, but if they succeed their efforts will only have proved that certification standards can never be a substitute for trust, commitment and individual integrity.

The only good news in this story is that it contradicts fundamentally the defeatist arguments of the WWF. Old-fashioned activist strategies, of shaming bad practice, boycotting products, and encouraging alternatives, do work. The market opportunity presently being exploited by WWF and company resulted from the success of these strategies, not their failure. Multinational corporations, we should conclude, really do fear activists, non-profits, informed consumers, and small producers all working together. ❑

Sources: Jonathan A. Foley et al. "Solutions for a Cultivated Planet," *Nature*, October 2011 (Nature.com); Jason Clay, "Economics, Behavior and Biodiversity Loss: Sustainability as a Pre-competitive Issue," March 25, 2011 (youtube.com); Food and Agriculture Organization of the United Nations, "Scarcity and degradation of land and water: growing threat to food security," November 28, 2011 (fao.org); State of the World's Land and Water Resources for Food and Agriculture (SOLAW), November 28, 2011 (fao.org); Mat McDermott, "More Dirty Deforestation: 55% of Indonesia's Logging Illegal + Cargill's Two Hidden Palm Oil Plantations," May 6, 2010 (treehugger.com); Earth Open Source (earthopensource.org); United Nations (UN; un.org); Roundtable on Sustainable Palm Oil (RSPO; rspo.org); Round Table on Responsible Soy (RTRS; responsiblesoy.org); Roundtable on Sustainable Biofuels (rsb.epfl.ch); Bonsucro (Bonsucro.com); WWF, "Save the Cerrado: What's happening in the Cerrado?" (wwf.org.uk); Gary Langer, "Behind the Label, Many Skeptical of Bio-engineered Food," June 19, 2001 (abcnews.com); Round Table on Responsible Soy, "Why certifying under the RTST Standard?" (responsiblesoy.org); Natural Resources Defense Council, "Atrazine: Poisoning the Well," May 2010 (nrdc.org); The *Capital-Journal* Editorial Board, "Time for action on rural depopulation," July 28, 2011 (cjonline.com); "State of the World's Indigenous Peoples Report, Chapter 7: Emerging Issues," January 2010 (un.org); "A Brief History of Rubber" (rainforests.mongabay.com); "Letter of critical opposition to the Round Table on Responsible Soy," April 2009 (bangmfood.org); Global Forest Coalition (globalforestcoalition.org); Public Declaration Against the Process of Certification of Industrial Shrimp Aquaculture, November 3, 2008 (mangroveactionproject.org); World Rainforest Movement, "Declarations against the Roundtable on Sustainable Palm Oil (RSPO) in Defence of Human Rights, Food Sovereignty," September 2008 (wrm.org); System of Rice Intensification (SRI-Rice; sri.ciifad.cornell.edu); Sarah Hills, "Coca-Cola snaps up first Bonsucro certified sugarcane," June 22, 2011 (foodnavigator.com); "Wal-Mart Unveils Global Sustainable Agriculture Goal," October 14, 2010 (walmartstores.com); "Largest Corporate Dairy, Biotech Firm and USDA Accused of Conspiring to Corrupt Rulemaking and Pollute Organics," January 23, 2012 (cornucopia.org); Dutch Ministry of Agriculture, "Nature and Food Quality Sustainable Food: Public Summary of Policy Document" (government.nl); Jonathan Latham and Allison Wilson, "How the Science Media Failed the IAASTD," April 7, 2008 (independentsciencenews.org).

Article 6.3

THE COSTS OF EXTREME WEATHER
Climate inaction is expensive—and inequitable.

BY HEIDI GARRETT-PELTIER
November/December 2011

Two thousand eleven has already been a record-setting year. The number of weather disasters in the United States whose costs exceed $1 billion—ten—is the highest ever. August witnessed one of the ten most expensive catastrophes in U.S. history, Tropical Storm Irene. An initial estimate put the damages from Irene at between $7 billion and $13 billion. In this one storm alone, eight million businesses and homes lost power, roads collapsed, buildings flooded, and dozens of people lost their lives. Meanwhile, Texas is experiencing its hottest year in recorded history: millions of acres in the state have burned, over 1,550 homes have been lost to wildfires as of early September, and tens of thousands of people have had to evacuate their homes. The devastation caused by the storms and droughts has left individuals and businesses wondering how they'll recover, and has left cash-strapped towns wondering how they'll pay for road and infrastructure repairs.

Extreme weather events like these are expected to become more frequent and more intense over the next century. That's just one of the impacts of climate change, which, according to the consensus of scientists and research organizations from around the world, is occurring with both natural and human causes, but mainly from the burning of fossil fuels. According to NASA, since 1950 the number of record high-temperature days has been rising while the number of record low-temperature days has been falling. The number of intense rainfall events has also increased in the past six decades. At the same time, droughts and heat waves have also become more frequent, as warmer conditions in drier areas have led to faster evaporation. This is why in the same month we had wildfires in Texas (resulting from more rapid evaporation and drought) and flooding in the Northeast (since warmer air holds more moisture and results in more intense precipitation).

In response to these dramatic weather changes, the courses of action available to us are *mitigation*, *adaptation*, and *reparation*. Mitigation refers to efforts to prevent or reduce climate change, for example, cutting fossil fuel use by increasing energy efficiency and using more renewable energy. *Adaptation* refers to changing our behaviors, technologies, institutions, and infrastructure to cope with the damages that climate change creates—building levees near flood-prone areas or relocating homes further inland, for example. And as the term implies, *reparation* means repairing or rebuilding the roads, bridges, homes, and communities that are damaged by floods, winds, heat, and other weather-related events.

Of these, mitigation is the one strategy whose costs and benefits can both be shared globally. Moving toward a more sustainable economy less reliant on the burning of fossil fuels for its energy would slow the rise in average global temperatures and make extreme weather events less likely. Mitigation will have the greatest impact with a shared worldwide commitment, but even without binding international agreements, countries can take steps to reduce their use of coal, oil, and natural gas.

According to the Intergovernmental Panel on Climate Change, even the most stringent mitigation efforts cannot prevent further impacts of climate change in the next few decades. We will still need to adapt and repair—all the more in the absence of such efforts. But the costs and burdens of adaptation and reparation are spread unevenly across different populations and in many cases the communities most affected by climate change will be those least able to afford to build retaining walls or relocate to new homes. Farmers who can afford to will change their planting and harvesting techniques and schedules, but others will have unusable land and will be unable to sustain themselves. Roads that are washed away will be more quickly rebuilt in richer towns, while poorer towns will take longer to rebuild if they can at all. The divide between rich and poor will only grow.

Given the high cost of damages we've already faced just this year, mitigation may very well be sound economic planning. But it is also the most humane and equitable approach to solving our climate problem. ❑

Sources: NOAA/NESDIS/NCDC, "Billion Dollar U.S. Weather/Climate Disasters 1980-August 2011"; Michael Cooper, "Hurricane Cost Seen as Ranking Among Top Ten," *New York Times*, August 30, 2011; "Hurricane Irene Damage: Storm Likely Cost $7 Billion to $13 Billion," *International Business Times*, August 29, 2011; Intergovernmental Panel on Climate Change, *Fourth Assessment Report: Climate Change 2007*, Working Group II ch. 19; NASA, "Global Climate Change: Vital Signs of the Planet—Evidence"; U.S. EPA, "Climate Change—Health and Environmental Effects, Extreme Events."

Article 6.4

LIVING UP TO RENEWABLE FUEL STANDARDS
BY HEIDI GARRETT-PELTIER
March/April 2012

Is reducing U.S. greenhouse gas emissions and independence on imported oil just a pipe dream? Without transforming the U.S transportation sector, which accounts for 34% of U.S. carbon dioxide emissions, it surely is.

The United States needs alternative forms of transportation: more public transit; more walking and biking; more carpooling; in short, just about any alternative to one person per vehicle. But the United States also needs to change its transportation energy, away from oil and toward biofuels and other alternatives. Currently petroleum accounts for 97.4% of U.S. transportation energy, and about half of it is imported.

The Renewable Fuel Standard was established under the Energy Inde-pendence and Security Act of 2007 and revised in 2010 by the Environmental Protection Agency to help make the shift toward petroleum alternatives. This revised standard, known as RFS2, could offer some hope. It mandates large increases in biofuels, which are required to have emissions of greenhouse gases 20% to 60% below that of gasoline, depending on their type.

But how much authentic progress has been made since 2007 and what is the promise that the RFS2 will bring about a genuine reduction in U.S. emissions of greenhouse gases and dependence on imported oil?

The key to the potential of the RFS2 to reduce greenhouse gas emissions lies in its promotion of the development and use of "advanced" biofuels. The biofuel that is most widely used in the U.S. today is corn-based ethanol, which is derived from the starch of the corn kernel. But the environmental benefits of corn ethanol are limited at best, and some studies have even found that the lifecycle greenhouse gas emissions from corn ethanol can be greater than from gasoline per unit of energy. The National Academy of Sciences has reviewed and conducted a number of studies on the sustainability of biofuels and has found that corn ethanol should be considered only a transitional biofuel, to be used until advanced biofuels are fully commercialized.

Advanced biofuels consist largely of cellulosic biofuels, which are fuels that are produced from non-food parts of plants. The materials used to produce these fuels include agricultural residues (such as corn stalks), dedicated energy crops such as grasses and fast-growing trees, forest resources, and municipal solid waste. Cellulosic fuels largely do not compete with food supplies and the National Academy of Sciences has estimated that by 2030, up to 40 billion gallons of cellulosic fuels could be produced annually in a sustainable manner.

There are other advanced biofuels, such as those made from algae, which also have the potential to dramatically reduce greenhouse gas emissions in comparison to petroleum. The trouble is, cellulosic and other advanced biofuels have not yet reached commercialization. If the United States is to reduce its greenhouse gas emissions in any meaningful way, advanced biofuels must reach commercial scale, and must do so quickly. Biofuels can be produced domestically, which means fewer oil imports. This, in turn, implies reduced military conflicts over oil, greater energy security, and less spending leaking out of the economy. Domestic production means domestic employment.

Whether we reach the point of producing billions of gallons per year of sustainably harvested cellulosic fuels depends on a number of factors, including how competitive the prices of biofuels are with gasoline, whether sufficient infrastructure is developed for the distribution of billions of gallons of biofuels annually, and whether there is continued public support to develop and commercialize these fuels. While the RFS2 could be one step in this direction, so far it has been insufficient. It mandates the volumes and emission reduction targets of biofuels, but in no way ensures price-competitiveness with gasoline. Advanced biofuels will continue to require subsidies as the industry gets off the ground, and the policy uncertainty that comes with on-again-off-again price subsidies can discourage some investors from building commercial-scale biofuel refineries.

The oil industry has benefited from public support in the form of subsidies and tax preferences for many decades. Advanced biofuels, mere infants in comparison, need the same kind of financial support to be able to compete. Given the potential for emissions reductions, as well as the economic benefits to the domestic economy, there are multiple reasons for supporting the growth of this industry. The RFS2 should be enforced, but we must pursue additional strategies to make cellulosic and other advanced biofuels viable options for transportation. ❑

Article 6.5

KEEP IT IN THE GROUND
An alternative vision for petroleum emerges in Ecuador. But will Big Oil win the day?

BY ELISSA DENNIS
July/August 2010

In the far eastern reaches of Ecuador, in the Amazon basin rain forest, lies a land of incredible beauty and biological diversity. More than 2,200 varieties of trees reach for the sky, providing a habitat for more species of birds, bats, insects, frogs, and fish than can be found almost anywhere else in the world. Indigenous Waorani people have made the land their home for millennia, including the last two tribes living in voluntary isolation in the country. The land was established as Yasuní National Park in 1979, and recognized as a UNESCO World Biosphere Reserve in 1989.

Underneath this landscape lies a different type of natural resource: petroleum. Since 1972, oil has been Ecuador's primary export, representing 57% of the country's exports in 2008; oil revenues comprised on average 26% of the government's revenue between 2000 and 2007. More than 1.1 billion barrels of heavy crude oil have been extracted from Yasuní, about one quarter of the nation's production to date.

At this economic, environmental, and political intersection lie two distinct visions for Yasuní's, and Ecuador's, next 25 years. Petroecuador, the state-owned oil company, has concluded that 846 million barrels of oil could be extracted from proven reserves at the Ishpingo, Tambococha, and Tiputini (ITT) wells in an approximately 200,000 hectare area covering about 20% of the parkland. Extracting this petroleum, either alone or in partnership with interested oil companies in Brazil, Venezuela, or China, would generate approximately $7 billion, primarily in the first 13 years of extraction and continuing with declining productivity for another 12 years.

The alternative vision is the simple but profound choice to leave the oil in the ground.

Environmentalists and indigenous communities have been organizing for years to restrict drilling in Yasuní. But the vision became much more real when President Rafael Correa presented a challenge to the world community at a September 24, 2007 meeting of the United Nations General Assembly: if governments, companies, international organizations, and individuals pledge a total of $350 million per year for 10 years, equal to half of the forgone revenues from ITT, then Ecuador will chip in the other half and keep the oil underground indefinitely, as this nation's contribution to halting global climate change.

The Yasuní-ITT Initiative would preserve the fragile environment, leave the voluntarily isolated tribes in peace, and prevent the emission of an estimated 407 million metric tons of carbon dioxide into the atmosphere. This "big idea from a small country" has even broader implications, as Alberto Acosta, former Energy Minister and one of the architects of the proposal, notes in his new book, *La Maldición de la Abundancia* (*The Curse of Abundance*). The Initiative is a *"punto de ruptura,"* he writes, a turning point in environmental history which "questions the logic of extractive (exporter of raw material) development," while introducing the possibility of global *"sumak kawsay,"* the indigenous Kichwa concept of "good living" in harmony with nature.

Ecuador, like much of Latin America, has long been an exporter of raw materials: cacao in the 19th century, bananas in the 20th century, and now petroleum. The nation dove into the oil boom of the 1970s, investing in infrastructure and building up external debt. When oil prices plummeted in the 1980s while interest rates on that debt ballooned, Ecuador was trapped in the debt crisis that affected much of the region. Thus began what Correa calls "the long night of neoliberalism:" IMF-mandated privatizations of utilities and mining sectors, with a concomitant decline of revenues from the nation's natural resources to the Ecuadorian people. By 1986, all of the nation's petroleum revenues were going to pay external debt.

Close to 40 years of oil production has failed to improve the living standards of the majority of Ecuadorians. "Petroleum has not helped this country," notes Ana Cecilia Salazar, director of the Department of Social Sciences in the College of Economics of the University of Cuenca. "It has been corrupt. It has not diminished poverty. It has not industrialized this country. It has just made a few people rich."

Currently 38% of the population lives in poverty, with 13% in extreme poverty. The nation's per capita income growth between 1982 and 2007 was only .7% per year. And although the unemployment rate of 10% may seem moderate, an estimated 53% of the population is considered "underemployed."

Petroleum extraction has brought significant environmental damage. Each year 198,000 hectares of land in the Amazon are deforested for oil production. A verdict is expected this year in an Ecuadorian court in the 17-year-old class action suit brought by 30,000 victims of Texaco/Chevron's drilling operations in the area northwest of Yasuní between 1964 and 1990. The unprecedented $27 billion lawsuit alleges that thousands of cancers and other health problems were caused by Texaco's use of outdated and dangerous practices, including the dumping of 18 billion gallons of toxic wastewater into local water supplies.

Regardless of its economic or environmental impacts, the oil is running out. With 4.16 billion barrels in proven reserves nationwide, and another half billion "probable" barrels, best-case projections, including the discovery of new reserves, indicate the nation will stop exporting oil within 28 years, and stop producing oil within 35 years.

"At this moment we have an opportunity to rethink the extractive economy that for many years has constrained the economy and politics in the country," says Esperanza Martinez, a biologist, environmental activist, and author of the book *Yasuní: El tortuoso camino de Kioto a Quito*. "This proposal intends to change the terms of the North-South relationship in climate change negotiations."

As such, the Initiative fits into the emerging idea of "climate debt." The North's voracious energy consumption in the past has destroyed natural resources in the South; the South is currently bearing the brunt of global warming effects like floods and drought; and the South needs to adapt expensive new energy technology for the future instead of industrializing with the cheap fossil fuels that built the North. Bolivian president Evo Morales proposed at the Copenhagen climate talks last December that developed nations pay 1% of GDP, totaling $700 billion/year, into a compensation fund that poor nations could use to adapt their energy systems.

"Clearly in the future, it will not be possible to extract all the petroleum in the world because that would create a very serious world problem, so we need to create measures of compensation to pay the ecological debt to the countries," says Malki Sáenz, formerly Coordinator of the Yasuní-ITT Initiative within the Ministry of Foreign Relations. The Initiative "is a way to show the international community that real compensation mechanisms exist for not extracting petroleum."

Indigenous and environmental movements in Latin America and Africa are raising possibilities of leaving oil in the ground elsewhere. But the Yasuni-ITT proposal is the furthest along in detail, government sponsorship, and ongoing negotiations. The Initiative proposes that governments, international institutions, civil associations, companies, and individuals contribute to a fund administered through an international organization such as the United Nations Development Program (UNDP). Contributions could include swaps of Ecuador's external debt, as well as resources generated from emissions auctions in the European Union and carbon emission taxes such as those implemented in Sweden and Slovakia.

Contributors of at least $10,000 would receive a Yasuní Guarantee Certificate (CGY), redeemable only in the event that a future government decides to extract the oil. The total dollar value of the CGYs issued would equal the calculated value of the 407 million metric tons of non-emitted carbon dioxide.

The money would be invested in fixed income shares of renewable energy projects with a guaranteed yield, such as hydroelectric, geothermal, wind, and solar power, thus helping to reduce the country's dependence on fossil fuels. The interest payments generated by these investments would be designated for: 1) conservation projects, preventing deforestation of almost 10 million hectares in 40 protected areas covering 38% of Ecuador's territory; 2) reforestation and natural regeneration projects on another one million hectares of forest land; 3) national energy efficiency improvements; and 4) education, health, employment, and training programs in sustainable activities like ecotourism and agro forestry in the affected areas. The first three activities could prevent an additional 820 million metric tons of carbon dioxide emissions, tripling the Initiative's effectiveness.

These nationwide conservation efforts, as well as the proposal's mention of "monitoring" throughout Yasuní and possibly shutting down existing oil production, are particularly disconcerting to Ecuadorian and international oil and wood interests. Many speculate that political pressure from these economic powerhouses was behind a major blow to the Initiative this past January, when Correa, in one of his regular Saturday radio broadcasts, suddenly blasted the negotiations as "shameful," and a threat to the nation's "sovereignty" and "dignity." He threatened that if the full package of international commitments was not in place by this June, he would begin extracting oil from ITT.

Correa's comments spurred the resignations of four critical members of the negotiating commission, including Chancellor Fander Falconí, a longtime ally in Correa's PAIS party, and Roque Sevilla, an ecologist, businessman, and ex-Mayor of Quito whom Correa had picked to lead the commission. Ecuador's Ambassador to the UN Francisco Carrion also resigned from the commission, as did World Wildlife Fund president Yolanda Kakabadse.

Correa has been clear from the outset that the government has a Plan B, to extract the oil, and that the non-extraction "first option" is contingent on the mandated monetary commitments. But oddly his outburst came as the negotiating team's efforts were bearing fruit. Sevilla told the press in January of commitments in various stages of approval from Germany, Spain, Belgium, France, and Switzerland, totaling at least $1.5 billion. The team was poised to sign an agreement with UNDP last December in Copenhagen to administer the fund. Correa called off the signing at the last minute, questioning the breadth of the Initiative's conservation efforts and UNDP's proposed six-person administrative body, three appointed by Ecuador, two by contributing nations, and one by UNDP. This joint control structure apparently sparked Correa's tirade about shame and dignity.

Within a couple of weeks of the blowup, the government had backpedaled, withdrawing the June deadline, appointing a new negotiating team, and reasserting the position that the government's "first option" is to leave the oil in the ground. At the same time, Petroecuador began work on a new pipeline near Yasuní, part of the infrastructure needed for ITT production, pursuant to a 2007 Memorandum of Understanding with several foreign oil companies.

Amid the doubts and mixed messages, proponents are fighting to save the Initiative as a cornerstone in the creation of a post-petroleum Ecuador and ultimately a post-petroleum world. In media interviews after his resignation, Sevilla stressed that he would keep working to ensure that the Initiative would not fail. The Constitution provides for a public referendum prior to extracting oil from protected areas like Yasuní, he noted. "If the president doesn't want to assume his responsibility as leader…let's pass the responsibility to the public." In fact, 75% of respondents in a January poll in Quito and Guayaquil, the country's two largest cities, indicated that they would vote to not extract the ITT oil.

Martinez and Sáenz concur that just as the Initiative emerged from widespread organizing efforts, its success will come from the people. "This is the moment to define ourselves and develop an economic model not based on petroleum," Salazar says. "We have other knowledge, we have minerals, water. We need to change our consciousness and end the economic dependence on one resource." ❑

Resources: Live Yasuni, Finding Species, Inc., liveyasuni.org; "S.O.S. Yasuni" sosyasuni.org; "Yasuni-ITT: An Initiative to Change History," Government of Ecuador, yasuni-itt.gov.ec.

Chapter 7

LABOR, UNIONS, AND WORKING CONDITIONS

Article 7.1

HOW HIGH COULD THE MINIMUM WAGE GO?
A 70% boost would help millions of workers, without killing jobs.

BY JEANNETTE WICKS-LIM
July/August 2012

The minimum wage needs a jolt—not just the usual fine-tuning—if it's ever going to serve as a living wage. Annual full-time earnings at today's $7.25 federal minimum wage are about $15,000 per year. This doesn't come anywhere near providing a decent living standard by any reasonable definition, for any household, least of all households with children. But among the seventeen states that either have active campaigns to raise their minimum wage or have raised them already this year, none have suggested raising the wage floor by more than 20%.

How high can the minimum wage go? As it turns out, a lot higher. Economists typically examine whether current minimum-wage laws hike pay rates up too high and cause employers to shed workers from their payrolls in response. But the current stockpile of economic research on minimum wages suggests that past increases have not caused any notable job losses. In other words, minimum wages in the United States have yet to be set too high. In fact, if we use past experience as a guide, businesses should be able to adjust to a jump in the minimum wage as great as 70%. That would push the federal minimum wage up to $12.30. In states with average living costs, full-time earnings at $12.30 per hour can cover the basic needs of the typical low-income working household (assuming both adults in two-adult households are employed).

Why is such a large increase possible? It's because minimum-wage hikes—particularly those in the 20-to-30% range adopted in the United States—impose very modest cost increases on businesses. This is true even for the low-wage, labor-intensive restaurant industry. And because these cost increases are so modest, affected businesses have a variety of options for adjusting to their higher labor costs that are less drastic than laying off workers.

Take, for example, the 31% rise in Arizona's state minimum wage in 2006, from $5.15 to $6.75. My colleague Robert Pollin and I have estimated that the average restaurant in Arizona could expect to see its costs rise between 1% and 2% of their sales revenue. What kind of adjustment would this restaurant need to make? A price hike of 1% or 2% would completely cover this cost increase. This would amount to raising the price of a $10.00 meal to $10.20.

To figure out what is the largest increase businesses can adjust to without laying off workers, we can take stock of what we know about how businesses have adjusted in the past and then figure out how much businesses can adjust along those lines.

Let's stick with the example of restaurants, since these businesses tend to experience the largest rise in costs. And let's start with a big increase in the minimum wage: 50%. If we add together all the raises mandated by such an increase in the minimum wage (assuming the same number of workers and hours worked), the raises employers would need to give workers earning wages above the minimum wage to maintain a stable wage hierarchy, and their higher payroll taxes, the total cost increase of a 50% minimum-wage hike would be 3.2% of restaurant sales.

The cost increase that these restaurants need to absorb, however, will actually be even smaller than 3.2% of their sales revenue. That's because when workers' wages rise, workers stay at their jobs for longer periods of time, saving businesses the money they would otherwise have spent on recruiting and training new workers. These savings range between 10% and 25% of the costs from raising the minimum wage. If the higher wage motivates workers to work harder, businesses would experience even more cost savings.

So what would happen if restaurants raised their prices to cover their minimum wage cost increases? One answer is that people may react to the higher prices by eating out less often and restaurant owners would lose business. With a large enough falloff in business, restaurants would have to cut back on their workforce. But it's unlikely that a price increase as small as 3% would stop people from eating out. Think about it: if a family is already willing to pay $40.00 to eat dinner out, it hardly seems likely that a price increase as small as $1.20 would to cause them to forgo all the benefits of eating out like getting together with family or friends and saving time in meal preparation, clean up, and grocery shopping.

Still, let's assume that a 3% price hike actually does influence people to eat out less. The key questions now are how much less and can restaurant owners make up their lost business activity? Economists have found that restaurant patrons do not react strongly to changes in menu prices (economists call this an "inelastic" demand). Estimates from industry research suggest that a price increase of 3% may reduce consumer demand by about 2%.

However, if these small price increases take place within a growing economy—even a slow-growing economy—restaurant owners will probably see basically no change in their sales. This is because as the economy expands and peoples' incomes rise, people eat out more. In an economy growing at a rate of 3% annually, which is slower than average for the U.S. economy, consumer demand for restaurant meals will typically rise by about 2.4%. This would boost sales more than enough to make up for any loss that restaurants may experience from a 3% price increase. In other words, consumers would still eat out more often even after a 50% minimum-wage hike.

After taking account of the ways that restaurants can adjust to the higher labor costs from a minimum wage hike, it turns out that the biggest minimum wage increase that restaurants can absorb while maintaining at least the same level of business activity is 70%. In 2004, Santa Fe, New Mexico, came close to this. Its citywide living-wage ordinance raised the wage floor by 65%—from $5.15 to $8.50. A city-commissioned report after it was put into effect found that "overall employment levels have been unaffected by the living wage ordinance."

However, even if the federal minimum rate were 70% higher, or $12.30, it would still fall short for two major groups of workers. First, one-worker families raising young children need generous income supports in addition to minimum wage earnings to help cover the high cost of raising children. Second, minimum-wage workers who live in expensive areas, such as New York City and Washington, D.C., require affordable housing programs.

A 70% minimum-wage hike is the biggest one-time increase that U.S. businesses can absorb without cutting jobs, but it's not the end of the story. In the future, the minimum wage can inch further upward. For example, it could rise in step with the expanding productive capacity of the U.S. economy, as it did in the 1950s and 1960s. A $12.30 minimum wage today rising each year with worker productivity would reach $17.00 in just over ten years (in 2011 dollars). This wage would be high enough so that a single parent with one child could support a minimally decent living standard. We would finally begin transforming the minimum wage into a living wage for all workers.

Policy discussions around the minimum wage need to move past the debate of whether or not it causes job loss. The evidence is clear: minimum wages, in the range of what's been adopted in the past, do not produce any significant job losses. Now it is time to focus on how we can use minimum wages to maximally support low-wage workers. Can we raise the minimum wage rate to a level we can call a living wage? By my reckoning, we can. ❑

Sources: Jeannette Wicks-Lim and Jeffrey Thompson, "Combining the Minimum Wage and Earned Income Tax Credit Policies to Guarantee a Decent Living Standard to All U.S. Workers" (Political Economy Research Institute, October 2010).

Article 7.2

CAMPUS STRUGGLES AGAINST SWEATSHOPS CONTINUE
Indonesian workers and U.S. students fight back against Adidas.

BY SARAH BLASKEY AND PHIL GASPER
September/October 2012

Abandoning his financially ailing factory in the Tangerang region of Indonesia, owner Jin Woo Kim fled the country for his home, South Korea, in January 2011 without leaving money to pay his workers. The factory, PT Kizone, stayed open for several months and then closed in financial ruin in April, leaving 2,700 workers with no jobs and owed $3.4 million of legally mandated severance pay.

In countries like Indonesia, with no unemployment insurance, severance pay is what keeps workers and their families from literal starvation. "The important thing is to be able to have rice. Maybe we add some chili pepper, some salt, if we can," explained an ex-Kizone worker, Marlina, in a report released by the Worker Rights Consortium (WRC), a U.S.-based labor-rights monitoring group, in May 2012.

Marlina, widowed mother of two, worked at PT Kizone for eleven years before the factory closed. She needs the severance payment in order to pay her son's high school registration fee and monthly tuition, and to make important repairs to her house.

When the owner fled, the responsibility for severance payments to PT Kizone workers fell on the companies that sourced from the factory—Adidas, Nike, and the Dallas Cowboys. Within a year, both Nike and the Dallas Cowboys made severance payments that they claim are proportional to the size of their orders from the factory, around $1.5 million total. But Adidas has refused to pay any of the $1.8 million still owed to workers.

Workers in PT Kizone factory mainly produced athletic clothing sold to hundreds of universities throughout the United States. All collegiate licensees like Adidas and Nike sign contracts with the universities that buy their apparel. At least 180 universities around the nation are affiliated with the WRC and have licensing contracts mandating that brands pay "all applicable back wages found due to workers who manufactured the licensed articles." If wages or severance pay are not paid to workers that produce university goods, then the school has the right to terminate the contract.

Using the language in these contracts, activists on these campuses coordinate nationwide divestment campaigns to pressure brands like Adidas to uphold previously unenforceable labor codes of conduct.

Unpaid back wages and benefits are a major problem in the garment industry. Apparel brands rarely own factories. Rather, they contract with independent manufacturers all over the world to produce their wares. When a factory closes for any reason, a brand can simply take its business somewhere else and wash its hands of any responsibilities to the fired workers.

Brands like Nike and Russell have lost millions of dollars when, pressed by United Students Against Sweatshops (USAS), universities haver terminated their contracts. According to the USAS website, campus activism has forced Nike to pay severance and Russell to rehire over 1,000 workers it had laid off, in order to avoid losing more collegiate contracts. Now many college activists have their sights set on Adidas.

At the University of Wisconsin (UW) in Madison, the USAS-affiliated Student Labor Action Coalition (SLAC) and sympathetic faculty are in the middle of a more than year-long campaign to pressure the school to terminate its contract with Adidas in solidarity with the PT Kizone workers.

The chair of UW's Labor Licensing Policy Committee (LLPC) says that Adidas is in violation of the code of conduct for the school's licensees. Even the university's senior counsel, Brian Vaughn, stated publicly at a June LLPC meeting that Adidas is "in breach of the contract based on its failure to adhere to the standards of the labor code." But despite the fact that Vaughn claimed at the time that the University's "two overriding goals are to get money back in the hands of the workers and to maintain the integrity of the labor code," the administration has dragged its feet in responding to Adidas.

Instead of putting the company on notice for potential contract termination and giving it a deadline to meet its obligations as recommended by the LLPC, UW entered into months of fruitless negotiations with Adidasin spring of 2012. In July, when these negotiations had led nowhere, UW's interim chancellor David Ward asked a state court to decide whether or not Adidas had violated the contract (despite the senior counsel's earlier public admission that it had). This process will delay a decision for many more months--perhaps years if there are appeals.

Since the Adidas campaign's inception in the fall of 2011, SLAC members have actively opposed the school's cautious approach, calling both the mediation process and the current court action a "stalling tactic" by the UW administration and Adidas to avoid responsibility to the PT Kizone workers. In response, student organizers planned everything from frequent letter deliveries to campus administrators, to petition drives, teach-ins, and even a banner drop from the administration building that over 300 people attended, all in hopes of pressuring the chancellor (who ultimately has the final say in the matter) to cut the contract with Adidas.

While the administration claims that it is moving slowly to avoid being sued by Adidas, it is also getting considerable pressure from its powerful athletics director, Barry Alvarez, to continue its contract with Adidas. As part of the deal, UW's sports programs receive royalties and sports gear worth about $2.5 million every year.

"Just look at the money—what we lose and what it would cost us," Alvarez told the *Wisconsin State Journal*, even though other major brands would certainly jump at the opportunity to replace Adidas. "We have four building projects going on. It could hurt recruiting. There's a trickle-down effect that would be devastating to our whole athletic program."

But Tina Treviño-Murphy, a student activist with SLAC, rejects this logic. "A strong athletics department shouldn't have to be built on a foundation of stolen labor," she told Dollars & Sense. "Our department and our students deserve better.".

Adidas is now facing pressure from both campus activists in the United States and the workers in Indonesia--including sit-ins by the latter at the German and British embassies in Jakarta. (Adidas' world headquarters are in Germany, and the company sponsored the recent London Olympics.) This led to a meeting between their union and an Adidas representative, who refused to admit responsibility but instead offered food vouchers to some of the workers. The offer amounted to a tiny fraction of the owed severance and was rejected as insulting by former Kizone workers.

In the face of intransigence from university administrations and multinational companies prepared to shift production quickly from one location to another to stay one step ahead of labor-rights monitors, campus activism to fight sweatshops can seem like a labor of Sisyphus. After more than a decade of organizing, a recent fundraising appeal from USAS noted that "today sweatshop conditions are worse than ever."

Brands threaten to pull out of particular factories if labor costs rise, encouraging a work environment characterized by "forced overtime, physical and sexual harassment, and extreme anti-union intimidation, even death threats," says Natalie Yoon, a USAS member who recently participated in a delegation to factories in Honduras and El Salvador.

According to Snehal Shingavi, a professor at the University of Texas, Austin who was a USAS activist at Berkeley for many years, finding ways to build links with the struggles of the affected workers is key. "What I think would help the campaign the most is if there were actually more sustained and engaged connections between students here and workers who are in factories who are facing these conditions," Shingavi told *Dollars & Sense*. Ultimately, he said, only workers' self-activity can "make the kind of changes that I think we all want, which is an end to exploitative working conditions."

But in the meantime, even small victories are important. Anti-sweatshop activists around the country received a boost in September, when Cornell University President David Skorton announced that his school was ending its licensing contract with Adidas effective October 1, because of the company's failure to pay severance to PT Kizone workers. The announcement followed a sustained campaign by the Sweatfree Cornell Coalition, leading up to a "study in" at the president's office. While the contract itself was small, USAS described the decision as the "first domino," which may lead other campuses to follow suit. Shortly afterwards, Oberlin College in Ohio told Adidas that it would not renew its current four-year contract with the company if the workers in Indonesia are not paid severance.

Perhaps just as significant are the lessons that some activists are drawing from these campaigns. "The people who have a lot of power are going to want to keep that power and the only way to make people give some of that up is if we make them," Treviño-Murphy said. "So it's really pressure from below, grassroots organizing, that makes the difference. We see that every day in SLAC and I think it teaches us to be not just better students but better citizens who will stand up to fight injustice every time." ❑

Sources: Worker Rights Consortium, "Status Update Re: PT Kizone (Indonesia)," May 15, 2012 (workersrights.org); Andy Baggot, "Alvarez Anxiously Awaits Adidas Decision," Wisconsin State Journal, July 13, 2012 (host.madison.com); United Students Against Sweatshops (usas.org), PT Kizone update, June 15, 2012 (cleanclothes.org/urgent-actions/kizoneupdate).

Article 7.3

FLORIDA TOMATO PICKERS DEMAND "FAIR FOOD"

BY DAN SCHNEIDER
November/December 2012

The Coalition of Immokalee Workers (CIW) celebrated another victory in October when Chipotle Mexican Grill announced that it would finally sign on to the group's Fair Food Program (FFP). The program guarantees that the company will buy tomatoes only from farms FFP-certified as observing fair labor practices, such as establishing health and safety boards and allowing worker-to-worker education sessions on company time. In addition, buyers like Chipotle agree to pay an extra "penny-per-pound premium" on tomatoes from FFP-certified farms.

The victory comes after years of pressure by CIW on the burrito chain. For years, Chipotle had refused to sign onto the FPP, claiming that the program would exert undue control over the company's business. In 2011, founder and CEO Steve Ells told *Coloradan* Magazine that dealing with CIW "would be like you giving to a charity, and then the charity protesting you for not signing a contract forcing you to do what the charity tells you to do in the future."

When Chipotle sidestepped CIW in 2009 and negotiated a "penny-per-pound" agreement directly with East Coast Growers and Packers, one of Florida's largest tomato growers, the group sent a protest letter with over 70 co-signers to Ells. Barry Estabrook, a Vermont farmer and author of the 2009 industry exposé *Tomatoland*, was one of the co-signers. "Their absence was noticeable, since Chipotle prides itself on being sustainable," Estabrook said. "The ultimate irony is that, how can something be sustainable if somebody who picks it can't sustain a lifestyle?"

CIW is based in Immokalee, Fla., in the heart of southwest Florida's tomato-growing country. The city's overwhelmingly Latino population provides a major portion of farm labor during tomato season, with 10,000 to 15,000 workers coming from the area. The average farmworker earns between $10,000 and $12,500 per year.

In 1993, laborer Lucas Benitez started CIW with a mission to improve industry conditions in four areas: low wages, wage theft, supervisor violence against workers, and a general lack of respect from employers. After nearly two decades, CIW has not only gotten eleven major fast-food chains to sign onto the Fair Food Program, but has also helped expose conditions little better than slavery for over 1,000 workers.

One of the CIW's greatest assets might seem like a weakness on the surface. The 1935 National Labor Relations Act (NLRA, or "Wagner Act") excludes farm workers. Unions covered by the NLRA, on the other hand, are barred from organizing "secondary boycotts," such as actions directed against an employer's suppliers or customers. Since CIW is not an NLRA union, it can take actions against big tomato buyers, like fast-food restaurants and grocery-store chains. In the past decade, it has organized high-profile boycotts of Taco Bell, Pizza Hut, and Burger King.

During the Chipotle campaign, the coalition did not go so far as to boycott the chain. It did, however, hold a rally, outside Chipotle's Denver headquarters. Protesters built a pyramid out of 153 tomato buckets, the number a field worker must fill in a day to make minimum wage. The announcement that Chipotle would sign on to the FFP came just two days before a planned mass demonstration at the Chipotle Cultivate Festival, a national gathering of chefs, farmers, and musicians. The protest likely would have drawn national attention to the CIW's cause—and negative publicity for Chipotle.

Gerardo Reyes, a farmworker and CIW staff member, told Dollars & Sense that although the "penny-per-pound" doesn't amount to a massive increase in worker pay—since 2001 it's yielded a total of $7 million for all of Florida's tomato pickers—the FFP is an essential step to improving working conditions in an industry rife with "slavery-like conditions."

"One of the important things to remember when people talk about sustainability is that there's always been a blind spot when it comes to farmworkers," Reyes said. "It's always about the environment, buying locally, and respecting the rights of animals. All of that of course is very important, but it's a little incomplete, because the reality is that without workers there is nothing." q

Sources: Coalition of Immokale Workers (ciw-online.org); Just Harvest USA (justharvestusa.org).

Article 7.4

WRONG ABOUT RIGHT-TO-WORK
Laffer throws another curve-ball.

BY JOHN MILLER
July/August 2011

> BOEING AND THE UNION BERLIN WALL
> Two policies have consistently stood out as the most important in predicting where jobs will be created and incomes will rise. First, states with no income tax generally outperform high income tax states. Second, states that have right-to-work laws grow faster than states with forced unionism.
>
> As of today there are 22 right-to-work states and 28 union-shop states. Over the past decade (2000-09) the right-to-work states grew faster in nearly every respect than their union-shop counterparts: 54.6% versus 41.1% in gross state product, 53.3% versus 40.6% in personal income, 11.9% versus 6.1% in population, and 4.1% versus -0.6% in payrolls.
>
> The Boeing incident makes it clear that right-to-work states have a competitive advantage over forced-union states. So the question arises: Why doesn't every state adopt right-to-work laws?
>
> —Arthur B. Laffer and Stephen Moore, *Wall Street Journal* op-ed, May 13, 2011

What do you get when you mix a *Wall Street Journal* editorial writer with a supply-side economist?

That's right: more of the same.

This time, however, it's right-to-work laws, not taxes, that come in for the full Laffer treatment (although without the illustration on the back of a cocktail napkin).

In May of this year, the National Labor Relations Board (NLRB) issued an injunction to stop defense giant Boeing from moving a jet production line from its unionized factories in Washington state to right-to-work South Carolina. The International Association of Machinists & Aerospace Workers union had filed a complaint that the planned move was in retaliation against strikes the union conducted over the last decade, and thus illegal.

The NLRB decision amounts to "a regulatory wall with one express purpose: to prevent the direct competition of right-to-work states with union-shop states," insist Arthur Laffer, the supply-side economist, and Stephen Moore, former head of the far-right economics think tank Club for Growth and now on the *Wall Street Journal*'s editorial board. Right-to-work laws enforced in 22 states, mostly in the southern and western United States, prohibit businesses and unions from agreeing to contracts that stipulate that an employer will hire only workers who join the union or pay union dues. In right-to-work states, unions confront a free-rider problem: they have to organize workers who can benefit from collective bargaining without joining (or staying in) the union or paying dues.

The disadvantages that right-to-work states impose on unions give those states a competitive advantage that will enrich them, according to Laffer and Moore. And their report, "Rich States, Poor States," has the numbers to prove it, or so they claim. Right-to-work states grow faster, add more income, create more jobs, and attract more people than states hamstrung by pro-union labor laws.

But it turns out that the claim that right-to-work laws lead states to prosper is no more credible than Laffer's earlier claim that cutting income taxes would spur such an explosion of economic growth that government revenues would actually rise despite the lower tax rates. Much like what Laffer had to say about tax cuts and economic growth, Laffer and Moore make the case for right-to-work laws as the key to economic prosperity through sleight of hand and half-truths.

Let's take a look at exactly where their story goes wrong.

Something Up Their Sleeve

To begin with, Laffer's and Moore's report needs to be read carefully. Their claim is that the economies of states with right-to-work laws grow faster, not that their citizens are better off.

And they are not. For instance, while it is true that both output and income have grown faster in right-to-work states than in other states over the last decade, the growth is from a much lower starting point. In fact, output and income in those states still lag well behind the levels in non-right-to-work states. Personal income per capita averaged $37,134 (in 2010) and real GDP per capita averaged $39,365 (in 2009) in right-to-work states, but $41,312 and $42,513 respectively in the other 28 states.

The positive job creation numbers that Laffer and Moore report for right-to-work states over the last decade haven't resulted in superior job prospects for those out of work. With their faster growing populations, right-to-work states had unemployment rates averaging 8.0% in April of this year, just below the 8.2% average in non-right-to-work states.

And in practice, right-to-work laws are very much "right-to-work-for-less" laws, as union critics call them. In a recent Economic Policy Institute briefing paper, economists Elise Gould and Heidi Shierholz looked closely at the differences in compensation between right-to-work and non-right-to-work states. Controlling for the demographic and job characteristics of workers as well as state-level economic conditions and cost-of-living differences across states, they found that in 2009:

- Wages were 3.2% lower in right-to-work states vs. non-right-to-work states—about $1,500 less annually for a full-time, year-round worker.

- The rate of employer-sponsored health insurance was 2.6 percentage points lower in right-to-work states compared with non-right-to-work states.

- The rate of employer-sponsored pensions was 4.8 percentage points lower in right-to-work states. On top of that, in 2008 the rate of workplace deaths was 57% higher in right-to-work states than non-right-to-work states, while the

2009, poverty rate in right-to-work states averaged 15.0%, considerably above the 12.8% average for non-right-to-work states.

But here is the real kicker: once their effect is isolated from the effects of other factors, right-to-work laws seem to have little or no impact even on economic growth itself. For instance, a 2009 study conducted by economist Lonnie Stevans concludes that:

> While … right-to-work states are likely to have more self-employment and less bankruptcies on average relative to non-right-to-work states, there is certainly no more business capital. … Moreover, from a state's economic standpoint, being right-to-work yields little or no gain in employment and real economic growth. Wages and personal income are both lower in right-to-work states, yet proprietors' income is higher.

Those lower wages and lower personal incomes are especially detrimental in today's fragile economic recovery, still plagued by a lack of consumer spending.

A Bad Move

The evidence above militates against the notion that right-to-work laws are the key to economic prosperity for state economies, and in favor of the notion that anti-union laws, much like deregulation and tax cuts targeted at the rich, are another mechanism for securing more and more for the well-to-do at the expense of most everyone else.

That is especially clear when it comes to Boeing's planned move from Washington state to South Carolina. Ironically, union-heavy Washington tops right-to-work South Carolina in Laffer's and Moore's Economic Outlook Rankings for 2010 and in their Economic Performance Rankings for 1998- 2008. Personal income, output, and employment all grew considerably faster in Washington state than in South Carolina from 1998 to 2008. And personal income per capita and GDP per capita in Washington state ($43,564 and $45,881 respectively) far exceed their levels in South Carolina ($33,163 and $30,845).

Beyond that, unemployment and poverty rates in Washington state are both well below those in South Carolina. By all those measures, Washington's economy is far and away the more vibrant of the two.

Working conditions are a lot better in Washington state too, something not lost on Boeing. Wage workers in Washington state on average make $11,020 a year more than their counterparts in South Carolina. Production workers in Washington state earn $5,560 a year more. South Carolina workers are 69% more likely to die on the job than workers in Washington. And not surprisingly, just 6.2% of wage and salary workers in right-to-work South Carolina were union members in 2010, versus more than 20% in Washington.

So then why does Boeing want to leave the Evergreen State for the Palmetto State? To benefit from a more vibrant economy? Or to take advantage of workers whose ability to organize is hindered by right-to-work laws, whose bargaining power has been eroded by high unemployment and poverty, who have few alternatives than to endure working in far more dangerous conditions while getting paid less than workers in Washington? The numbers speak for themselves.

No wonder the NLRB filed an injunction against Boeing's planned move. Labor board members saw it for what it is: not a mere relocation, but an exercise of raw power intended to bust a union. ❑

Sources: Arthur B. Laffer and Stephen Moore, "Rich States, Poor States: ALEC-Laffer State Economic Competitiveness Index, 3rd edition," *Wall Street Journal*, April 7, 2010; Lonnie K. Stevans, "The Effect of Endogenous Right-to-Work Laws on Business and Economic Conditions in the United States: A Multivariate Approach," *Review of Law & Economics*, Vol. 5, Issue 1, 2009; Elise Gould and Heidi Shierholz, "The Compensation Penalty of 'Right-to-Work' Laws," Economic Policy Institute Briefing Paper #299, February 17, 2011 (epi.org); Gordon Lafar, "'Right-to-Work': Wrong in New Hampshire," Economic Policy Briefing Paper #302, April 5, 2011 (epi.org); Carl Horowitz, "NLRB Sues Boeing; Seeks End to Commercial Jet Production in South Carolina," National Legal and Policy Center, May 4, 2011 (nlpc.org).

Article 7.5

WAL-MART MAKES THE CASE FOR AFFIRMATIVE ACTION
Lessons from the Supreme Court's Ruling on Sex Discrimination

BY JEANNETTE WICKS-LIM
September/October 2011

On June 20, 2011, the Supreme Court put an end to what would have been the largest class-action lawsuit in U.S. history. The lawsuit, filed on behalf of more than 1.5 million current and former female Wal-Mart employees, alleged that Wal-Mart supervisors routinely discriminated against female workers by promoting and paying them less than their male counterparts.

That's too bad, because the facts presented by the plaintiffs describe a situation that surely calls out for redress.

Wal-Mart has a bare-bones policy telling managers how to dole out promotions. Eligible workers need only meet three basic criteria: 1) an above-average performance rating, 2) at least one year of job tenure, and 3) a willingness to relocate. Among these candidates, local supervisors have full discretion over whom to promote.

With the door wide open for supervisors to act on their subjective preferences, it may be no surprise that men dominate the company's management team. In 2001 women made up only 33% of Wal-Mart's managers, according to labor economist Richard Drogin, even though they made up 70% of its hourly workforce. Compare that with Wal-Mart's peer companies, where 57% of managers were women.

Wal-Mart also gives its (mostly male) managers significant wiggle room in setting their supervisees' wages. The result? Drogin reported that in 2001, Wal-Mart women earned consistently less than their male counterparts even after controlling for such factors as job performance and job tenure. He concluded that "… there are statistically significant disparities between men and women at Wal-Mart … [and] these disparities … can be explained only by gender discrimination."

The trouble is that these disparities exist even though no part of Wal-Mart's wage or promotion policy directs managers to make biased decisions. In fact, Wal-Mart has an anti-discrimination policy on its books.

With no "smoking gun" corporate policy, the Supreme Court blocked the women of Wal-Mart from lodging a collective complaint against the company. In the majority opinion, Justice Antonin Scalia writes: "Other than the bare existence of delegated discretion, respondents have identified no 'specific employment practice' … Merely showing that Wal-Mart's policy of discretion has produced an overall sex-based disparity does not suffice."

In other words, the majority of Supreme Court justices intend to take a narrow view of which employment practices justify class-action discrimination lawsuits. Potential plaintiffs will have to show exactly how an employer discriminated. And as the Wal-Mart case demonstrates, this can boil down to the murky business of trying to expose employers' unspoken intentions.

What this means is that the traditional, complaint-driven approach to enforcing the 1964 Civil Rights Act cannot protect workers from discrimination. Deprived of class-action lawsuits as a tool, the women behind the Wal-Mart case and other workers in plainly discriminatory workplaces will now have to pursue their claims individually—at best putting them into a much weaker position with fewer resources.

To eliminate workplace discrimination and achieve true equality, policies have to focus squarely on the pattern of outcomes of employers' decisions. In a phrase, on the question of whether an employer discriminates, "the proof is in the pudding." President Lyndon Johnson recognized this more than 40 years ago when his administration first put such policies into action under the rubric of affirmative action.

What does affirmative action require? First, the employer keeps a record of whether the race and gender make-up of its workforce is proportional to the wider pool of eligible workers. If not, the employer develops a plan to act "affirmatively"—with goals and timetables—to improve female and minority representation.

Affirmative action plans may include sexual harassment awareness training for supervisors, for instance, or directing recruitment efforts toward minority and women's organizations. Rigid quotas—the most controversial aspect of affirmative action policies—can only be used in the context of a court-ordered or -approved plan in response to a discrimination suit.

The Wal-Mart case demonstrates why workers need affirmative action policies to eradicate discrimination. As President Johnson put it in 1965, affirmative action represents "… the next and more profound stage of the battle for civil rights. We seek … not just equality as a right and a theory, but equality as a fact and as a result." ❑

Sources: "Statistical analysis of gender patterns in Wal-Mart workforce," Expert testimony by Richard Drogin, Ph. D., February 2003 (walmartclass.com); "The representation of women in store management at Wal-Mart Stores, Inc.," Expert testimony by Marc Bendick, Jr., Ph.D., January 2003 (walmartclass.com); Supreme Court of the United States, *Wal-Mart Stores, Inc., petitioner v. Betty Dukes et al.* (No. 10–277) June 20, 2011.

Article 7.6

UNIONS AND ECONOMIC PERFORMANCE

BY ARTHUR MACEWAN
November/December 2011

> Dear Dr. Dollar:
> I know unions have shrunk in the United States, but by how much? And how best to respond to my right-wing friends who claim that unions are bad for the economy? —*Rich Sanford, Hardwick, Mass.*

Take a look at the graph below. The two lines on the graph show for the period 1917 through 2007 (1) labor union membership as a percentage of the total U.S. work force and (2) the percentage of all income obtained by the highest 1% of income recipients. So the lines show, roughly, the strength of unions and the distribution of income for the past century. (John Miller and I developed this graph for our book *Economic Collapse, Economic Change*.)

The picture is pretty clear. In periods when unions have been strong, income distribution has been less unequal. In periods when unions have been weak, income distribution has been more unequal. In the post-World War II era, union members were about 25% of the labor force; today the figure is about 10%. In those postwar years, the highest-income 1% got 10% to 12% of all income; today they get about 25%.

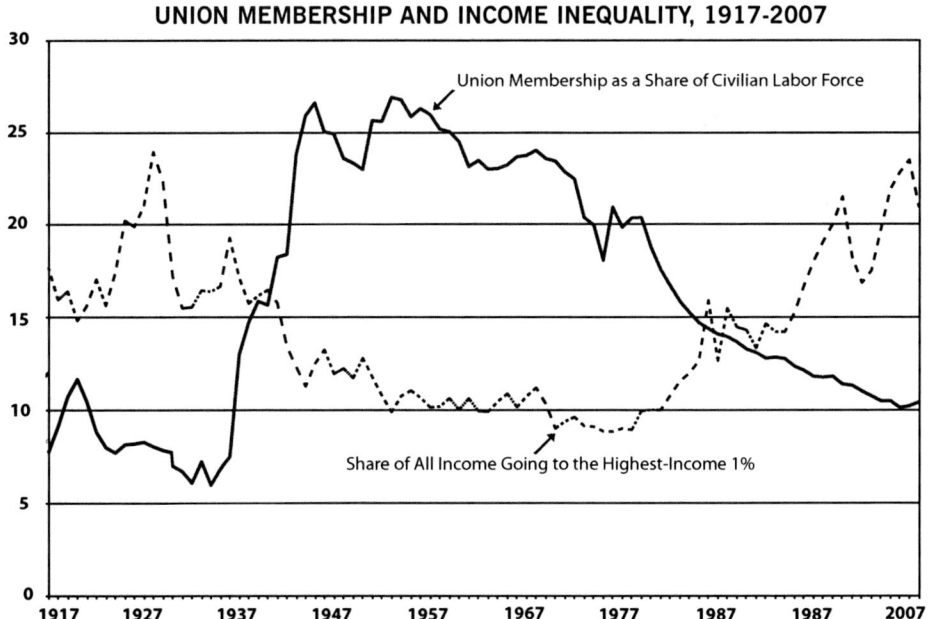

Source: Arthur MacEwan and John A. Miller, *Economic Collapse, Economic Change: Getting to the Root of the Crisis* (M.E. Sharpe, 2011).

The causation between union strength and income distribution is not simple. Nonetheless, there are some fairly direct connections. For example, when unions are strong, they can push for higher wages and thus we see a more equal distribution of income. Also, strong unions can have an impact on the political process, bringing about policies that are more favorable to workers.

But causation can work in the other direction as well. Great income inequality puts more power in the hands of the rich, and they can use that power to get policies put in place that weaken unions—for example, getting people who are hostile to unions appointed to the National Labor Relations Board.

And then there are other factors that affect both union strength and income distribution—for example, the changing structure of the global economy, which places U.S. workers in competition with poorly paid workers elsewhere. Yet the structure of the global economy is itself affected by the distribution of political power. For example, the "free trade" agreements that the United States has established with other countries generally ignore workers' rights (to say nothing of the environment) and go to great lengths to protect the rights of corporations. So, again, causation works in complex ways, and there are certainly other factors that need to be taken account of to explain the relationship shown in the graph.

However one explains the relationship, it is hard to imagine that we can return to a more equal distribution of income while unions remain weak. This means, at the very least, that the interests of unions and of people at the bottom of the income distribution are bound up with one another. Building stronger unions is an important part of fighting poverty—and the hunger and homelessness that are the clear manifestations of poverty.

One important thing to notice in the graph: In the post-World War II years, economic growth was the best we have seen. Certainly no one can claim that it is impossible for strong unions and a more equal distribution of income to co-exist with fairly rapid economic growth. Indeed, we might even argue that strong unions and a more equal distribution of income create favorable conditions for economic growth!

Stronger unions, it turns out, could be good preventive medicine for much of what ails our economy. ❑

Chapter 8

Spotlight
PUBLIC-SECTOR WORKERS

Article 8.1

AMERICA'S PUBLIC-SECTOR WORKERS UNDER ATTACK
It's not about their pay and benefits—it's about what they do.

BY GERALD FRIEDMAN
November/December 2011

From California to Massachusetts, from Texas to Wisconsin, whether by fiat or through bargaining, state governments would balance their budgets by taking a meat ax to public employee wages, benefits, and jobs. Behind the headlines, the relative strength of public-sector unions has long made them a target for economists and conservatives hostile to all forms of working-class collective action and any regulation of the capitalist marketplace. Labor economist Leo Troy set the tone for many when he warned in 1994 of "A New Society" that was emerging, dominated by unions of public employees and a redistributive state. While market competition had beaten back the threat of private-sector unionism, public employee unions, in his view, had renewed the socialist challenge to free enterprise.

Ideologues like Troy inspired an ongoing attack on public-sector unions to defend America from socialism. When he accepted the Republican presidential nomination in 1996, for example, Bob Dole singled out the teachers' unions for attack. While this was a great applause line, Dole lost the election. This has been the outcome of most of the right's attack on public-sector workers and unions: applause from the far right and some of the media but little resonance among a public that generally supports public services and those who provide them.

It may be that those who would attack public employees and their unions as sponsors of incipient socialism have learned to conceal their real motives. Instead of attacking public services, they present themselves as advocates for private-sector workers and insist that they only seek to eliminate inequities between private- and public-sector workers. New Jersey Gov. Chris Christie denounces public-sector unions as creating "two classes of citizens: one that receives rich health and pension benefits, and all the rest who are left to pay for them."

It is odd to find such touching concern for equity among those who have campaigned relentlessly to widen disparities between rich and poor and between managers and workers. In any case, such equity concerns should be relieved by the growing body of empirical studies showing that public-sector workers are *not* overpaid compared with private-sector workers. Nor is there evidence that public-sector unions have been diverting national income towards their exorbitant salaries and staffing. State and local taxes took 9% of income in 1990 and 9% in 2007. As a share of national income, state and local employee compensation has fallen since the 1990s despite rising demands on the public sector—to improve education, repair infrastructure, clean up the environment, and provide health care to growing numbers left out of our private health care system.

When neither evidence nor popular opinion can deflect political attacks on public-sector workers, then we should look for some deeper ideological hostility rather than rational explanation. Public-sector workers and their unions are not under attack because their salaries have grown, because of a groundswell of popular hostility, nor because their pay and employment benefits are swamping the capacity of the public. They are under attack because their very existence and the commitment of public-sector workers to provide services without regard to ability to pay or the market distribution of income challenges the legitimacy of markets. Public schools, public health services, public roads and parks, even public police and fire protection offend those who would restrict such services to those who can pay for them, denying them to the poor, the young, and the disabled. Their view may be shaped by racial and gender animosity: not only are a disproportionate share of public employees women and people of color, but so are their young and low-income clientele.

If the reactionaries are now winning where Dole had earlier failed, it may be because they have new allies, enablers who have turned against public employees in a misguided attempt to protect public services and liberal values. Republicans have been the face of the attack on public employees but Democrats, even liberals, have been right there with them. New York's Governor Andrew Cuomo, Massachusetts's Deval Patrick and California's Jerry Brown have all found political advantage in attacking public employee unions. Indeed, in his 2011 state of the state address, Christie found support for his anti-worker stance in the words of Cuomo and Brown, whose calls for austerity and wage cuts, Christie declared, were inspired by New Jersey's example. By lending credibility to reactionaries like Christie, liberals like Brown and Cuomo provide political cover for attacks on public-sector workers.

But there is more here than simple political opportunism. The anti-public employee rhetoric from Cuomo, Patrick, and other liberals reflects the frustration of pro-government liberals five years into the worst economic recession since the 1930s. Years of falling revenues and rising state and local deficits have forced liberal politicians to make agonizing choices among competing needs. After cutting schools to save road repair and cutting Medicaid to save drug rehabilitation programs, liberal politicians have come to look covetously at public employee salaries and benefits. In the labor-intensive work of education and providing social services, everything liberals want to do comes up against the cost of paying workers; and a chance to reduce those costs means a chance to save services in times of austerity. As Assemblyman Angel Fuentes, a Camden Democrat who represents one of the neediest cities in the United States, said in endorsing Governor Christie's program, "These reforms are unquestionably bitter pills for us to swallow, but they are reasonable and they are necessary" because "towns across this state" are laying off workers to pay for health benefits for their employees.

One can understand how these liberal enablers would try to protect spending even by cutting public employee pay. The problem is that they have accepted a false choice that pits public services against each other rather than against other uses of the public's money, including private consumption. There is no economic logic in taking the pool of government revenue as fixed rather than considering whether public services should be preserved by reducing *private* expenditure by raising taxes. But if we are to argue that liberals are wrong to accept the need to cut government spending, then we need to develop alternatives to austerity. We need to articulate not only a defense of the work of the public sector, but also a coherent way to fund it.

Here's how:

- "Flip" the state and federal tax systems. A recent report by United for a Fair Economy demonstrates how shifting the tax burden so that the wealthiest would pay the rates currently borne by the poorest would eliminate state budget deficits; under such a plan, for example, New Jersey would raise some $12 billion in additional revenue, more than enough to restore all of Governor Christie's spending cuts while dramatically increasing state support for communities like Camden. Since 1979, federal tax cuts have saved households in the top 0.1% nearly $90 billion a year. Reversing those cuts would supply enough revenue to balance state budget deficits for the current fiscal year.

- Federal revenue sharing. This program was established during the Nixon administration, repealed under Reagan and brought back briefly and under a different name under Obama. It could eliminate the need for state and local spending cuts by sharing with these governments the abundant revenues of the national government and its capacity to borrow.

- Upgrade Social Security and establish universal, single-payer health coverage. By dramatically reducing their labor costs, improved national pensions and health insurance would immediately solve the fiscal problems of states and localities. Even enacted on a state level, universal pensions and single-payer health systems would realize huge savings. For example, a single-payer health insurance program on the state level, such as Vermont is currently establishing, could save between 15% and 30% of the current cost of health care, savings of between 3% and 6% of state income. In addition to being a boon for business and consumers, this would produce huge savings throughout state and local governments. In Massachusetts, for example, cities and towns could save over $320 million on their current health care spending and the state government would save over $2 billion, more than this year's budget deficit.

It is time to stop playing defense against the often absurd and always misguided attacks on public employees. There are alternatives to austerity. All that we need is the political will to demand them. ❑

Sources: Michael Cooper and Megan Thee-Brenan, "Majority in Poll Back Employees in Public Sector Unions," *New York Times*, February 28, 2011; David M. Halbfinger, "Gov. Chris Christie of New Jersey Lays Out Tight Budget," *New York Times*, February 22, 2011; Jeffrey Keefe, "Debunking the Myth of the Overcompensated Public Employee: The Evidence," Economic Policy Institute, September 15, 2010; Karen Kraut, Shannon Moriarty, and Dave Shreve, *Flip it to Fix it: An Immediate, Fair Solution to State Budget Shortfalls,* United for a Fair Economy, May 25, 2011; Elizabeth McNichol, Phil Oliff, and Nicholas Johnson, "States Continue to Feel Recession's Impact," Center on Budget and Policy Priorities, June 17, 2011; Richard Pérez-Peña, "N.J. Legislature Moves to Cut Benefits for Public Workers," *New York Times*, June 23, 2011; Jeffrey Thompson and John Schmitt, "The Wage Penalty for State and Local Government Employees in New England," Political Economy Research Institute and CEPR, September 2010; Leo Troy, *The New Unionism in the New Society: Public Sector Unions in the Redistributive State*, Fairfax, Va.: George Mason University Press, 1994.

Article 8.2

STATE WORKERS FACE A COMPENSATION PENALTY
BY ETHAN POLLACK
March/April 2011

The campaign against state and local workers is often justified with claims that they are privileged relative to their private-sector peers or have somehow been cushioned from the effects of the recent recession and slow recovery. Data from Wisconsin as well as Indiana, New Jersey, and Ohio prove that these claims are clearly false.

In Wisconsin, which has become a focal point in this debate, public servants already take a pretty hefty pay cut just for the opportunity to serve their communities, according to findings by Rutgers economist Jeffrey Keefe. The figure below shows that when comparing the total compensation (which includes non-wage benefits such as health care and pensions) of workers with similar education, public-sector workers consistently make less than their private-sector peers. Workers with a bachelor's degree or more—who make up nearly 60% of the state and local workforce in Wisconsin—are compensated between $20,000 a year less (if they just have a bachelor's degree) to over $82,000 less (if they have a professional degree).

True apples-to-apples comparisons require controlling for worker characteristics such as education in order to best measure a worker's potential earnings in a different sector or industry. Controlling for a larger range of earnings predictors—including not just education but also age, experience, gender, race, etc., Wisconsin public-sector workers face an annual compensation penalty of 11%. Adjusting for the slightly fewer hours worked per week on average, these workers still face a compensation penalty of 5% for choosing to work in the public sector.

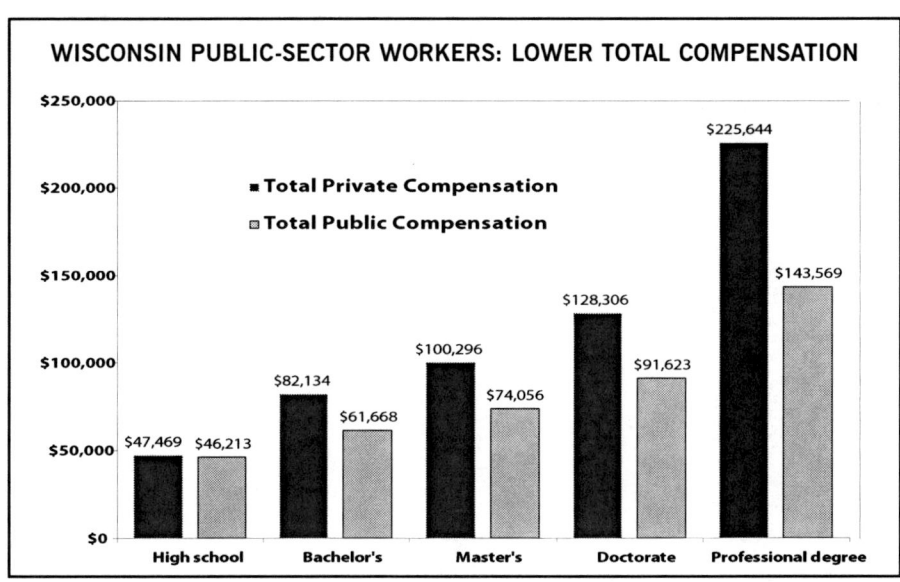

PUBLIC- AND PRIVATE-SECTOR WORKERS COMPARED					
	Public-sector Penalty	Job experience		% w/ 4-yr degree	
		Public	Private	Public	Private
Indiana	7.5%	24.1 years	21.6	49%	24%
New Jersey	4.1%	24	22	57%	40%
Ohio	6%	23.2	21.7	49%	26%
Wisconsin	11%	22.5	21.3	59%	30%

The story is similar in Indiana, New Jersey, and Ohio. Public-sector workers in all of these states also face an annual compensation penalty—of 7.5%, 4.1%, and 6%, respectively. As in Wisconsin, a higher percentage of public-sector workers than private-sector workers in these states have a four-year college degree, as well as more job experience on average (see table above).

The deficit that these states face is caused by the economic downturn and, in Wisconsin, a recent tax-cut package. It has nothing to do with the compensation of the people that educate our children, keep the streets safe and clean, keep dangerous chemicals out of our water, and keep insurance companies from taking advantage of us. These public servants are already paid less than those in the private sector, and nationally, this gap has actually been increasing over the past few decades, according to a report by University of Wisconsin-Milwaukee economists Keith Bender and John Heywood.

Instead of opportunistically using these hard times to target workers who—because of their public service—already take a substantial pay cut, state politicians should focus on creating jobs and boosting the incomes of all workers. ❑

A version of this article originally appeared as a "Snapshot" at the Economic Policy Institute website (epi.org).

Sources: Keith Bender and John Heywood, "Out of Balance: Comparing Public and Private Sector Compensation over 20 Years," National Institute on Retirement Security, Washington, D.C., April 2010, (sige.org); Jeffrey H. Keefe, "Are Wisconsin Public Employees Overcompensated?," Economic Policy Institute, Washington, D.C., February 10, 2011 (epi.org); Economic Policy Institute, Reports on public-sector worker undercompensation in Ohio, Indiana, and New Jersey, Washington, D.C., February 18, 2011 (epi.org).

Article 8.3

THE BETRAYAL OF PUBLIC WORKERS

It's not only bad politics for states to use their budget crises to bust unions—it's bad economics.

BY ROBERT POLLIN AND JEFFREY THOMPSON
March 2011; The Nation

The Great Recession and its aftermath are entering a new phase in the United States, which could bring even more severe assaults on the living standards and basic rights of ordinary people than we have experienced thus far. This is because a wide swath of the country's policy- and opinion-making elite have singled out public sector workers—including schoolteachers, healthcare workers, police officers and firefighters—as well as their unions and even their pensions as deadweight burdens sapping the economy's vitality.

The Great Recession did blow a massive hole in state and municipal government finances, with tax receipts—including income, sales and property taxes—dropping sharply along with household incomes, spending and real estate values. Meanwhile, demand for public services, such as Medicaid and heating oil assistance, has risen as people's circumstances have worsened. But let's remember that the recession was caused by Wall Street hyper-speculation, not the pay scales of elementary school teachers or public hospital nurses.

Nonetheless, a rising chorus of commentators charge that public sector workers are overpaid relative to employees in comparable positions in the private sector. The fact that this claim is demonstrably false appears not to matter. Instead, the attacks are escalating. The most recent proposal gaining traction is to write new laws that would allow states to declare bankruptcy. This would let them rip up contracts with current public sector employees and walk away from their pension fund obligations. Only by declaring bankruptcy, Republican luminaries Jeb Bush and Newt Gingrich argued in the *Los Angeles Times*, will states be able to "reform their bloated, broken and underfunded pension systems for current and future workers."

But this charge is emanating not only from the Republican right; in a front-page story on January 20, the *New York Times* reported on a more general trend spreading across the country in which "policymakers are working behind the scenes to come up with a way to let states declare bankruptcy and get out from under crushing debts, including the pensions they have promised to retired public workers."

Considered together, state and local governments are the single largest employer in the US economy. They are also the country's most important providers of education, healthcare, public safety and other vital forms of social support. Meanwhile, the official unemployment rate is stuck at 9%—a more accurate figure is 16.1%—a full eighteen months after the recession was declared over. How have we reached the point where the dominant mantra is to dismantle rather than shore up state and local governments in their moment of crisis?

Why States Need Support During Recessions

The Wall Street–induced recession clobbered state and local government budgets. By 2009, state tax revenues had fallen by fully 13% relative to where they were in 2007, and they remained at that low level through most of last year. By comparison, revenues never fell by more than 6% in the 2001 recession. Even during the 1981–82 recession, the last time unemployment reached 9%, the decline in state tax revenues never exceeded 2%. These revenue losses, starting in 2008, when taken together with the increased demand for state services, produced an average annual budget gap in 2009–11 of $140 billion, or 21% of all state spending commitments.

Unlike the federal government, almost all state and local governments are legally prohibited from borrowing money to finance shortfalls in their day-to-day operating budgets. The state and local governments do borrow to finance their long-term investments in school buildings, roads, bridges, sewers, mass transit and other infrastructure projects. They have established a long record of reliability in repaying these debt obligations, even during the recession. Nevertheless, these governments invariably experience a squeeze in their operating budgets during recessions, no matter how well they have managed their finances during more favorable economic times.

If, in a recession, states and municipalities are forced to reduce their spending in line with their loss in tax revenues, this produces layoffs for government employees and loss of sales for government vendors. These cutbacks, in turn, will worsen conditions in the private market, discouraging private businesses from making new investments and hiring new employees. The net impact is to create a vicious cycle that deepens the recession.

As such, strictly as a means of countering the recession—on behalf of business interests as well as everyone else in the community—the logic of having the federal government providing stimulus funds to support state and local government spending levels is impeccable. The February 2009 Obama stimulus—the American Recovery and Reinvestment Act (ARRA)—along with supplemental funds for Medicaid, has provided significant support, covering about one-third of the total budget gap generated by the recession. But that leaves two-thirds to be filled by other means. ARRA funds have now run out, and the Republican-controlled House of Representatives will almost certainly block further funding.

In 2010 roughly another 15% of the budget gap was covered by twenty-nine states that raised taxes and fees-for-services. In general, raising taxes during a recession is not good policy. But if it must be done to help fill deepening budgetary holes, the sensible way to proceed is to focus these increases on wealthier households. Their ability to absorb such increases is obviously strongest, which means that, unlike other households, they are not likely to cut back on spending in response to the tax hikes. In fact, ten states—New York, Illinois, Connecticut, North Carolina, Wisconsin, Oregon, Hawaii, Vermont, Rhode Island and Delaware—have raised taxes progressively in some fashion.

Of course, the wealthy do not want to pay higher taxes. But during the economic expansion and Wall Street bubble years of 2002–07, the average incomes of the richest 1% of households rose by about 10% per year, more than three times that for all households. The richest 1% received fully 65% of all household income growth between 2002–07.

One charge against raising state taxes in a progressive way is that it will encourage the wealthy to pick up and leave the state. But research on this question shows that this has not happened. We can see why by considering, as a hypothetical example, the consequences of a 2% income tax increase on the wealthiest 5% of households in Massachusetts. This would mean that these households would now have $359,000 at their disposal after taxes rather than $370,000—hardly enough to affect spending patterns significantly for these households, much less induce them to relocate out of the state. At the same time, a tax increase such as this by itself will generate about $1.6 billion for the state to spend on education, healthcare and public safety.

But even with the ARRA stimulus funds and tax increases, states and municipalities have had to make sharp cuts in spending. More severe cuts will be coming this year, with the ARRA funds now gone. These include cuts that will reduce low-income children's or families' eligibility for health insurance; further cuts in medical, homecare and other services for low-income households, as well as in K–12 education and higher education; and layoffs and furloughs for employees. The proposed 2012 budgets include still deeper cuts in core areas of healthcare and education. In Arizona, the governor's budget would cut healthcare for 280,000 poor people and reduce state support for public universities by nearly 20%. In California, Governor Brown is proposing to bring spending on the University of California down to 1999 levels, when the system had 31% fewer students than it does today.

State and Local Government Workers Are Not Overpaid

Even if state and local government employees are not responsible for the budgetary problems that emerged out of the recession, are they nevertheless receiving bloated wage and benefits packages that are holding back the recovery? Since the recession began, there has been a steady stream of media stories making such claims. One widely cited 2009 Forbes cover article reported, "State and local government workers get paid an average of $25.30 an hour, which is 33% higher than the private sector's $19.... Throw in pensions and other benefits and the gap widens to 42%."

What figures such as these fail to reflect is that state and local government workers are older and substantially better educated than private-sector workers. Forbes is therefore comparing apples and oranges. As John Schmitt of the Center for Economic Policy Research recently showed, when state and local government employees are matched against private sector workers of the same age and educational levels, the public workers earn, on average, about 4% less than their private counterparts. Moreover, the results of Schmitt's apples-to-apples comparison are fully consistent with numerous studies examining this same question over the past twenty years. One has to suspect that the pundits who have overlooked these basic findings have chosen not to look.

State Pension Funds Are Not Collapsing

Not surprisingly, state and local government pension funds absorbed heavy losses in the 2008–09 Wall Street crisis, because roughly 60% of these pension fund assets were invested in corporate stocks. Between mid-2007 and mid-2009, the total value of these pension funds fell by nearly $900 billion.

This collapse in the pension funds' asset values has increased their unfunded liabilities—that is, the total amount of benefit payments owed over the next thirty years relative to the ability of the pension funds' portfolio to cover them. By how much? In reality, estimating the total level of unfunded liabilities entails considerable guesswork. One simply cannot know with certainty how many people will be receiving benefits over the next thirty years, nor—more to the point—how much money the pension funds' investments will be earning over this long time span. The severe instability of financial markets in the recent past further clouds the picture.

Thus, these estimates vary by huge amounts, depending on the presumed rate of return for the funds. The irony is that right-wing doomsayers in this debate, such as Grover Norquist, operate with an assumption that the fund managers will be able to earn returns only equal to the interest rates on riskless US Treasury securities. Under this assumption, the level of unfunded liabilities balloons to the widely reported figure of $3 trillion. To reach this conclusion, the doomsayers are effectively arguing that the collective performance of all the Wall Street fund managers—those paragons of free-market wizardry—will be so anemic over the next thirty years that the pension funds may as well just fire them and permanently park all their money in risk-free government bonds. It follows that the profits of private corporations over the next thirty years will also be either anemic or extremely unstable.

But it isn't necessary to delve seriously into this debate in order to assess the long-term viability of the public pension funds. A more basic consideration is that before the recession, states and municipalities consistently maintained outstanding records of managing their funds. In the 1990s the funds steadily accumulated reserves, such that by 2000, on average, they were carrying no unfunded liabilities at all. Even after the losses to the funds following the previous Wall Street crash of 2001, the unfunded share of total pension obligations was no more than around 10%. By comparison, the Government Accountability Office holds that to be fiscally sound, the unfunded share can be as high as 20% of the pension funds' total long-term obligations.

A few states are facing more serious problems, including New Jersey, Illinois and California. New Jersey is in the worst shape. But this is not because the state has been handing out profligate pensions to its retired employees. The average state pension in New Jersey pays out $39,500 per year. The problem is that over the past decade, the state has regularly paid into the system less than the amount agreed upon by the legislature and governor and stipulated in the annual budgets. For 2010 the state skipped its scheduled $3.1 billion payment altogether. However, even taking New Jersey's worst-case scenario, the state could still eliminate its unfunded pension fund liabilities—that is, begin running a 100% fully funded pension fund—if it increased the current allocation by about 4% of the total budget, leaving 96% of the state budget allocation unchanged.

In dollar terms, this worst-case scenario for New Jersey would require the state to come up with roughly $4 billion per year to cover its pension commitments in an overall budget in the range of $92 billion. Extracting this amount of money from other programs in the budget would certainly cause pain, especially when New

Jersey, like all other states, faces tight finances. But compare this worst-case scenario with the bankruptcy agenda being discussed throughout the country.

To begin with, seriously discussing a bankruptcy agenda will undermine the confidence of private investors in all state and municipal bonds—confidence that has been earned by state and municipal governments. When the markets begin to fear that states and municipalities are contemplating bankruptcy, this will drive up the interest rates that governments will have to pay to finance school buildings, infrastructure improvements and investments in the green economy.

Then, of course, there is the impact on the pensioners and their families. For the states and municipalities to walk away from their pension fund commitments would leave millions of public sector retirees facing major cuts in their living standards and their sense of security. Something few Americans understand is that roughly one-third of the 19 million state and local employees—i.e., those in fifteen states, including California, Texas and Massachusetts—are not eligible for Social Security and will depend exclusively on their pensions and personal savings in retirement. In addition, public sector pensions are not safeguarded by the federal Pension Benefit Guaranty Corporation. Unlike Wall Street banks, state pensioners will receive no bailout checks if the states choose to abrogate their pension fund agreements.

Getting Serious About Reforming State Finances

Of course, there are significant ways the public pension systems, as well as state and local finances more generally, can be improved. The simplest solution, frequently cited, involves "pension spiking"—that is, practices such as allowing workers to add hundreds of hours of overtime at the end of their careers to balloon their final year's pay and their pensions. This has produced serious additional costs to pension obligations in some states and municipalities, but it is still by no means a major factor in explaining states' current fiscal problems.

But states and municipalities also have to follow through on the steps they have taken to raise taxes on the wealthy households that are most able to pay. They should also broaden their sources of tax revenue by taxing services such as payments to lawyers, as well as by taxing items purchased over the Internet. And they have to stop giving out large tax breaks to corporations as inducements to locate in their state or municipality instead of neighboring locations. This kind of race to the bottom generates no net benefit to states and municipalities.

Finally, state and local governments are in the same boat as the federal government and private businesses in facing persistently rising healthcare costs. As was frequently noted during the healthcare debates over the past two years, the United States spends about twice as much per person on healthcare as other highly developed countries do, even though these other countries have universal coverage, longer life expectancies and generally healthier populations. These costs weigh heavily on the budgets of state and local governments, which finance a large share of Medicaid and health benefits for state employees. The problem is that we spend far more than other countries on medications, expensive procedures and especially insurance and administration. We also devote less attention to prevention. It remains to be seen how much the Obama healthcare reform law—the 2010 Patient Protection and Affordable Care Act—will remedy this situation. It is certainly the case that more must be done, especially in establishing effective controls on the drug and insurance industries.

These are some of the long-run measures that must be taken to bolster the financing of education, healthcare, public safety and other vital social services, as well as to support investments in infrastructure and the green economy. If states declare bankruptcy they will break their obligations to employees, vendors, pensioners and even bondholders, which will undermine the basic foundations of our economy. As we emerge, if only tentatively, from the wreckage of the Great Recession, this is precisely the moment we need to strengthen, not weaken, the standards of fairness governing our society. ❑

Article 8.4

TEACHERS, SECRETARIES, AND SOCIAL WORKERS: THE NEW WELFARE MOMS?

BY RANDY ALBELDA
May/June 2011

Conservatives have had their sights on public-sector workers for a while and for good reason. Public-sector workers represent two favorite targets: organized labor and government. I am a public-sector employee and union member, so I can't help but take these attacks and struggles personally. I am also a veteran of the welfare "reform" battles of the 1990s, and the debates over public-sector workers are strikingly similar.

Like welfare moms, public-sector workers have been painted as greedy [fill-in-the-blank barnyard animals], feeding from the public trough and targeted as the primary source of what's wrong with government today.

Like 1990s welfare-reform debates, this one is dominated by more fiction than fact. For example, previous and recent research consistently shows public-sector workers actually earn less than private-sector workers with comparable skills and experience. While many, but not all, public-sector workers who work long enough for the public sector have a defined-benefit pension, the unfunded portions of those pensions are often due to bad state policy, not union negotiations.

In some states, like my own, Massachusetts, current workers are paying most of their pension costs through their own contributions into interest-bearing pension funds. Because state and local governments with defined pensions do not contribute to social security, there are currently cost savings. The upshot is that the cost of pensions may not be as high as some are arguing.

It is true that health-insurance costs for current retirees are expensive and worrisome. But this is because of the rising costs in private health insurance. Making workers pay more for their health-care benefits will erode the compensation base of public-sector workers, but it won't get at the real problem of escalating health-care costs.

During the welfare debates, one of the arguments used to justify punitive legislative changes was spun around the fact that welfare moms who did get low-wage employment could also get child-care assistance—while other moms could not. Sound familiar? Public-sector workers do have employer-sponsored benefits many private-sector workers no longer get. But benefits haven't improved in the public sector over the last 20 years; indeed most public-sector workers are paying more for the same benefits.

Over the same period, many private-sector workers have been stripped of their employer-provided benefits even as profits have soared. Instead of asking why corporate America is stripping middle-class workers of decent health-care coverage and retirement plans, the demand is to strip public-sector workers of theirs.

The new Cadillac-driving welfare queens are the handful of errant politicians who game the pension system and a few highly paid administrators getting handsome pensions. Sure they exist, but are hardly representative. The typical public-sector worker is a woman, most often working as a teacher, secretary or social worker. Women comprise 60% of all state and local workers (compared to their 47% representation in the private work force). And those three occupations make up 40% of the state and local work force.

Shaking down public-sector unions may make some feel better about solving government fiscal problems, but the end result will be more lousy jobs for educated and skilled workers. It will also not stem the red ink that is causing states to disinvest in much-needed human and physical infrastructure with budget cuts. But eroding wages and benefits combined with public-sector bashing will send a very loud market signal to the best and brightest currently thinking about becoming teachers, librarians, or social workers to do something else.

Wisconsin Governor Scott Walter is leading the attack on public-sector workers today. In the 1990s it was another Wisconsin governor, Tommy Thompson, who was a leader in demanding and implementing punitive changes to his state's welfare system. His plan became a model for the rest of the states and federal welfare legislation in 1996. Then there were horror stories and welfare bashing, but not much in the way of discussing the real issue of decent paying jobs that poor and low-income mothers on and off welfare needed to support their families. The main result of welfare reform was the growth in working-poor moms.

There is one important difference. Public-sector workers, unlike welfare moms, have unions and a cadre of supporters behind them. ❑

Article 8.5

MAKING LABOR PAY
Recent battles in Wisconsin and San Jose show why we need universal pensions.

BY KATHERINE SCIACCHITANO
September/October 2012

The political economy of the recovery is making the United States even more unequal than it was during the bubble years. Incomes fell across the board during the crisis: median family income is 6.3% below what it was in 2001. But the top 1% garnered 93% of income growth in the first year of recovery. Housing, still the main source of wealth for middle-income families, remains depressed while stocks are close to pre-crash highs. Moreover, the drive for more tax cuts for the wealthy continues. And policy initiatives to cut Social Security, Medicare, and Medicaid would weaken the safety net even as it is most needed.

A spate of attacks on state and local public-sector pensions now threatens to make inequality even more entrenched and painful, and to undermine both short- and long-term economic growth.

The power of labor is dead center in this agenda. Despite a long-term decline in workers covered by union contracts, unions have over 16 million members: they are still the social force most capable of combating the assault on workers' incomes and militating for greater equality. Crippling their political power therefore remains both a tactical and a strategic objective on the right. With only 6.9% of workers in the private sector covered by union contracts, versus 37% in the public sector, public-sector unions are bearing the brunt of the attacks. And public pensions are the battering ram.

Attacking Unions, Eroding Pensions

The trip wire for the assault on pensions was the combined fall in state and local revenues from the bursting of the housing bubble, and the steep losses suffered by pension funds during the resulting stock market slide of 2007-2009: by 2010 there were widely acknowledged public pension funding shortfalls totaling nearly $800 billion.

While pension funds are slowly making back market losses, conservative advocates like Andrew Biggs at the American Enterprise Institute are arguing for new measures of shortfalls that would bring them to over $4 trillion, and using this $4 trillion figure to call for a national movement to slash both public-sector pensions and union rights. The implicit threat is that taxpayers will have to pay these trillions now and into the future, even though they themselves may not have pensions. The stated policy objective is to convince taxpayers and politicians that defined benefit pensions are too expensive in the public sector and should be replaced with defined contribution plans.

Defined benefit pensions are a form of deferred compensation—pay for work performed; they provide guaranteed lifetime payments in retirement. Defined-contribution plans give workers tax breaks for individual savings; workers invest these savings and then pray they don't run out. Over the past three decades, defined benefit pensions have been nearly eradicated in the private sector for non-union workers; their abandonment in the public sector would effectively end defined benefit pensions as a norm for retirement security and shift the burden of retirement savings almost entirely to individuals.

Abandoning public defined benefit pensions would also erode the more than $3 trillion in investment capital controlled and invested by public-sector funds—aggregated capital that gives the funds both a critical role in long-term economic investment and an important shareholder voice in reforming corporate governance and pushing for re-regulation of the financial sector.

While unions remain a powerful voice in defending universal programs like Social Security, declining union density makes defending benefits like defined benefit pensions that are mainly enjoyed by union workers more difficult. Union benefits no longer spill over into the non-union sector as they did when non-union employers had to complete with union employers for workers. While 70% of private-sector union workers and almost all public-sector workers still have access to defined benefit pensions, only 14% of private-sector non-union workers do, opening the way for a divide-and-conquer strategy for conservative politicians to exploit.

Cutting Edge in Wisconsin

Wisconsin governor Scott Walker is the poster child for the dual attack on public-sector unions and pensions. Elected in late 2010 in a Republican sweep, Walker immediately pushed through over $140 million in tax cuts targeted to corporations and the wealthy, then turned around and blamed an alleged $137 million state budget deficit on public employee pensions and unions. In early February, he introduced legislation to eviscerate state workers' bargaining rights, triggering the now-famous months-long occupation of the state capitol by hundreds of thousands of outraged union and non-union workers.

The facts were with the demonstrators: there were no shortfalls in pension funding for taxpayers to make up, and unions had already offered higher worker contributions to help pay for benefits.

When the Republican legislature nevertheless passed legislation eviscerating public-sector bargaining rights and unilaterally raising worker pension contributions, unions launched a yearlong effort to recall the governor.

In the 1930s, Wisconsin had been the birthplace of AFSCME, the nation's largest public-sector union; in the 1950s, it had passed the first state legislation authorizing public-sector bargaining. Yet public pensions remained a wedge issue throughout the campaign.

Wisconsin was once a private-sector union manufacturing stronghold as well, but more recently workers there have been battered with job and benefit losses. As one activist put it, the Walker campaign's uninterrupted message was "cut taxes, create jobs, don't pay for other peoples' pensions." Union workers were almost as vulnerable to the argument as non-union workers: 38% of union households in the state had at least one member who voted to keep Walker in office, handing him a 53% to 47% victory.

Scapegoating in San Jose

The same day as the failed Wisconsin recall, voters in largely Democratic San Jose, California, approved drastic cuts to city workers' pay and pensions with an equally shocking 69% yes vote.

A wealthy community in the heart of Silicon Valley, where the average annual wage is $95,472, San Jose began an ill-timed "Decade of Investment" at the height of the dot-com bubble. Severely limited both in the property tax revenues it could collect, by California's long-standing Proposition 13, and in raising other taxes to compensate, San Jose was buffeted over the next ten years by two recessions, high unemployment, sharp drops in revenue from sales taxes, and repeated budget shortfalls. While city leaders managed to more than double capital expenditures during this decade, spending on services increased less than 1.5% per year (not adjusted for inflation). By 2011, San Jose had endured cumulative workforce reductions of 20% and repeated cuts in services, including closings of 22 community centers.

Having paid for virtually its entire FY 2011-2012 budget shortfall with cuts to payroll, with its FY 2012-2013 budget finally projected to be in balance, the city promptly set about restoring services by slashing pensions.

Like most pension funds, San Jose's were heavily invested in the stock market and suffered large losses from 2007 through 2009, bringing the funds from roughly 90% funded to 75% funded. Although the drop in funding necessitated increased contributions by the city to compensate, the size of the contributions could have been kept reasonable by spreading them out over a longer period of time and bargaining with city unions for appropriate adjustments to benefits and employee contributions.

Instead, San Jose Mayor Chuck Reed magnified pension funding problems to scapegoat workers for revenue shortfalls. Over an 18-month period that coincided with the turmoil in Wisconsin, Reed repeatedly described the city's pension costs as a "cancerous growth" and talked about imminent disaster if benefits weren't cut.

Reed's "Exhibit A" was a figure—eventually exposed by NBC reporters as having been pulled "off the top of the head" of a city retirement official —purporting to show that city pension contributions would more than double over four years, reaching $650 million annually by FY 2015-2016. Forced to do math, the city cut its estimate to $430 million, but still failed to factor in savings from negotiated pay cuts of 10% to 12% and workforce reductions.

The city's final figure—published a year into Reed's campaign, well after the $650 million figure was burned into peoples' brains—was $320 million, less than half the city's original claim. Even this figure included the costs of a voluntary undertaking by the city to pre-fund retiree health care benefits, as well as changed assumptions about future investment returns that increased the size of city pension contributions to be made in the short term – decisions that AFSCME researcher Dan Doonan publicly described as "comically bad timing" for a city recovering from the most severe economic downturn since the Great Depression.

Numbers Games

The pension fight in San Jose highlights the role seemingly arcane actuarial assumptions play in calculating pension shortfalls, and how such assumptions can provide ammunition for public pension battles.

Pension boards invest contributions made by employers and workers and use the returns on these investments to pay for benefits to retirees. They regularly assess the adequacy of returns in relation to benefits that will have to be paid. If pension boards anticipate lower returns over an extended period, they may decide to increase contributions to compensate.

If increased contributions are required, pension boards have several options for minimizing disruptions. They can average gains and losses over a five-year period—a practice called "smoothing." They can lengthen the number of years—or amortization period—over which payments are spread. Lengthening the amortization period is similar to what homeowners do when they choose between a thirty-year mortgage, which spreads payments out over a longer period to keep each payment lower, and a fifteen-year mortgage, which saves money over the long-term, but increases the size of required monthly payments. If boards decide the anticipated rate of return on investments needs to be lowered, they can do that gradually too.

The consequences for taxpayers of these decisions about timing can be enormous. Postponing additional required contributions for too long may mean that small shortfalls become unmanageable. But front-loading payments increases their size, and may force unnecessary tax increases and service cuts, benefit reductions, or all three.

San Jose front-loaded its payments. Pension trustees lowered estimates of future returns without easing in the change. They declined to lengthen the amortization period, spreading increased contributions over a shorter amortization period than they had to. And the city made an enormously expensive decision to pre-fund retiree health care rather than funding it on a pay-as-you-go basis as most other jurisdictions do, voluntarily increasing its immediate payroll costs for retiree health care to 17% of pay, and 15.5% for employees.

Together with the city's earlier inflated estimates of the contributions that would be required to compensate for investment losses, these choices allowed San Jose to magnify pension shortfalls and intensify pressures to reduce benefits.

Pensions and Economic Recovery

San Jose's pension cuts are currently in litigation. If they are upheld, the price for city workers will range from just under 30% to just over 40% of take-home pay: 15.5% for retiree health care; additional contributions for pensions of up to 16%; and a 10% to 12% pay cut—all *in addition* to existing contributions of 13% of pay. Alternatively, city workers, who like many public-sector workers don't participate in Social Security, may be able to opt for a lower tier of benefits being created for new employees, provided the scheme is approved by the IRS. Not surprisingly, San Jose is now having trouble retaining and recruiting personnel.

The price for city residents has also been severe. In addition to what Doonan characterizes as "wrecking the labor market," Reed's divisive campaign increased mistrust of the city by its unions, and of unions by city residents, many of whom might well have worked in coalition with city workers for solutions, including a one-quarter-of-one-cent sales tax increase that could have avoided the bloodletting and improved the city's fiscal position as well. As Bob Brownstein of San Jose-based Working Partnerships USA put it, "When you have a perfect fiscal storm from capital projects you can't staff, a bad economy, falling revenues, and investment losses, then any chance you get to push expenditures off to the future or bring revenues forward, you should probably take. Anytime is going to be better than now."

It's in the context of these votes in Wisconsin and San Jose, and another similar result in San Diego, that AEI's Andrew Biggs is calling for a national movement for to cut public employee pensions by referenda in order to bring them "closer in line with what stressed private sector workers can expect in the 21st century"—a cruel joke, since most private-sector workers have no pensions.

The price of such widespread take-backs would be enormous, not just for future retirees, but for economic recovery and future growth. The real estate bubble was the last stage of a decades-long transformation in which the contribution of manufacturing profits and employment to the U.S. economy fell and the role of the finance industry and debt expanded. The transition was disastrous, both for workers' wages and economic stability. Five years into a severe downturn, the official unemployment rate is still 8.2%. The youth unemployment rate is 16.4%. The critical challenge is economic growth to reduce unemployment and raise wages, not further tax reductions.

Far from just supporting retirees, defined-benefit pensions contribute to economic recovery by providing a long-term, stable source of counter-cyclical spending—spending that continues even during economic downturns. The National Institute on Retirement Security calculates that each dollar of benefits from a defined benefit pension supports $2.37 in economic output. In 2009, defined benefit pension dollars spent in the economy supported 6.5 million jobs nationally, or 4.2% of the labor force.

To the extent that pension funds use dividend income from investments to pay benefits, they also redistribute income that would normally go to high-income investors, making income more equal across the economy. This in turn boosts spending, since lower-income workers spend much more of their income than the wealthy do.

Finally, as David Marchick, managing director of the Carlyle Group, has explained to Congress, defined-benefit funds have a responsibility to actively invest their capital in order to produce long-term returns, not just short-term profits. As a result, they are a critical source of the long-term, patient investment and venture capital needed for sustainable growth and job creation, a role that has been even more vital during the crisis and recovery.

Neither defined-contribution plans nor other kinds of individual savings provide these same benefits. Because workers have to worry about outliving the income from these accounts, they are more reluctant to spend it, limiting its stimulus effect. Small individual accounts don't provide the opportunity for the large-scale, targeted, job-creating investments that pension funds routinely make. And because defined contribution plans are tied to individual savers who have shorter investment horizons and can afford to take fewer risks than professional managers in large funds, they characteristically have 20% to 40% lower returns over their life than defined benefit plans. They also have higher fees.

As a result, defined benefit plans cost half as much to fund as defined contribution plans. Put another way, each dollar contributed to a defined contribution plan delivers half the benefits of a dollar contributed to a defined benefit plan.

Any further large-scale switch from defined benefit to defined contribution plans as currently structured would thus not only undermine retirement security and overall, or aggregate, demand in the economy, it would place heavier burdens on future generations of taxpayers. On the one hand, saving more to achieve the same benefits lowers spending and aggregate demand today, hurting the recovery. On the other hand, *not* saving more and ending up with lower benefits reduces aggregate demand—what will be spent—in the future, hurting long-term growth. To the extent that lower benefits fail to meet basic needs for retirement security, they pave the way for higher poverty rates, raising the need for public assistance down the line, creating longer-term fiscal problem for state and the federal governments—and taxpayers.

The Real Crisis: Retirement Insecurity

Economist Dean Baker of the Center for Economic and Policy Research has calculated that virtually the entire shortfall in public pension funding was caused by the sudden drop in the stock market and cutbacks in contributions during the downturn. The Center for Retirement Research in Boston estimates that if markets continue to recover, pensions are likely to rebound from their crisis low of 75% funded in 2011 to 82% by 2015. The Center for Budget and Policy Priorities calculates that most states can correct remaining shortfalls by easing in increased contributions of up to 1.2% of their budgets over the next five years and modestly scaling back benefits. The exceptions are the handful of states—Illinois, Kentucky, and New Jersey among them—that took "contribution holidays" during the bubble or that promised benefit increases without funding them, where more substantial measures will be needed.

The real pension crisis isn't the acknowledged $800 billion in public pension shortfalls. It's the estimated $6.6 trillion gap in private savings that Retirement USA estimates workers need to achieve retirement security.

Since Social Security's establishment during the Depression, policy makers have viewed retirement security as a "three-legged stool" composed of Social Security, employer pensions, and private savings. Today, less than half of all private-sector workers participate in pensions of any sort. Median-income households with 401(k)s and a head-of-household between 60 and 62 (a group that has lived through two recent stock-market crashes and the bursting of the housing bubble) have saved just one quarter of what they need to maintain their standard of living in retirement. Younger workers face another lost decade of economic growth before they can start saving. In California, 55% of workers aged 25 to 44 can expect to retire on less than $22,000 a year.

The best way to address the real retirement crisis while supporting recovery is to preserve and strengthen Social Security without cutting benefits; defend defined benefit pensions where they exist; and build a universal system to strengthen individual saving among the increasing number of workers who have no pensions.

Saving individually for retirement maximizes three types of risk: longevity risk—the risk of outliving savings; investment risk—the risk of poor diversification or investment choices; and what is referred to as market risk—the risk of retiring in a severe market downturn.

As a result, most proposals for universal coverage start by pooling individual investment accounts into professionally managed funds that can more effectively diversify investments, share longevity risk, and spread gains and losses over much longer periods than individuals can. These techniques for managing risk allow the funds to take appropriate risk to achieve much higher returns, making retirement savings more efficient for individuals and for society.

Senator Tom Harkin of (D-Iowa) has disseminated a proposal for a national system of pooled accounts that would pay annuities based on a combination of the individual contributions workers make and the performance of the investments. To encourage saving, the system would enroll workers automatically, but allow them to opt out or contribute less than the automatic minimum. Because Harkin's program is national, it would be completely portable. Harkin's plan also strengthens Social Security by tailoring its cost-of-living allowance to cover seniors' basic needs, removing the cap on wages subject to the Social Security payroll tax, and modestly boosting benefits by approximately $60 a month for most workers.

Pension economist Teresa Ghilarducci has made proposals for state and national level plans that overlap with Harkin's but would guarantee a minimum return above inflation. Because most tax breaks aimed at encouraging pension saving currently subsidize 401(k) contributions by higher-income savers, Ghilarducci's proposals re-weight assistance towards middle- and low-income savers who would otherwise not be able to save for retirement.

Because of the current political climate that makes expansion of government benefits highly contested, both Ghilarducci's and Harkin's plans are structured to avoid government payment of benefits and to work in tandem with Social Security and existing defined benefit pensions. A number of states, including California, are also developing proposals for universal private-sector pension plans.

Recasting the Debate

A robust defense of pensions is no longer possible without a robust fight for universal coverage linked to the broader fight for economic growth. As Jelger Kalmijn, president of a California local of the Communication Workers of America, put it, "Just fighting to keep the defined benefit plans is like fighting to keep the people who are currently in unions in unions. If you only fight to keep the contracts we have and don't organize anyone new, we've all agreed that's a loser."

The biggest challenge in building a universal pension system is to begin. The challenge in defending existing pensions is to broaden the fight so most workers have a positive stake in winning,

When viewed against the realities of pension economics or the broader macroeconomy, the facts in Wisconsin and San Jose don't support the electoral results achieved. But the electoral results do match the political reality on the ground: the profound anxiety and suffering caused by decades of job losses in manufacturing jobs across the country, the stagnation of hourly wages, and the shredding of benefits. Without concrete solutions many of these workers are holding on to what little they have, which in too many cases comes down to their tax dollars. It's up to unions to lead the fight for those solutions, even though the solutions go beyond traditional union membership or coverage under a contract.

As union density shrinks, fighting for universal benefits will broaden the political playing field. While the educational and political battles will be long, making the fight a concrete one now by making it about pensions for all is what it will take to change the terms of the debate and move from playing defense to playing offense. ❏

Selected sources: California State Auditor, "City of San Jose: Some Retirement Cost Projections Were Unsupported Although Rising Retirement Costs Have Led to Reduced City Services," Bureau of State Audits, August 2012 (bsa.ca.gov); Jenna Susko, et al., "San Jose Pension Estimates Questioned," April 27, 2012 (nbcbayarea.com); Ilana Boivie, "Pensionomics 2012: Measuring the Economic Impact of DB Pension Expenditures," National Institute on Retirement Security, March 2012, (nirsonline.org); Alicia H. Munell, et al., "The Funding of State and Local Pensions: 2011-2015," Center for Retirement Research, Boston College (crr.bc.edu); David Marchick, "The Power of Pensions: Building a Strong Middle Class and Strong Economy," Testimony Before the Senate Committee on Health, Education, Labor and Pensions, July 12, 2011 (help.senate.gov); "The Retirement Income Deficit," Retirement USA (retirement-usa.org); Diane Oakley, Executive Director, National Institute on Retirement Security, "The Power of Pensions: Building a Strong Middle Class and Strong Economy," Testimony before the United States Senate Committee on Health, Education, Labor and Pensions, July 12, 2011 (help.senate.gov); Tom Harkin, Chair, United States Senate Committee on Health, Education, Labor and Pensions, "The Retirement Crisis and a Plan to Solve It" (harkin.senate.gov); Teresa Ghilarducci, "Guaranteed Retirement Accounts: Toward Retirement Income Security," Economic Policy Institute, EPI Briefing Paper #204, November 20, 2007 (gpn.org); Alicia H. Munnell, et al., "The Pension Coverage Problem in the Private Sector," Center for Retirement Research, September 2012 (crr.bc.edu); Alicia H. Munell, et al., "How Would GASB Proposals Affect State and Local Pensions," Center for Retirement Research, Boston College (crr.bc.edu).

For a full list of sources, visit dollarsandsense.org.

Chapter 9

POVERTY AND WEALTH

Article 9.1

THE 99%, THE 1%, AND CLASS STRUGGLE

BY ALEJANDRO REUSS
November/December 2011

Between 1979 and 2007, the income share of the top 1% of U.S. households (by income rank) more than doubled, to over 17% of total U.S. income. Meanwhile, the income share of the bottom 80% dropped from 57% to 48% of total income. "We are the 99%," the rallying cry of the Occupy Wall Street movement, does a good job at calling attention to the dramatic increase of incomes for those at the very top—and the stagnation of incomes for the majority.

This way of looking at income distribution, however, does not explicitly focus on the different *sources* of people's incomes. Most people get nearly all of their incomes—wages and salaries, as well as employment benefits—by working for someone else. A few people, on the other hand, get much of their income not from work but from ownership of property—profits from a business, dividends from stock, interest income from bonds, rents on land or structures, and so on. People with large property incomes

GROWING GAP BETWEEN PRODUCTIVITY AND PAY, 1947-2010

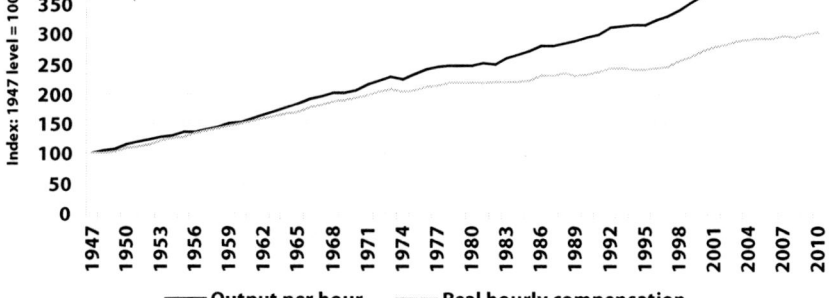

Source: Bureau of Labor Statistics, Real Hourly Compensation, Private Business Sector, Series ID number: PRS84006153; Bureau of Labor Statistics, Output Per Hour, Private Business Sector, Series ID number: PRS84006093.

may also draw large salaries or bonuses, especially from managerial jobs. Executive pay, though treated in official government statistics as labor income, derives from control over business firms and really should be counted as property income.

Over the last forty years, the distribution of income in the United States has tilted in favor of capitalists (including business owners, stock- and bondholders, and corporate executives) and against workers. Between the 1940s and 1960s, U.S. workers' hourly output ("average labor productivity") and workers' real hourly compensation both grew at about 3% per year, so the distribution of income between workers and capitalists changed relatively little. (If the size of a pie doubles and the size of your slice also doubles, your share of the pie does not change.) Since the 1970s, productivity has kept growing at over 2% per year. Average hourly compensation, however, has stagnated—growing only about 1% per year (see figure below). As the gap between what workers produce and what they get paid has increased, workers' share of total income has fallen, and capitalists' share has increased. Since income from property is overwhelmingly concentrated at the top of the income scale, this has helped fuel the rising income share of "the 1%."

The spectacular rise in some types of income—like bank profits or executive compensation—has provoked widespread outrage. Lower financial profits or CEO pay, however, will not reverse the trend toward greater inequality if the result is only to swell, say, profits for nonfinancial corporations or dividends for wealthy shareholders. Focusing too much on one or another kind of property income distracts from the fact that the overall property-income share has been growing at workers' expense.

Workers and employers—whether they like it or not, recognize it or not, prepare for it or not—are locked in a class struggle. Employers in the United States and other countries, over the last few decades, have recognized that they were in a war and prepared for it. They have been fighting and winning. Workers will only regain what they have lost if they can rebuild their collective fighting strength. In the era of globalized capitalism, this means not only building up labor movements in individual countries, but also creating practical solidarity between workers around the world.

A labor resurgence could end workers' decades-long losing streak at the hands of employers and help reverse the tide of rising inequality. Ultimately, though, this struggle should be about more than just getting a better deal. It should be—and can be—about the possibility of building a new kind of society. The monstrous inequalities of capitalism are plain to see. The need for an appealing alternative—a vision of a cooperative, democratic, and egalitarian way of life—is equally stark. ❑

Sources: Bureau of Labor Statistics, Real Hourly Compensation, Private Business Sector, Series ID number: PRS84006153; Bureau of Labor Statistics, Output Per Hour, Private Business Sector, Series ID number: PRS84006093; Congressional Budget Office, Trends in the Distribution of Household Income Between 1979 and 2007 (October 2011) (www.cbo.gov); James Heintz, "Unpacking the U.S. Labor Share," *Capitalism on Trial: A Conference in Honor of Thomas A. Weisskopf*, Political Economy Research Institute, University of Massachusetts-Amherst (September 2011).

Article 9.2

NO THANKS TO THE SUPER-RICH
We don't owe them gratitude for their "superior productivity."

BY ALEJANDRO REUSS
January/February 2012

> "Look at the industries that have dramatically improved over the past several decades, and you'll see a pattern: certain super-productive individuals have led the way. These individuals invariably fall under the 1% of income earners--often the 1% of the 1%. …
>
> "In no other country are high achievers as free to have a vision, to act on it, to reap the rewards, and to accumulate and reinvest capital--even when they are unpopular, even when 'the 99%' disagree or are resentful or envious.
>
> "So, at a time when the 1% are the easy scapegoats, it's fitting this Thanksgiving to take a moment to thank the 1%--and to be grateful that our country rewards success. And as we approach the new year, let's resolve to keep it that way."
>
> —Alex Epstein, "Let's Give Thanks for the One Percent," FoxNews.com, November 23, 2011

Leave it to Fox News to publish an opinion piece, on the eve of Thanksgiving, titled "Let's Give Thanks for the One Percent." Author Alex Epstein, a former fellow of the Ayn Rand Institute, argues that most of "the 1%" (the Occupy Wall Street movement's designation of the richest 1% of the population) "earn their success—through superior productivity that benefits us all."

Is it true that the United States "fosters and rewards productivity like no other," as Epstein argues? Is greater inequality the price we pay for greater economic dynamism? As a first cut, let's compare Gross Domestic Product (GDP) per capita in different high-income countries. Here, the United States ranks second among large industrial countries (excluding small, oil-rich countries, city-states, etc.) behind only Norway. In 2010, Norway's GDP per capita was nearly $56,000, compared to just under $47,000 for the United States. This difference was not a one-year anomaly—Norway's GDP per capita has exceeded that of the United States for over twenty years. One doubts that Epstein would see Nordic social democracy as the kind of society—in which "high achievers [are] free to have a vision, to act on it, to reap the rewards, and to accumulate and reinvest capital"—that fosters high productivity. Yet the GDP figures suggest that it does just that.

Still, second place is not bad. The United States does outpace most of Western Europe on GDP per capita. So maybe Norway is an anomaly, and the more general picture is that the United States and its incentives to "high achievers" vastly outperform Western European "socialism" in fostering productivity. Here, we need to look at a more refined measure, GDP per hour worked, in place of GDP per capita. Average work hours per year vary dramatically among different countries. Workers in many Western European countries enjoy a shorter work week and much longer vacations than workers in the United States. Employed U.S. workers work an average of over 1700 hours per year. Their counterparts in France, Germany, the Netherlands, and Norway, in contrast, average just over 1400 hours. These differences in hours worked explain much of the variation in GDP per capita among these high-income countries. Shifting from GDP per capita to GDP per hour worked, we find that the United States (at about $59/hour) still ranks second to Norway (about $74/hour). The big difference in the rankings, however, is that the gap between the United States and several Western European countries all but disappears. Ireland, The Netherlands, Belgium, and France (yes, France!) all boast figures of over $57/hour, belying the idea that the United States "fosters ... productivity like no other" country (see Figure 1 below).

The idea that greater inequality fosters greater productivity is a widely held article of faith in the United States, and not only among conservatives. Even liberals may accept the idea that there is a tradeoff between equality and productivity, though they may see some loss in productivity as a price worth paying for greater equality. In fact, some countries may enjoy high labor productivity *because of*, not despite, their higher degree of economic equality (both in terms of the distribution of private incomes and the provision of public services). Near-universal access to education and health care, for example, helps people develop greater productive capabilities. Greater overall economic security (including an extensive social safety net and full-employment policies) can make it easier for people to take risks and attempt new ventures. Maybe these are some of the reasons that greater equality in many Western European countries is compatible with such high material standards of living.

While the United States does little better (or, in one case, worse) than five different Western European countries on productivity, we are clearly number one when it comes

FIGURE 1: GDP PER HOUR WORKED, HIGH-INCOME COUNTRIES

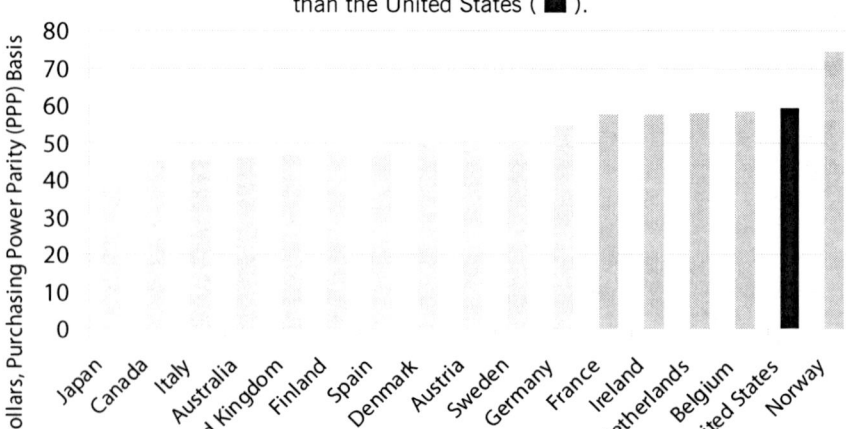

Which is the country that "fosters productivity like no other"? Five European countries ( ) have levels of GDP per hour worked very similar to or greater than the United States ( ).

Source: Bureau of Labor Statistics, International Comparisons of GDP per Capita and per Hour, 1960-2010, Real GDP per hour worked, by country, 1960-2010, Table 3a. Converted to U.S. dollars using 2010 PPPs (2010 dollars).

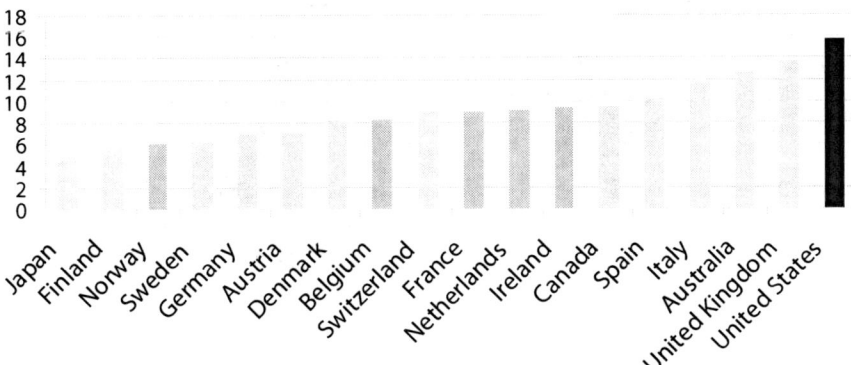

FIGURE 2: INCOME INEQUALITY—RATIO OF TOP 10% TO BOTTOM 10%
Countries (▨) with similar levels of productivity to the United States (■) boast much lower levels of income inequality.

High-income countries, per capita income > US$30,000 PPP, 2007.

Source: United Nations Development Programme (UNDP), Human Development Report 2009, Table M: Economy and inequality, Share of income or expenditure, Richest 10%, Poorest 10%, p. 195 (hdr.undp.org/en/media/HDR_2009_EN_Complete.pdf).

to income inequality. One way to measure income inequality is to compare the share of total income going to the top 10% of the population, by income ranking, to the share going to the bottom 10%. (Using other measures does not change the basic story.) In the United States, the top 10% receives nearly 16 times as much income as the bottom 10%. In the four countries with GDP per hour very similar to the United States'—Belgium, France, Ireland, and Holland—this ratio is less than ten to one. These countries are all in the middle of the pack, in terms of income inequality, among high-income industrial economies. Norway, the country with the highest GDP per hour, has a ratio of just six to one. By this measure, it boasts the third-lowest level of income inequality among these high-income countries (see Figure 2).

Average labor productivity in the U.S. economy, measured by output per hour in the private business sector, has nearly doubled over the last thirty years. Part of the increase is explained by an increase in the education and skills of U.S. workers; part, by the fact that they are working with more and better tools. Most of the increase in income inequality in the United States is not due to an increasing gap in incomes between highly educated (and supposedly more productive) workers and less-educated workers. It is due, rather, to an increase in incomes from property (profits, rent, dividends, interest, capital gains, etc.) at the expense of incomes from labor, and to an increase in the incomes of top corporate executives (which derive from corporate control, and should be classified as part of property income).

That one person's income is higher than another's does not prove that the former is more productive than the latter. If a particular person or group's income is rising, this does not prove that they are being "rewarded" for their increasing productivity. Gains in productivity, like those in the United States in recent decades, must go to someone or other. It is the way that these gains have been split up among different groups that explains the United States' high and rising income inequality—and that has less to do with changes in the relative productivity of different people than shifts in the balance of power between owners and workers.

That does call for a response from the majority, but it's not "thank you." ❑

Sources: Alex Epstein, "Let's Give Thanks for the One Percent," FoxNews. com, November 23, 2011; Bureau of Labor Statistics, International Comparisons of GDP per Capita and per Hour, 1960-2010, Real GDP per hour worked, by country, 1960-2010, Table 3a. Converted to U.S. dollars using 2010 PPPs (2010 dollars), (bls.gov); Bureau of Labor Statistics, Output Per Hour, Private Business Sector, Series ID number: PRS84006093 (bls.gov); United Nations Development Programme, *Human Development Report 2009*, Table M: Economy and inequality, Share of income or expenditure, Richest 10%, Poorest 10%, p. 195 (undp.org).

Article 9.3

THE GREAT RECESSION IN BLACK WEALTH
BY JEANNETTE WICKS-LIM
January/February 2012

The Great Recession produced the largest setback in racial wealth equality in the United States over the last 25 years. In 2009 the average white household's wealth was 20 times that of the average black household, nearly double that in previous years, according to a 2011 report by the Pew Research Center.

Driving this surge in inequality is a devastating drop in black wealth. The typical black household in 2009 was left with less wealth than at any time since 1984 after correcting for inflation.

It's important to remember wealth's special role—different from income—in supporting a household's economic well-being. Income pays for everyday expenses—groceries, clothes, and gas. A family's wealth, or net worth, includes all the assets they've built up over time (e.g., savings account, retirement fund, home, car) minus any money they owe (e.g., school loans, credit card debt, mortgage). Access to such wealth determines whether a layoff or medical crisis creates a bump in the road, or pushes a household off a financial cliff. Wealth can also provide families with financial stepping-stones to advance up the economic ladder—such as money for college tuition, or a down payment on a house.

Racial wealth inequality in the United States has always been severe. In 2004, for example, the typical black household had just $1 in net worth for every $11 of a typical white household. This is because families slowly accumulate wealth over their lifetime and across generations. Wealth, consequently, ties the economic fortunes of today's households to the explicitly racist economic institutions in America's past—especially those that existed during key phases of wealth redistribution. For example, the Homesteading Act of 1862 directed the large-scale transfer of government-owned land nearly exclusively to white households. Also starting in the 1930s, the Federal Housing Authority made a major push to subsidize home mortgages—for primarily white neighborhoods. On top of that, Jim Crow Laws—in effect until the mid-1960s—and racial violence severely curtailed efforts by the black community to start their own businesses to generate their own wealth.

The housing market crisis and the Great Recession made racial wealth inequality yet worse for two reasons. First, the wealth of blacks is more concentrated in their

MEDIAN HOUSEHOLD NET WORTH (2009 DOLLARS)

	1984	1988	1991	1993	1995	2004	2009
White	$76,951	$75,403	$68,203	$67,327	$68,520	$111,313	$92,000
Black	$6,679	$7,263	$7,071	$6,503	$9,885	$9,823	$4,900
Ratio of White to Black	12	10	10	10	7	11	19

Source: Taylor et al., *Twenty-to-One: Wealth Gaps to Rise to Record High Between Whites, Blacks and Hispanics*, Pew Research Center.

homes than the wealth of their white counterparts. Homes of black families make up 59% of their net worth compared to 44% among white families. White households typically hold more of other types of assets like stocks and IRA accounts. So when the housing crisis hit, driving down the value of homes and pushing up foreclosure rates, black households lost a much greater share of their wealth than did white households.

Second, mortgage brokers and lenders marketed subprime mortgages specifically to black households. Subprime mortgages are high-interest loans that are supposed to increase access to home financing for risky borrowers—those with a shaky credit history or low income. But these high-cost loans were disproportionately peddled to black households, even to those that could qualify for conventional loans. One study estimated that in 2007 nearly double the share of upper-income black households (54%) had high-cost mortgages compared to low-income white households (28%).

Subprime mortgages drain away wealth through high fees and interest payments. Worse, predatory lending practices disguise the high-cost of these loans with initially low payments. Payments then shoot up, often leading to default and foreclosure, wiping out a family's home equity wealth. In 2006, Mike Calhoun, president of the Center for Responsible Lending, predicted that the surge of subprime lending within the black community would "…likely be the largest loss of African-American wealth that we have ever seen, wiping out a generation of home wealth building." It was a prescient prediction.

To reverse the rise in racial wealth inequality, we need policies that specifically build wealth among black households, such as the "baby bonds" program proposed by economists William Darity of Duke University and Darrick Hamilton of The New School. Baby bonds would be federally managed, interest-bearing trusts given to the newborns of asset-poor families, and could be as large as $50,000 to $60,000 for the most asset-poor. By using a wealth means-test, this program would disproportionately benefit black communities, while avoiding the controversy of a reparations policy. When recipients reach age 18, they could use the funds for a house down payment, tuition, or to start a business. This program would cost about $60 billion per year, which could easily be covered by letting the Bush-era tax cuts expire for the top 1% of income earners. ❑

Sources: Amaad Rivera, Brenda Cotto-Escalera, Anisha Desai, Jeannette Huezo, and Dedrick Muhammad, *Foreclosed: State of the Dream 2008*, United for a Fair Economy, 2008; Citizens for Tax Justice, "The Bush Tax Cuts Cost Two and a Half Times as Much as the House Democrats' Health Care Proposal," CTJ Policy Brief, September 9, 2009; Darrick Hamilton and William Darity, Jr., "Can 'Baby Bonds' Eliminate the Racial Wealth Gap in Putative Post-Racial America?" *Review of Black Political Economy*, 2010; Paul Taylor, Rakesh Kochhar, Richard Fry, Gabriel Velasco, and Seth Motel, *Twenty-to-One: Wealth Gaps to Rise to Record High Between Whites, Blacks and Hispanics*, Washington DC: Pew Research Center, 2011.

Article 9.4

HOW IMPORTANT IS *CITIZENS UNITED*?

BY ARTHUR MacEWAN
March/April 2012

Dear Dr. Dollar:
People in the Occupy movement and many others are quite concerned about "corporate personhood," and especially about the Citizens United decision. Did that Supreme Court decision in fact make a crucial difference with regard to the role of money in elections? —*Dan Schneider, Boston, Mass.*

Crucial? No, I wouldn't say crucial. The *Citizens United* decision of 2010 was, however, one more important link in the long chain securing the role of money in U.S. politics.

In *Citizens United v. the Federal Election Commission*, the U.S. Supreme Court, dividing along well-recognized conservative-liberal lines, voted to strike down restrictions that limited corporate (and union) donations to political action committees, so-called "super PACs." Plus, the ruling made it possible for the donors to keep their identities secret. The impact of *Citizens United* has been evident in 2012, with huge amounts of corporate cash flowing into the super PACs, which use the money for a deluge of campaign ads that are ostensibly independent of the candidates they support.

The Court's majority based its case on the First Amendment, arguing that corporations (and unions) have the same rights as individuals to take part in election-related activities. While the majority's argument does not use the term "corporate personhood," it was based on the long-established position of corporations as legal persons.

Corporate personhood is of course nonsense. A corporation is a legal entity in which investors pool their money and share ownership. The owners obtain corporate status from the government, and this status gives them limited liability, which means they are not liable for the financial obligations of the firm beyond their investments in the firm. Corporations have long been "legal people," in the sense that they have had the right to enter into contracts, sue and be sued—all necessary to engage in commerce. But to jump from this to the idea that corporations are just like real people is, well, nonsense.

However, through the late 19th century and up to *Citizens United*, the courts have extended the rights of these "legal people," treating them increasingly like real people. One particularly important step prevented local communities from treating outside corporations differently than local (non-corporate) firms. *Citizens United* has been another important step.

Yet corporations are not treated the same as people in many realms—they are treated better! For example, corporations are subject to very different bankruptcy laws than are real people, giving them advantages that real people don't have. Also, tax laws provide many advantages to corporations that real people don't enjoy. (By the way, because the government has the authority to grant the privilege of corporate status, even with corporate personhood, much could be done to limit corporations in return for this privilege—if the government would do so.)

The concept of corporate personhood is odious and the *Citizens United* decision harmful. Yet the huge, undemocratic role of money in politics is not dependent on either. Between 1999 and 2009, lobbying expenditures grew by 89%, in inflation adjusted terms, to $3.51 billion. In 2009 alone, health-care firms spent $552 million on lobbying. All before *Citizens United*. Add to this the direct campaign contributions from the wealthy, and the way politicians, top aides, regulators, and other policy makers move from government to high-paying positions with private firms.

Then there's the influence of money and corporate power on the way the media shape ideas about political affairs. As a former president and CEO of the *New York Times* reminded us in 2002: "Today's news media are themselves frequently a part of large, often global corporations dependent on advertising revenue that, increasingly, comes from other large corporations.… It is both impractical and unrealistic to expect news media companies, including newspaper firms, to retreat from their positions as increasingly large, diversified business enterprises."

One could add the way large foundations controlled by very wealthy individuals (e.g., the Gates Foundation) have dominated the "school reform" movement. This movement that has spread the idea that teachers' unions and government bureaucracies are what damage the education of our children. The damaging impact of poverty? Not on the agenda.

Perhaps most important, the power of large corporations lies in their role of making decisions about investments and jobs. Policy makers believe that they must do the bidding of corporations in order to keep the economy going. So we get excessive tax breaks and other favors for these powerful firms and their owners.

Getting rid of corporate personhood and overturning *Citizens United* would be good, important steps towards democracy. However, the problems run deeper. Ultimately, we cannot have democracy when we have such an unequal distribution of income and wealth. ❑

Article 9.5

WHO ARE THE "47%"?
And Why Don't They Pay (Income) Taxes?

BY GERALD FRIEDMAN
November/December 2012

"There are 47% of the people ... who are dependent upon government, who believe that they are victims, who believe the government has a responsibility to care for them, who believe that they are entitled to health care, to food, to housing, to you-name-it... These are people who pay no income tax."

While Mitt Romney did not intend for the general public to hear his candid remarks to his wealthy donors, his dismissal of nearly half of the American public as irresponsible dependents mooching off hard-working taxpayers is common among American conservatives. It is also wrong. Virtually all of those who pay no federal income tax pay other taxes, including federal payroll taxes and state and local sales and property taxes, and many pay a higher share of their income in taxes than do Mitt Romney and his wealthy friends. (The latter avoid payroll taxes and much of their income tax by taking their salary as capital gains.) Furthermore, most of "the 47%" owe no federal income tax for good and sensible reasons: they are disabled, elderly, or have a very low income.

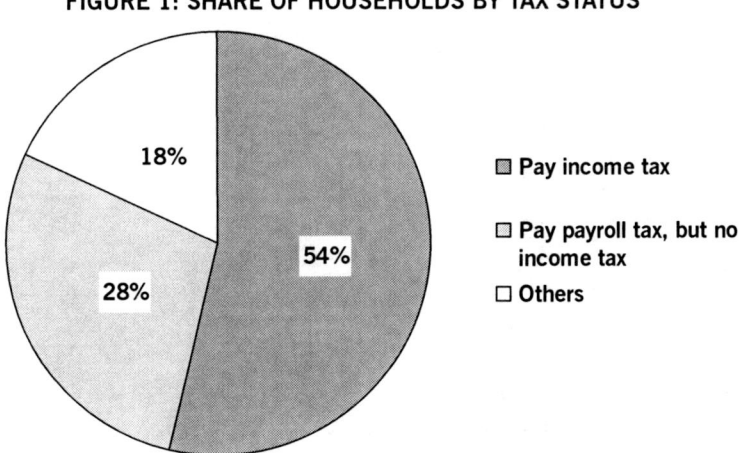

FIGURE 1: SHARE OF HOUSEHOLDS BY TAX STATUS

■ Pay income tax
□ Pay payroll tax, but no income tax
□ Others

While just over 46% of Americans paid no income tax last year, over half of them (over 28% of the total) paid payroll taxes (e.g., Social Security and Medicare taxes), most paid federal excise taxes (on phones and other services), and almost all paid sales and other state and local taxes.

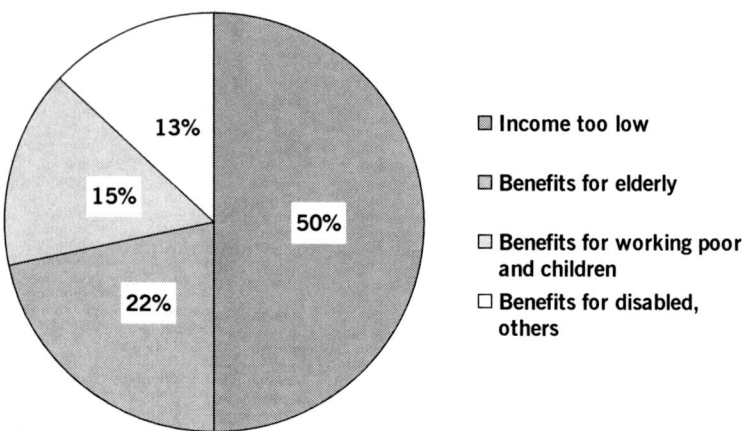

FIGURE 2: REASONS FOR NOT PAYING INCOME TAX

Those who are not paying income tax include the elderly, the disabled, many children, and the poorest Americans. Almost a third have household incomes under $10,000, and almost two thirds have incomes under $20,000. Only 5% have household incomes of as much as $50,000.

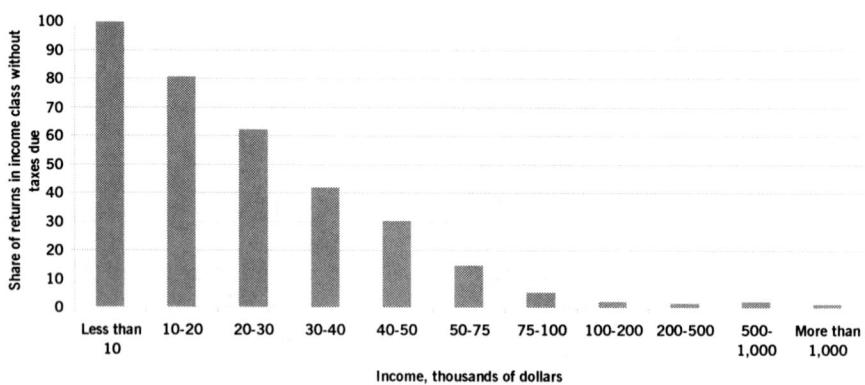

FIGURE 3: PERCENTAGE NOT PAYING INCOME TAX, BY INCOME CLASS

The proportion of returns without income tax liability falls quickly from almost 100% for the lowest incomes down to a negligible percentage for high income returns.

Many Americans do not pay income tax because of provisions inserted into the tax code, including some under Republican icons like Richard Nixon and Ronald Reagan, to encourage low income Americans to seek paid work— such as the Earned

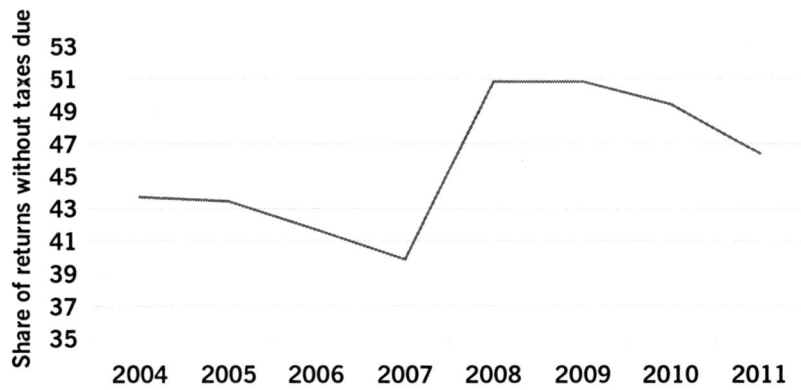

FIGURE 4: TAX RETURNS WITH ZERO OR NEGATIVE INDIVIDUAL INCOME TAX

Income Tax Credit and the high minimum income threshold before income taxes are due. Because of provisions like these, when incomes fall, the income of a larger share of Americans falls below the level at which they pay income taxes. This is why the share not paying income tax increased sharply during the Great Recession, and has been decreasing (slowly) with the (slow) recovery since.

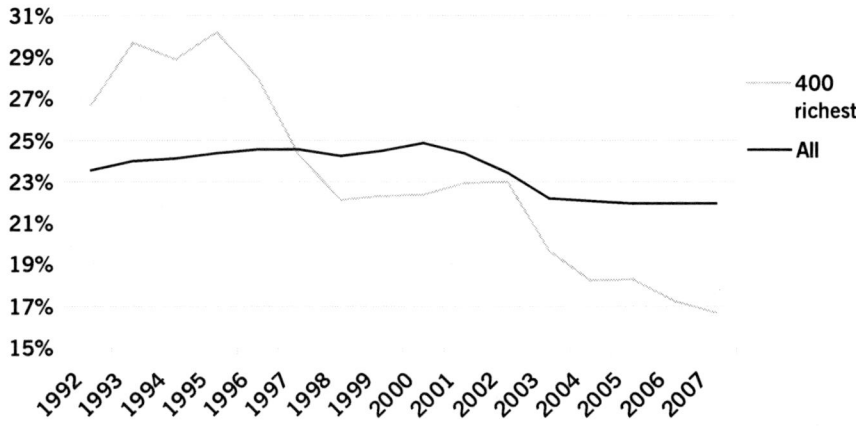

FIGURE 5: FEDERAL TAX RATES AS A SHARE OF ADJUSTED GROSS INCOME, 1992-2007 (INCOME AND PAYROLL TAXES)

The real tax evaders are not the disabled, elderly, or the poor who earn too little to pay federal income tax. They are the super-rich who shift income into tax shelters, offshore accounts, and get paid in capital gains taxed at a preferential rate. Such evasions have allowed the wealthiest Americans to lower their total federal tax bill to well below the rate paid by other Americans. ❏

Source: Tax Policy Center.

Article 9.6

FAMINE MYTHS
Five Misunderstandings Related to the 2011 Hunger Crisis in the Horn of Africa

BY WILLIAM G. MOSELEY
March/April 2012

The 2011 famine in the horn of Africa was one of the worst in recent decades in terms of loss of life and human suffering. While the UN has yet to release an official death toll, the British government estimates that between 50,000 and 100,000 people died, most of them children, between April and September of 2011. While Kenya, Ethiopia, and Djibouti were all badly affected, the famine hit hardest in certain (mainly southern) areas of Somalia. This was the worst humanitarian disaster to strike the country since 1991-1992, with roughly a third of the Somali population displaced for some period of time.

Despite the scholarly and policy community's tremendous advances in understanding famine over the past 40 years, and increasingly sophisticated famine early-warning systems, much of this knowledge and information was seemingly ignored or forgotten in 2011. While the famine had been forecasted nearly nine months in advance, the global community failed to prepare for, and react in a timely manner to, this event. The famine was officially declared in early July of 2011 by the United Nations and recently (February 3, 2012) stated to be officially over. Despite the official end of the famine, 31% of the population (or 2.3 million people) in southern Somalia remains in crisis. Across the region, 9.5 million people continue to need assistance. Millions of Somalis remain in refugee camps in Ethiopia and Kenya.

The famine reached its height in the period from July to September, 2011, with approximately 13 million people at risk of starvation. While this was a regional problem, it was was most acute in southern Somalia because aid to this region was much delayed. Figure 1 provides a picture of food insecurity in the region in the November-December 2011 period (a few months after the peak of the crisis).

The 2011 famine received relatively little attention in the U.S. media and much of the coverage that did occur was biased, ahistorical, or perpetuated long-held misunderstandings about the nature and causes of famine. This article addresses "famine myths"—five key misunderstandings related to the famine in the Horn of Africa.

Myth #1: Drought was the cause of the famine.

While drought certainly contributed to the crisis in the Horn of Africa, there were more fundamental causes at play. Drought is not a new environmental condition for much of Africa, but a recurring one. The Horn of Africa has long experienced erratic rainfall. While climate change may be exacerbating rainfall variability, traditional livelihoods in the region are adapted to deal with situations where rainfall is not dependable.

The dominant livelihood in the Horn of Africa has long been herding, which is well adapted to the semi-arid conditions of the region. Herders traditionally ranged widely across the landscape in search of better pasture, focusing on different areas depending on meteorological conditions.

The approach worked because, unlike fenced in pastures in America, it was incredibly flexible and well adapted to variable rainfall conditions. As farming expanded, including large-scale commercial farms in some instances, the routes of herders became more concentrated, more vulnerable to drought, and more detrimental to the landscape.

Agricultural livelihoods also evolved in problematic ways. In anticipation of poor rainfall years, farming households and communities historically stored surplus crop production in granaries. Sadly this traditional strategy for mitigating the risk of drought was undermined from the colonial period moving forward as households were encouraged (if not coerced by taxation) to grow cash crops for the market and store less excess grain for bad years. This increasing market orientation was also encouraged by development banks, such as the World Bank, International Monetary Fund, and African Development Bank.

FIGURE 1: FOOD INSECURITY IN THE HORN OF AFRICA REGION, NOVEMBER-DECEMBER 2011.

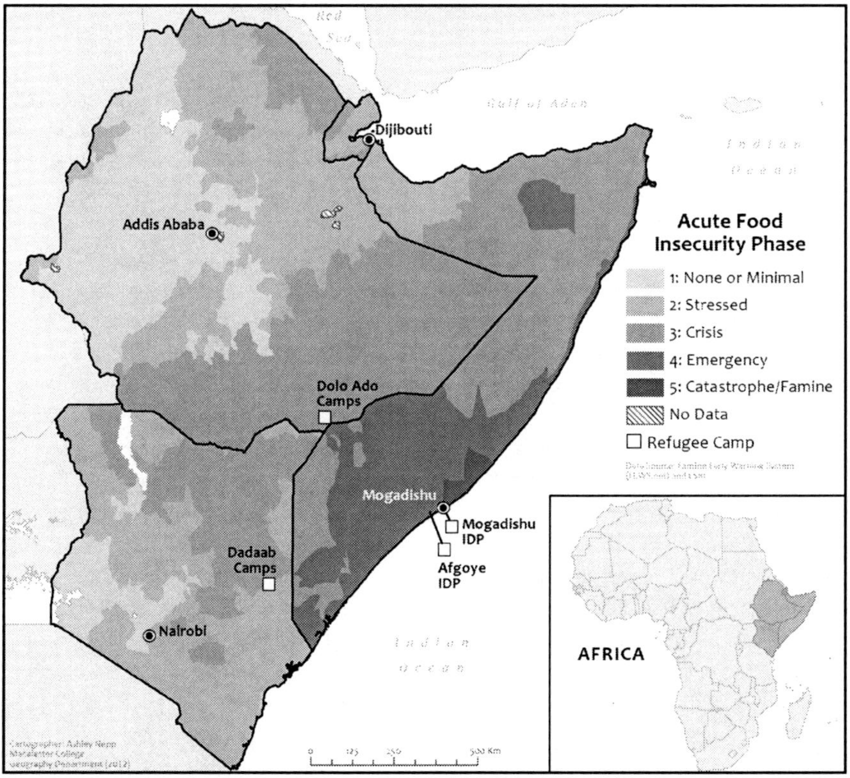

Based on data and assessment by FEWS-Net (a USAID-sponsored program).
Cartography by Ashley Nepp, Macalester College.

The moral of the story is that famine is not a natural consequence of drought (just as death from exposure is not the inherent result of a cold winter), but it is the structure of human society which often determines who is affected and to what degree.

Myth #2: Overpopulation was the cause of the famine.

With nearly 13 million people at risk of starvation last fall in a region whose population doubled in the previous 24 years, one might assume that these two factors were causally related in the Horn of Africa. Ever since the British political economist Thomas Malthus wrote "An Essay on the Principle of Population" in 1798, we have been concerned that human population growth will outstrip available food supply. While the crisis in Somalia, Ethiopia and Kenya appeared to be perfect proof of the Malthusian scenario, we must be careful not to make overly simplistic assumptions.

For starters, the semi-arid zones in the Horn of Africa are relatively lightly populated compared to other regions of the world. For example, the population density of Somalia is about 13 persons per sq. kilometer, whereas that of the U.S. state of Oklahoma is 21.1. The western half of Oklahoma is also semi-arid, suffered from a serious drought in 2011, and was the poster child for the 1930s Dust Bowl. Furthermore, if we take into account differing levels of consumption, with the average American consuming at least 28 times as much as the average Somali in a normal year, then Oklahoma's population density of 21.1 persons per sq. kilometer equates to that of 591 Somalis.

Despite the fact that Oklahoma's per capita impact on the landscape is over 45 times that of Somalia (when accounting for population density and consumption

---

Land Grabs in Africa

Long term leases of African land for export-oriented food production, or "land grabs," have been on the rise in the past decade. Rather than simply buying food and commodity crops from African farmers, foreign entities increasingly take control of ownership and management of farms on African soil. This trend stems from at least two factors. First, increasingly high global food prices are a problem for many Asian and Middle Eastern countries that depend on food imports. As such, foreign governments and sovereign wealth funds may engage in long-term leases of African land in order to supply their own populations with affordable food. Secondly, high global food prices are also seen as an opportunity for some Western investors who lease African land to produce crops and commodities for profitable global markets.

In the Horn of Africa, Ethiopia (which has historically been one of the world's largest recipients of humanitarian food aid) has made a series of long-term land leases to foreign entities. The World Bank estimates that at least 35 million hectares of land have been leased to 36 different countries, including China, Pakistan, India and Saudi Arabia. Supporters of these leases argue that they provide employment to local people and disseminate modern agricultural approaches. Critics counter that these leases undermine food sovereignty, or people's ability to feed themselves via environmentally sustainable technologies that they control.

levels), we don't talk about overpopulation in Oklahoma. This is because, in spite of the drought and the collapse of agriculture, there was no famine in Oklahoma. In contrast, the presence of famine in the Horn of Africa led many to assume that too many people was a key part of the problem.

Why is it that many assume that population growth is the driver of famine? For starters, perhaps we assume that reducing the birthrate, and thereby reducing the number of mouths to feed, is one of the easiest ways to prevent hunger. This is actually a difficult calculation for most families in rural Africa. It's true that many families desire access to modern contraceptives, and filling this unmet need is important. However, for many others, children are crucial sources of farm labor or important wage earners who help sustain the family. Children also act as the old-age social security system for their parents. For these families, having fewer children is not an easy decision. Families in this region will have fewer children when it makes economic sense to do so. As we have seen over time and throughout the world, the average family size shrinks when economies develop and expectations for offspring change.

Second, many tend to focus on the additional resources required to nourish each new person, and often forget the productive capacity of these individuals. Throughout Africa, some of the most productive farmland is in those regions with the highest population densities. In Machakos, Kenya, for example, agricultural production and environmental conservation improved as population densities increased. Furthermore, we have seen agricultural production collapse in some areas where population declined (often due to outmigration) because there was insufficient labor to maintain intensive agricultural production.

Third, we must not forget that much of the region's agricultural production is not consumed locally. From the colonial era moving forward, farmers and herders have been encouraged to become more commercially oriented, producing crops and livestock for the market rather than home consumption. This might have been a reasonable strategy if the prices for exports from the Horn of Africa were high (which they rarely have been) and the cost of food imports low. Also, large land leases (or "land grabs") to foreign governments and corporations in Ethiopia (and to a lesser extent in Kenya and Somalia) have further exacerbated this problem. These farms, designed solely for export production, effectively subsidize the food security of other regions of the world (most notably the Middle East and Asia) at the expense of populations in the Horn of Africa.

Myth #3: Increasing food production through advanced techniques will resolve food insecurity over the long run.

As Sub-Saharan Africa has grappled with high food prices in some regions and famine in others, many experts argue that increasing food production through a program of hybrid seeds and chemical inputs (a so-called "New Green Revolution") is the way to go.

While outsiders benefit from this New Green Revolution strategy (by selling inputs or purchasing surplus crops), it is not clear if the same is true for small farmers and poor households in Sub-Saharan Africa. For most food insecure households on the continent, there are at least two problems with this strategy. First, such an approach to farming is energy intensive because most fertilizers and pesticides are petroleum based. Inducing poor farmers to adopt energy-intensive farming methods is short sighted, if not unethical, if experts know that global energy prices are likely to rise. Second, irrespective of energy prices, the New Green Revolution approach requires farmers to purchase seeds and inputs, which means that it will be inaccessible to the poorest of the poor, i.e., those who are the most likely to suffer from periods of hunger.

If not the New Green Revolution approach, then what? Many forms of bio-intensive agriculture are, in fact, highly productive and much more efficient than those of industrial agriculture. For example, crops grown in intelligent combinations allow one plant to fix nitrogen for another rather than relying solely on increasingly expensive, fossil fuel-based inorganic fertilizers for these plant nutrients. Mixed cropping strategies are also less vulnerable to insect damage and require little to no pesticide use for a reasonable harvest. These techniques have existed for centuries in the African context and could be greatly enhanced by supporting collaboration among local people, African research institutes, and foreign scientists.

Myth #4: U.S. foreign policy in the Horn of Africa was unrelated to the crisis.

Many Americans assume that U.S. foreign policy bears no blame for the food crisis in the Horn and, more specifically, Somalia. This is simply untrue. The weakness of the Somali state was and is related to U.S. policy, which interfered in Somali affairs based on Cold War politics (the case in the 1970s and 80s) or the War on Terror (the case in the 2000s).

During the Cold War, Somalia was a pawn in a U.S.-Soviet chess match in the geopolitically significant Horn of Africa region. In 1974, the U.S. ally Emperor Haile Selassie of Ethiopia was deposed in a revolution. He was eventually replaced by Mengistu Haile Mariam, a socialist. In response, the leader of Ethiopia's bitter rival Somalia, Siad Barre, switched from being pro-Soviet to pro-Western. Somalia was the only country in Africa to switch Cold War allegiances under the same government. The U.S. supported Siad Barre until 1989 (shortly before his demise in 1991). By doing this, the United States played a key role in supporting a long-running dictator and undermined democratic governance.

More recently, the Union of Islamic Courts (UIC) came to power in 2006. The UIC defeated the warlords, restored peace to Mogadishu for the first time in 15 years, and brought most of southern Somalia under its orbit. The United States and its Ethiopian ally claimed that these Islamists were terrorists and a threat to the region. In contrast, the vast majority of Somalis supported the UIC and pleaded with the international community to engage them peacefully. Unfortunately, this peace did not last. The U.S.-supported Ethiopian invasion of Somalia begun in December 2006 and displaced more than a million people and killed close to 15,000 civilians. Those displaced then became a part of last summer and fall's famine victims.

The power vacuum created by the displacement of the more moderate UIC also led to the rise of its more radical military wing, al-Shabaab. Al-Shabaab emerged to engage the Transitional Federal Government (TFG), which was put in place by the international community and composed of the most moderate elements of the UIC (which were more favorable to the United States). The TFG was weak, corrupt, and ineffective, controlling little more than the capital Mogadishu, if that. A low-grade civil war emerged between these two groups in southern Somalia. Indeed, as we repeatedly heard in the media last year, it was al-Shabaab that restricted access to southern Somalia for several months leading up to the crisis and greatly exacerbated the situation in this sub-region. Unfortunately, the history of factors which gave rise to al-Shabaab was never adequately explained to the U.S. public. Until July 2011, the U.S. government forbade American charities from operating in areas controlled by al-Shabaab—which delayed relief efforts in these areas.

Myth #5: An austere response may be best in the long run.

Efforts to raise funds to address the famine in the Horn of Africa were well below those for previous (and recent) humanitarian crises. Why was this? Part of it likely had to do with the economic malaise in the U.S. and Europe. Many Americans suggested that we could not afford to help in this crisis because we had to pay off our own debt. This stinginess may, in part, be related to a general misunderstanding about how much of the U.S. budget goes to foreign assistance. Many Americans assume we spend over 25% of our budget on such assistance when it is actually less than one percent.

Furthermore, contemporary public discourse in America has become more inward-looking and isolationist than in the past. As a result, many Americans have difficulty relating to people beyond their borders. Sadly, it is now much easier to separate ourselves from them, to discount our common humanity, and to essentially suppose that it's okay if they starve. This last point brings us back to Thomas Malthus, who was writing against the poor laws in England in the late 18th century. The poor laws were somewhat analogous to contemporary welfare programs and Malthus argued (rather problematically) that they encouraged the poor to have more children. His essential argument was that starvation is acceptable because it is a natural check to over-population. In other words, support for the poor will only exacerbate the situation. We see this in the way that some conservative commentators reacted to last year's famine.

The reality was that a delayed response to the famine only made the situation worse. Of course, the worst-case scenario is death, but short of death, many households were forced to sell off all of their assets (cattle, farming implements, etc.) in order to survive. This sets up a very difficult recovery scenario because livelihoods are so severely compromised. We know from best practices among famine researchers and relief agencies in that you not only to detect a potential famine early, but to intervene before livelihoods are devastated. This means that households will recover more quickly and be more resilient in the face of future perturbations.

Preventing Famines

While the official famine in the horn of Africa region is over, 9.5 million people continue to need assistance and millions of Somalis remain in refugee camps in

Ethiopia and Kenya. While this region of the world will always be drought prone, it needn't be famine prone. The solution lies in rebuilding the Somali state and fostering more robust rural livelihoods in Somalia, western Ethiopia and northern Kenya. The former will likely mean giving the Somali people the space they need to rebuild their own democratic institutions (and not making them needless pawns in the War on Terror). The latter will entail a new approach to agriculture that emphasizes food sovereignty, or locally appropriate food production technologies that are accessible to the poorest of the poor, as well as systems of grain storage at the local level that anticipate bad rainfall years. Finally, the international community should discourage wealthy, yet food-insufficient, countries from preying on poorer countries in Sub Saharan African countries through the practice of land grabs. ❑

Sources: Alex de Waal, *Famine That Kills: Darfur, Sudan*, Oxford University Press, 2005; William G. Moseley, "Why They're Starving: The man-made roots of famine in the Horn of Africa," *The Washington Post*. July 29, 2011; William G. Moseley and B. Ikubolajeh Logan, "Food Security," in B. Wisner, C. Toulmin and R. Chitiga (eds)., *Toward a New Map of Africa*, Earthscan Publications, 2005; Abdi I. Samatar, "Genocidal Politics and the Somali Famine," Aljazeera English, July 30, 2011; Amartya Sen, *Poverty and Famines*, Oxford/Clarendon, 1981; Michael Watts and Hans Bohle, "The space of vulnerability: the causal structure of hunger and famine," *Progress in Human Geography*, 1993.

Chapter 10

RESISTANCE AND ALTERNATIVES

Article 10.1

RANK-AND-FILE ECONOMICS
Fighting for a Jobs- and Wage-Led Recovery

BY KATHERINE SCIACCHITANO
September/October 2011

Riddle 1: When is a recovery not a recovery?
Answer: When profits are at record levels, corporations are sitting on $1.7 trillion in cash, and unemployment is still at 9.2% and rising.

Riddle 2: When is a stimulus not a stimulus?
Answer: When it's less than one-fourth the size of the hole in the economy it is intended to fill.

Riddle 3: When will it be possible to rebuild the economy?
Answer: When the U.S. labor movement joins with community and international labor allies to demand global economic development, jobs, and rising wages.

When the U.S. housing bubble burst in 2008, putting jobs first was a no-brainer. Global unions demanded immediate action. The G-20—the group of 20 nations charged with coordinating a global response to the crisis—agreed. Governments rushed to do stimulus spending. The worst was prevented.

Then in the spring of 2010 the Greek debt crisis hit. Markets plummeted. The G-20 pulled back and told countries to cut spending. Greece, Ireland, Spain, Portugal, and the U.K. have since enacted austerity packages with drastic spending and wage cuts.

The global jobs crisis is now worse than ever. Between 2007 and 2010, 30 million workers lost their jobs worldwide. In the United States, GDP is falling, jobs have declined since the recovery started, and the unemployment rate is rising again as federal stimulus funds fade and layoffs mount in the states. The Brookings Institution estimates it will take over ten years to return to normal employment levels, even at pre-crisis growth rates. Now, real wages are falling as well.

Union reps negotiating contracts with state and local governments are on the frontlines of the resulting battles. Flanked as they are by terrified members on one side, and angry tax payers and state legislatures attacking wages, benefits, and bargaining rights on the other, their problems go far beyond what can be solved at the bargaining table.

The out-of-the-box solution would be to organize for a comprehensive program of job creation. Blueprints for jobs-based recoveries do exist. But such blueprints need "rank-and-file economists" to turn them into brick and mortar. With Democrats and Republicans actively vying to impose austerity, those rank-and-file economists—community organizers as well as union reps—must tell, not ask, our elected representatives what we need. Then they have to engage in the drawn-out battle to make what we need a reality.

A major obstacle to struggle is the widespread belief—even among many union members—that there is little that government can do besides cut spending, and that only the private sector can create jobs.

Yet the fact that so many are frustrated with government over the high unemployment is evidence that on some level people do believe government action is not only possible but necessary. A rank-and-file economics needs to channel that frustration and nurture that belief. It needs to explain why the "free market" isn't going to create the jobs that are needed. It needs to educate people about the real causes of the crisis. And it needs to convince community and union members that a positive agenda for long-term growth still exists.

First, we have to arm ourselves by educating ourselves.

The Private Sector Can't Do It Alone

Here in the United States, people are surrounded by the narrative that only the private sector can create jobs. Even those who acknowledge that we need to rebuild our infrastructure and that rebuilding would create jobs are likely to say that we can't afford public investment right now. Instead, the argument goes, we should cut taxes and let corporations create the jobs and the investment we need: too much public spending got us where we are; every tax dollar spent by the government is one less dollar business could be used to create jobs.

There are three main responses to these arguments.

First, *corporations already have enough cash to invest; tax cuts for corporations and the wealthy aren't going to lead to more job creation.*

The Bush tax cuts didn't boost job creation, they didn't boost wages, and they didn't boost investment in the real economy. What they boosted was corporate profits and the deficit. Today businesses are sitting on record profits and $1.7 trillion in cash that they don't *want* to invest. What investment is being done is aimed at boosting productivity and cutting labor costs—that is, cutting jobs. The jobs problem is *not* due to businesses not having enough cash to invest. Further enriching corporations with tax cuts isn't going to fix it.

Second, *the deficit didn't cause the crisis; the crisis caused the deficit.*

Calls to cut government spending in order to spur growth ignore the fact that the economic crisis we're in has nothing to do with government spending. The deficit didn't cause the crisis. The crisis caused the deficit. The spike in the deficit is principally due to the drop in revenues as people lost jobs and businesses lost sales. What additional spending we have done in the past three years—for the stimulus program and for TARP—was temporary. And as economist Dean Baker from the Center for Economic and Policy Research (CEPR) has calculated, in the long run the U.S. budget deficit would virtually disappear if it brought its health-care spending in line with other industrialized countries, all of which have universal health coverage.

Third, *there are times when government spending is essential to help the economy over a crisis and when failure to spend will make the deficit worse.*

In the short term, the best way to reduce the deficit without increasing unemployment is to recover from the crisis, not cut spending and create more joblessness while the economy is still weak. This is a lesson we should have learned from the last great global economic collapse, the Depression of the 1930s.

Before the 1930s, most economists believed that economies recovered naturally from recessions: in a downturn, either prices would fall and stimulate spending, or wages would fall and stimulate hiring, or both. But when consumers and businesses stopped spending during the Depression, falling wages and prices made the economy worse. It took the New Deal to get the economy growing. From 1933 through the end of the Depression, GDP rose and fell with government spending. By 1936 unemployment had fallen from 23% to 9%. But in 1937 unemployment rose again after Roosevelt cut the budget to reduce the deficit. After that it took massive spending for World War II to return the economy to full employment.

Stimulus Isn't Enough Either

Given the lessons from the Depression of the 1930s, why didn't the Obama stimulus plan work better than it did?

One reason is that the housing bubble drained nearly $1.4 trillion in annual spending, yet the Obama administration proposed a stimulus that was only $825 billion spread over several years. Congressional Republicans then reduced that number to $727 billion. They also cut proposed spending for infrastructure, green energy, and aid to states so they could increase tax cuts, even though tax cuts are known to create fewer jobs.

But the deeper reason the Obama stimulus failed is that the administration misunderstood the nature of the crisis. The country needs more than stimulus spending for recovery. It needs a sustained program for rebuilding the real economy and raising wages. The problem isn't just that cutbacks over the past decades have left us with a shortage of over two trillion dollars in infrastructure spending. It's that growing inequality has created too big a hole in demand.

During the boom following World War II, the United States regularly used government spending to ease recessions. The idea was that instead of waiting for unemployment to push down wages in the hopes that low wages would boost hiring, the government should boost job creation, and hence wages, by plugging holes in private consumption with public expenditures.

This worked because during the post-war boom, wages as a matter of policy rose with productivity. Recessions were due to short-term policy missteps or the "business cycle"—production temporarily getting ahead of demand. When that happened, businesses made fewer profits and investment would fall. Government spending would boost demand. And demand would spur investment.

In the current economy, stimulus spending can't accomplish what it did in the post-war economy. Not only have we just had a massive financial crisis rather than a dip in the business cycle, but the crisis happened after decades of stagnating wages. Since the 1980s, demand has been based not on rising wages, as it was in the post-war era, but on household debt backed by the rising prices of assets such as stocks and real estate.

With the bursting of the housing bubble, 28% of homeowners are now under water. Under these circumstances, households that get a temporary bump in disposable income from a stimulus package are as likely to pay down debt as they are to increase spending. Even households that aren't in debt may save instead of spending because of fear of unemployment. The economy may get a small boost. But businesses correctly see that demand isn't there and hold back from investing. The economy remains in a hole unless the government embarks on a sustained program of rebuilding wages, jobs, and the real economy.

How We Unlearned Equality

To understand what it will take to rebuild the economy, we have to understand the strength of the post-war economy and how it was reversed.

The great economic lesson of the post-war era was the importance of equality for economic growth and stability. The period before the Great Depression had been marked by steep inequality, debt, and bubbles. Following World War II, the governments of the United States and most of Western Europe made commitments to full employment and rising wages in order to avoid another similar collapse. Global growth reached record rates. Inequality declined. And there were no serious global financial crises.

In the United States, real hourly wages roughly doubled during this period. The policies that made this wage growth and stability possible included corporate acceptance of collective bargaining; a strong social safety net; high quality public services; regulation of business; progressive tax systems—where corporations and the wealthy are taxed at higher rates—to help pay for public services and the cost of regulation; deficit spending to stimulate the economy during economic downturns, thereby preventing wages from falling; and a willingness to lower interest rates when unemployment rose.

Corporate tolerance for these pro-labor policies was transitory and grudging: it lasted as long as the extraordinary post-war levels of profit lasted. Once global profit rates slowed, corporations fought to reverse wage growth and restore profit rates under the guise of the policy mix that came to be known as neoliberalism. They attacked labor rights, the minimum wage, and unemployment insurance. They pushed to reduce taxes on corporations and the wealthy, shifting the tax burden to working people instead. They lobbied to privatize public services and deregulate industries—opening opportunities for profits, denigrating the role of government, and increasing the likelihood of financial crises. The rhetoric of balanced budgets and self-reliance replaced support for a strong safety net and stimulus spending to stabilize wages during recessions. And interest rate hikes were used to minimize inflation—now touted as a primary threat to living standards—by *raising* unemployment and keeping wages low.

Going Global: Coordination, not Competition

Jobs debates tend to focus on national needs. We're told repeatedly that competition is the key to a country's economic success: increase productivity, decrease labor costs, hone our technology, and we'll beat out the other guy to get the jobs. But the kind of development the world needs for recovery isn't a zero-sum game. U.S. labor needs healthy manufacturing and wage growth in other countries every bit as much as we need a revival of manufacturing and wages in the United States.

Achieving the objectives proposed in this article—rising wages, demand-led growth, and global development—will require both struggle and international coordination. Labor is familiar with many of the economic tools that will be needed to achieve these core objectives, but it is used to applying them in a national context only, not advocating for their use as part of a global development agenda. Here are a few of the most familiar tools that will be needed and what labor can add by pressing for international coordination:

Fiscal and monetary policy to support employment growth. Governments need to return to wider use of fiscal and monetary policy to stimulate demand and put a floor on unemployment. But in a global economy, stimulus spending can end up "leaking" out of a country when consumers buy imports. Stimulus is most effective when countries act together so one country can't "steal" demand from another by keeping its wages and demand low while another country raises wages and expands demand.

Labor rights and employment regulation to raise wages. Using fiscal and monetary policy to put a floor on unemployment can help keep wages from falling. But wage growth needs a vigorous commitment to collective bargaining, social benefits such as health care and pensions, minimum and living wage laws, and a strong safety net for unemployed and underemployed workers. These policies are most effective when widely adopted, both because widespread adoption raises global demand and also because it discourages low-wage competition.

Tax reform to provide adequate revenues. Tax reform is needed to ensure that the wealthy and corporations pay their share of the costs for the economic crisis, and to provide revenue for rebuilding and development. Corporate tax reform in particular needs to be coordinated to prevent corporations from gaming differences in countries' tax rates by relocation or transfer pricing. Since the crisis began, a vigorous global movement has sprung up for a financial transaction tax, which could raise hundreds of billions globally from the finance industry.

Industrial policy to nurture high-wage manufacturing sectors. Ultimately, strong job growth is needed to support strong wage growth. Countries that have developed successfully—including the United States and Britain in their early years, Europe and Japan after World War II, the Asian Tigers in the 1980s, and now China—have done so by using industrial policies to nurture infant industries and growth. These policies have included such measures as regulation of the movement of capital in and out of the country; government investment in infrastructure, education, research and development; requirements that corporations purchase inputs locally and train local workforces; and facilitating the availability of credit for key industries and sectors. Since the eighties and nineties, neoliberal policies and trade agreements have sought to ban many of these policies and make countries dependent on transnational corporations instead. International labor campaigns to eliminate these bans will be critical for reversing this dependence and the advantage it gives corporations over labor. Freeing countries to use industrial policy will in turn be critical for the growth of green manufacturing and energy production as the world grapples with climate change.

Sources: Damian Paletta and David Enrich, "Banks Gain in Rules Debate," *Wall Street Journal*, July 15, 2010; Damian Paletta and David Enrich, "Risks Rulebooks Is Nearly Done—Key Aspects of Banks' New Restraints Are Agreed Upon," *Wall Street Journal*, July 27, 2010; Damien Paletta, "Banks Get New Restraints," *Wall Street Journal*, September 13, 2010.

There were changes in international policy as well. After World War II, U.S. trade policy had focused on opening up markets for U.S. exports, which meant not only higher profits but higher domestic employment. Under neoliberalism, boosting profits meant moving production to lower cost areas overseas and exporting back to the United States. It meant cutting jobs at home as well as and pushing down wages abroad.

In short, while the post-war strategy supported rising incomes in the United States and much of the rest of the world, the strategy from the 1980s onward was built on stagnating or falling wages for workers generally. The result was that the global rate of profit rose while hourly wages stagnated or fell, with few exceptions, throughout the globe—not just in the United States and developing countries, but in Europe as well.

To compensate for stagnating purchasing power, U.S. consumers borrowed, and the finance industry made credit more available: between 1981 and 2007, the last year of the housing bubble, household debt doubled as a percentage of GDP. The U.S. consumer became the consumer of last resort for the world. And the global economy balanced precariously on U.S. consumer debt and the dollar.

By the early 2000s, balancing on U.S. consumer debt meant balancing on the housing bubble: dollars exited the country to pay for imports and were recycled back, not as demand for U.S. exports, but as demand for investment in U.S. mortgage securities and other financial assets. The world found out how painful a balancing act this was when the U.S. housing bubble burst, homeowners defaulted on mortgages, and the banking system nearly collapsed, cutting off the supply of easy credit. Global demand plummeted. It hasn't recovered since.

Tackling Inequality Head-on

In its own terms, neoliberalism worked: it increased profits, suppressed wages, and shifted tax burdens from the wealthy to lower income workers. Proponents have seized on the deficits created by the crisis to slash social spending, helping insure against future tax increases for those at the top.

The contradictions *should* be obvious to all: suppressing wages suppresses demand, and balancing consumer spending on debt rather than wages destabilizes the U.S. economy *and* the global economy. Cutting government spending before we rebuild private demand will throw the country and the world back into recession. It will keep U.S. unemployment at Depression-era levels. And it will result in larger, not smaller, deficits.

Yet the contradictions don't register because people have a deep-seated belief that the very inequality that is crashing the system is essential to growth and jobs—that by limiting inequality we are limiting our ability to generate wealth.

To build momentum for a jobs- and wage-based recovery, the labor movement has to tackle the belief in inequality head on. It needs to show that the jobs crisis can only be addressed by rebuilding and rebalancing the national and global economies with higher wages and greater equality.

Rebuild and Rebalance

A broad consensus is developing within the global labor movement on how this rebuilding and rebalancing needs to take place. There are three main goals:

Raise wages, raise demand. The most pressing economic problem today isn't government debt or deficits. It's the hole in demand left by 30 years of wage suppression, and the danger of another period of bubble-fueled growth. To be sustainable, demand has to be based on wages, not on household debt. Inequality isn't just painful for workers. It's destabilizing for the global economy. Correcting inequality isn't a matter of charity. It's a matter of economic survival.

First and foremost, rebalancing the global economy means correcting the global wage imbalance by creating jobs and raising wages. This imbalance isn't primarily about high- versus low-income countries. It's about the share of national incomes going to workers wages and the share going to profit. Since 1980, the share of income going to labor has fallen steadily in all regions of the world, with the possible exceptions of East and Central Asia. The decline hasn't been due to shifts to low-wage occupations. It hasn't been limited to low-wage countries. And it has occurred at all income levels. It's also getting worse. In the current recovery, U.S. corporations captured a whopping 88% of the growth in national income through the beginning of 2010, while only 1% went to labor. Compare that to the recovery after the 1991 recession, when 50% of the growth in national income went to labor.

Replace growth based on low-wage exports with wage- and demand-led growth around the world. As U.S. corporations moved overseas in the eighties and nineties, the U.S. government used the carrot and the stick—as well as its powers over the IMF and the World Bank—to persuade destination countries to cut government spending, let wages fall, remove regulations on movement of foreign capital known as "capital controls," and "devalue" currencies to artificially force down the price of exports. The result was intensified global competition and the emergence of an "export-led" model of growth: economies grew not because rising wages grow domestic demand, but because suppressed wage growth (or falling wages) pushed down the price of exports. Regardless of their income level, countries that adopt the export-led model suppress both wage growth and demand for imports. They export more than they import. And they run permanent trade surpluses while their trading partners lose jobs and run deficits.

European countries that are sharply reducing deficits to deal with the current crisis and letting wages stagnate or fall are turning to the export-led growth model in hopes of becoming "more competitive." This kind of "competitiveness" as a primary strategy for global growth isn't the solution for lagging incomes. It's a recipe for an intensified race to the bottom and permanently depressed wages. It's also impossible for a majority of the world to "export" its way out of the crisis and back to growth; for every country that exports, another must be able to import. The solution, whether in Europe or the developing world, is to trade in the model of export-led growth for one based on rising wages and domestic demand.

Create a global model for economic development and decent work. The idea of stimulus spending is that it "jumpstarts" a cycle of demand, investment, and job creation when a basically healthy economy stalls. Today, living on the "other side" of the export-led model the United States helped create, U.S. consumers are too mired in debt, corporations too addicted to outsourcing and cutting jobs and wages, and the country too far behind in infrastructure spending for this kind of stimulus to be effective. We need to rebuild, not "jumpstart," the U.S. economy. The same is true overseas. Developing countries mired in the export-led model also suffer from a long-term lack of public investment and infrastructure.

To replace the export-led growth model unions need to demand a global agenda for decent work. This in turn requires a program for sustainable development that includes support for public services such as education and health care, funds for infrastructure, and support for sustainable manufacturing and green energy in both advanced and developing countries. The jobs and wages created by this investment will in turn build the base of demand needed for sustained demand-led growth.

Closer Than We Think

There are ways out of the current jobs crisis. Budget-cutting, austerity, and intensified wage competition aren't among them. Unionists need to keep their eyes on the ball: The chief barrier to recovery is the lack of global demand. A main cause of the current crisis is a multi-decade, multi-pronged strategy of wage suppression across the world. And the response must include global coordination for economic development—a global New Deal.

Governments committed to neoliberal policies won't be the prime movers behind a global New Deal. That's labor's job. So is forging the ties with other labor movements that will be needed to carry on the struggle both nationally and internationally. (See sidebar, p. 201.)

This struggle must take place country by country. Over the past decade U.S. unionists have fought successful battles for living wage ordinances. They have won community benefits agreements from corporations receiving public funds, locking in pledges to create jobs and respect labor rights. They've renewed the battle for single-payer health care and made common cause with immigrant workers working at the margins of the U.S. economy. There is crucial organizing for a national infrastructure bank, withdrawal from Iraq and Afghanistan, putting a floor on foreclosures, and taxing the wealthy. Learning new strategies is not going to be the hard part of U.S. labor. Nor will forging international linkages with unions in other countries—a process which will deepen understanding of common problems and exponentially increase the energy and clarity of struggle.

The hard part will be unlearning the indoctrination we've received about the crisis, the role of government in the economy, and the free market. Once we do that, we can build successful movements at home and abroad. We're closer than we think to the army of rank-and-file economists that we need. ❑

Sources: Gerald Friedman, "Bernanke's Bad Teachers," *Dollars & Sense*, July/August 2009 (stimulus spending during the Depression); Michael Greenstone and Adam Looney, "The Great Recession's Toll on Long-Term Unemployment," Brookings Institution UP Front Blog, November 5, 2010; Dean Baker, "The Economic Illiterates Step Up Attacks on Social Security and Medicare," August 2, 2011, cepr.net (inadequate size of the Obama stimulus); Dean Baker, "Barack Obama's Big Stimulus," *The Guardian*, Jan 19th, 2009 (original composition of the Obama stimulus); Katherine Sciacchitano, "W(h)ither the Dollar?," *Dollars & Sense*, May/June 2010; Resolution on a Sustainable and Just Development Model for the 21st Century, International Trade Union Confederation, 2nd World

Congress, Vancouver, 21-25 June 2010 (2CO/E/6.4 final); Francisco Rodriguez and Arjun Jayadev, "The Declining Share of Labor Income," UNDP Human Development Research Paper 2010/36; Steven Greenhouse, "The Wageless, Profitable Recovery," *New York Times*, June 30th, 2011; Andrew Sum, Ishwar Khatiwada, Joseph McLaughlin and Sheila Palma, "The 'Jobless and Wageless' Recovery from the Great Recession of 2007- 2009: The Magnitude and Sources of Economic Growth Through 2011 I and Their Impacts on Workers, Profits, and Stock Values," Center for Labor Market Studies Northeastern University Boston, Massachusetts, May 2011; National Infrastructure Development Bank press release, May 20, 2009; Ha Joon Chang, Bad Samaritans: The Myth of Free Trade and the Secret History of Capitalism (Bloomsbury Press, 2008); Thomas I. Palley, "The Rise and Fall of Export-led Growth," Levy Economics Institute of Bard College, Working Paper No. 675, July 2011.

Article 10.2

FULL EMPLOYMENT AS THE ANSWER FOR EUROPE
BY ROBERT POLLIN
March/April 2011

The economic crisis in Western Europe today—including, most seriously, Greece, along with the other PIIGS economies, Portugal, Ireland, Italy, and Spain—is fundamentally a crisis of neoliberalism. Neoliberalism is the package of economic measures whose guiding principles include deregulation of financial markets and the displacement of full employment, in favor of inflation control, as the central concern of macroeconomic policy.

Financial market titans have always been the biggest cheerleaders for neoliberalism. Of course, they never appreciated having government regulators tell them how to run their businesses. Big-time financiers also know that inflation will almost always lower the value of the financial assets they own and manage for their clients. Even moderate inflation therefore cuts into their profits.

Neoliberal policies have been ascendant throughout the world since the mid-1970s, and especially since Margaret Thatcher took office in the United Kingdom in 1979 and Ronald Reagan became the U.S. president in 1980. Over this 35-year span, neoliberalism has produced persistent financial crises, along with greater unemployment and sharply rising inequality throughout the world. But there has also always been a solution to crises readily at hand within the neoliberal recipe book: to impose austerity on the majority of middle- and working-class families and the poor—squeezing their incomes and social services to find the funds to clean up the mess created by ruling elites.

The European crisis should be properly seen as marking yet another failure of neoliberalism. But this failure has not created a demand for a return to an economic policy framework centered around full employment. This is despite the fact that creating an economy with an abundance of decent employment opportunities—a "full-employment" economy, as we are using the term—is a matter of basic ethics. Without full employment, the fundamental notion of equal rights for everyone—the core idea emanating from the Enlightenment and elaborated upon in both the liberal and socialist traditions—faces insurmountable obstacles in practical implementation.

Rather, to date, the crisis has only elicited ever more severe variants on the standard neoliberal austerity policies, even with political parties in power that are socialist in name, as in Greece, Portugal, and Spain. The main justification for such measures is that—in the spirit of Margaret Thatcher's famous dictum of the late 1970s—"there is no alternative."

In fact, as the Greek experience is demonstrating every day, austerity policies are self-defeating. By imposing severe cuts in incomes for ordinary people, they reduce the ability of these people to spend money, which in turn means fewer sales for businesses. Without seeing strong market opportunities ahead of them, businesses then become less willing to invest in expanding their operations and, in particular, hiring new workers.

It is true that constructing a viable full-employment agenda is always a challenge, but most especially so out of the wreckage created by neoliberalism. To begin with, full employment is not simply a matter of everyone spending their days trying to scratch out a living. If that were our definition of full employment, austerity would work perfectly, by forcing people to become "employed"—doing anything to stave off destitution. A meaningful definition of full employment entails an abundance of decent jobs.

What kind of full-employment policy could work in Europe in the current globalized age? Such a policy should strive for an officially measured unemployment rate below 4%. To achieve this would entail channeling more public and private investments to those industries that both generate high levels of social benefit and also produce an abundance of jobs anchored to the domestic economy.

Two clear areas of interest here are energy and education. Building a clean-energy economy—i.e., an economy powered by solar power, wind, and other renewable energy sources and that achieves high levels of energy efficiency—is highly effective for generating jobs per euro of spending. And by a significant margin, education is the *most* effective source of domestic job-creation per euro of spending.

There are two reasons for this. The first is labor intensity, i.e. how much of the total increase in new spending is devoted to hiring workers as opposed to spending on buildings, machines, land, and energy itself. The second factor is relative domestic content per euro of overall spending—that is, how much of total spending remains within the Greek, Spanish, or other EU economies as opposed to leaking out of the domestic economy through imports and outsourcing. With education, by far the largest share of total spending is for people working directly in local communities.

With renewable energy and energy efficiency, the employment boost is not as high as with education, but it is far higher than spending the same amount of money on oil imports. Consider, for example, an economy-wide project to increase the energy efficiency of the country's existing stock of buildings. This would create major energy savings throughout each of the oil-importing EU economies, and each euro saved would be one that is not spent on imported oil.

Of course, investments in education and clean energy also deliver major social and environmental benefits. Spending on education is the foundation for building a productive economy over the long term. Investments in energy efficiency will both lower greenhouse gas emissions and save money for both businesses and consumers over time. These investments, along with those to build a renewable energy infrastructure, will also diminish the country's dependence on foreign oil.

Of course, one has to figure out how to pay for the full-employment economy. Technically speaking, the problem is actually simpler to solve than it appears. In the short term, the European Central Bank only has to emulate what Ben Bernanke has already undertaken at the Federal Reserve. Under the banner of "quantitative easing," the Fed is now buying up long-term U.S. Treasury bonds, as a way to lower long-term interest rates and stimulate private borrowing. If the ECB would undertake basically the same operation now on a scale similar to the Fed, the result would be a two-fold benefit. It would contribute toward lowering interest rates on long-term European government bonds. It would also remove a significant share of the toxic sovereign debt from the balance sheets of the private European banks.

This would allow the private banks to refocus on making loans for productive investments and job creation rather than obsessing over crisis management. But the banks would then also have to be prepared to make loans to support job creation, rather than hyper-speculation. This means that, along with full employment, Europe needs to establish a new, viable system of financial regulations, committed to supporting the productive economy and job creation. In short, the real solution to the crisis in Europe today is to abandon the failed policies of austerity and neoliberalism, and begin the long transition toward establishing full employment and financial stability as the centerpieces of economic renewal. ❑

Article 10.3

THE CASE FOR A NATIONAL INFRASTRUCTURE BANK
A bank could be a recession-proof source of jobs.

BY HEIDI GARRETT-PELTIER
November/December 2010

Tragic events in recent years, such as the Minnesota bridge collapse or New Orleans' failed levees, combined with the daily aggravations of pot holes and power failures, underscore the need for improved infrastructure across the United States. The American Society of Civil Engineers gave the United States a "D" on its most recent *Report Card for America's Infrastructure*; the organization estimates that it will cost $2.2 trillion over the next five years to bring our infrastructure up to "good" condition.

Besides helping prevent disasters, infrastructure improvements create jobs. Maintenance, repair, and new construction of roads, buildings, water, and energy systems create jobs for engineers, construction crews, machinery manufacturers, and bookkeepers, among others.

Infrastructure improvements also have so-called positive externalities: their social benefits are greater than the financial gains earned by the parties who fund them. Improving roads, bridges, and transit systems can increase productivity, lower the cost of maintaining cars and buses, and reduce carbon emissions. Energy investments can increase productivity, and if directed toward energy efficiency and renewables, can also promote environmental sustainability. Investments in water systems lead to better health and lower health care costs.

Private companies cannot reap financial rewards from all of these indirect benefits. For instance, a private rail company could not feasibly charge a fee to everyone who enjoys less-congested roads or cleaner air thanks to a new rail line. So infrastructure projects have traditionally been publicly funded, primarily at the local level with some state and federal assistance.

Public infrastructure funding often falls short, however. In a recession, state and local tax revenues fall, making it harder to fund infrastructure projects precisely at a time when they could help the economy recover. Another problem is that during downturns and recoveries alike, higher-income localities are better able to fund their own roads or water systems than poorer ones. So available funds do not necessarily go to the projects providing the greatest benefits.

Today the United States invests in infrastructure at only half the level the ASCE recommends. One proposal for an innovative method to finance infrastructure is currently garnering bipartisan interest—a national infrastructure bank (NIB). An NIB would be a quasi-public agency whose function would be to use some federal funds to leverage a much larger amount of state, local, and private money which it would then provide to infrastructure projects.

An NIB could use various tools to finance infrastructure. It could sell bonds to private investors. It could be set up as a revolving loan fund, whereby an initial pool of funds is lent, and future loans made only once the earlier ones are repaid. It could even make grants for certain projects.

There are merits and drawbacks to any of these financing models. Some would make the NIB entirely self-sustaining, and so compel it to prioritize projects with a revenue stream, for instance from tolls, that would go to paying back the loan. Such a model would limit the bank's ability to choose projects with greater social benefits but less ability to repay funds quickly: it might fund construction of a toll road to a wealthy suburb rather than an upgrade to a municipal water system despite the latter's greater benefit. Other models would require more federal spending, but would give the bank greater flexibility to fund projects with less revenue potential.

In any case, a national infrastructure bank would make an important contribution to upgrading and expanding the country's infrastructure. It would boost the overall level of infrastructure spending. By leveraging private investment, it could continue to fund infrastructure projects even during recessions. Plus, it would make infrastructure spending more equitable since it would raise funds from a geographically distributed population, then target those funds toward the areas of greatest need. ❏

Article 10.4

SAVING ENERGY CREATES JOBS

BY HEIDI GARRETT-PELTIER
May/June 2009

Improving energy efficiency—using less energy to do the same amount of work—saves money and cuts pollution. But today, the other benefit of investing in energy efficiency may be the best draw: saving energy creates jobs.

Let's look at energy use in residential and commercial buildings. In the United States, buildings account for 40% of all energy use and are responsible for 38% of U.S. carbon emissions. Homes and other buildings lose energy through wasted heat, air-conditioning, and electricity. Following Jimmy Carter's suddenly fashionable example, we can turn down the thermostat in the winter and put on a sweater. We can unplug appliances that aren't used and save "phantom" power.

Beyond these personal changes, though, lie massive opportunities for systematic energy efficiency gains. These include insulating buildings, replacing old windows, and updating appliances and lighting. All of these generate new economic opportunities—read, jobs—in construction, manufacturing, and other sectors.

For instance, retrofitting existing homes, offices, and schools to reduce heating- and cooling-related energy waste (also known as weatherization) creates jobs of many kinds. Recent media attention has spotlighted "green jobs" programs that are hiring construction workers to add insulation, replace windows, and install more efficient heating systems. Perhaps less visible, retrofitting buildings also creates jobs for the engineers who design the new windows and furnaces, the factory workers who build them, and the office workers who make the appointments and handle the bookkeeping.

In fact, retrofitting creates more than twice as many jobs per dollar spent than oil or coal production, according to a detailed study that my colleagues and I at the Political Economy Research Institute conducted in 2008. For each $1 million spent, retrofitting creates about 19 jobs while spending on coal creates nine jobs and oil only six. Retrofitting also creates more jobs per dollar spent than personal consumption on typical items such as food, clothing, and electronics. Personal consumption does better than fossil fuels, but not as well as retrofitting, generating about 15 jobs per $1 million spent.

Why does retrofitting create more jobs? First, retrofitting is more labor-intensive than fossil-fuel production, meaning that more of each dollar spent goes to labor and less to machinery and equipment. Retrofitting also has higher domestic content than either fossil fuels or consumer goods; in other words, more of the supplies used to retrofit buildings are produced in the United States. In fact, about 95% of spending on retrofits stays in the domestic economy, versus only 80% of spending on oil (including refining and other related activities). Since more of its inputs are produced in the United States, retrofitting employs more U.S. workers. And this raises its multiplier effect: when those workers spend their earnings, each retrofitting dollar leads to yet more demand for goods and services.

To be fair, not all energy efficiency improvements will create jobs. When a more energy-efficient appliance or window design is widely adopted, the manufacturing worker who produced a less efficient good yesterday is simply producing a more efficient good today, with no net increase in employment. On the other hand, many retrofitting activities are pure job creators. Insulating attics and caulking leaky windows are activities that necessitate new workers—not just a shift from producing one good to another. With the collapse of the housing bubble and the huge rise in construction industry unemployment, retrofitting is an activity that could put tens of thousands of people back to work.

The Obama administration's stimulus package contains a wide variety of energy efficiency incentives, from 30% rebates for home insulation and for installing efficient windows, to rebates for builders of energy-efficient new homes and commercial buildings. These provisions will drive energy-saving improvements, accelerating the transition to a low-carbon economy while also creating jobs. ❑

Sources: U.S. Department of Energy, EERE Building Technologies Program; Robert Pollin, Heidi Garrett-Peltier, James Heintz, and Helen Scharber, "Green Recovery," Political Economy Research Institute, September 2008.

Article 10.5

TURNING TOWARD SOLUTIONS
It's time to occupy and reorganize production.

BY RICHARD D. WOLFF
January/February 2012

Since last September, the 99% have been wielding the weapon of criticism against the 1%. They are effective because they act in a new, collective, and organized way. Occupy Wall Street (OWS) and its many offshoots expose basic truths and demand basic changes. They struggle peacefully to reach, inform, and mobilize public opinion. They keep winning huge numbers of hearts and minds. In reaction, the U.S. 1% copied their counterparts in Tunisia, Egypt, Syria, and Bahrain. They limited media access needed by the movement to reach its growing audience. That failed. Their police intimidated, but that failed. Democratic Party operatives tried to convert Occupiers into Obama enthusiasts for the 2012 election. That failed, too.

Then, the 99%'s weapon of criticism suffered the counter-criticism of weapons. The 1%— frequent preachers of non-violence to others—resorted to coordinated police violence in cities across the country. As elsewhere, to cover up its failure to win hearts and minds, the U.S. government resorted to violence. Chickens raised abroad returned home to roost. Internet images flashed of New York Police Department machines and personnel bulldozing the free library in Zuccotti Park. Many recalled the famous 1930s photographs of police burning the books of those the Nazis feared or hated and therefore demonized.

New York's newly renamed billionaire mayor—*Mubarak* Bloomberg—gave the order to "clear and clean" Zuccotti Park. Having presided over some of the world's filthiest subway tunnels and stations, Bloomberg suddenly became obsessed with cleanliness. In New York, where income distribution is even more unequal than in the nation as a whole, the 1% mayor tried to silence OWS criticisms of that inequality and its capitalist roots. As OWS matures into a national movement, will that lead to renaming the President—as *Mubarak* Obama?

The conditions causing OWS include deepening economic inequality, the moneyed corruption of politics, and the collapsing fortunes and prospects of the mass of Americans. Neither Bloomberg nor Obama are changing them. The U.S. Census Bureau recalculated poverty last November (as requested and reported by the *New York Times,* November 19, 2011). The new calculation divided poverty into three types: "deep" (earning 50% or less of the official poverty level), "poor" (earning 50-100 % of the poverty level) and "near poor" (earning 100-150% of the poverty level). The new calculation took into account regional cost of living differences, government benefits (transfer payments) and income lost to taxation, health care and work expenses.

The Census Bureau's conclusion: *one-third of the United States was in or near poverty.* Over 100 million of our fellow citizens live at poverty levels hard to imagine, let alone endure. What this capitalist system delivers contradicts most Americans' notions of fairness, expectations of "middle-class" rewards for hard work, and hopes for their children. Business and political leaders had refused to see, debate, or change these conditions for decades. Most mainstream media and academics were similarly in denial. The system thus kept reproducing the causes of poverty (unemployment that precluded wage increases, "deficit reductions" that cut government transfer payments to the needy, foreclosures yielding more homeless people alongside more abandoned homes, etc.). The capitalist system became increasingly intolerable to increasing numbers of people. It produced a mass movement like OWS that shook and disrupted the national consensus on denial. Today, the criticism of weapons (police) risks losing to the weapon of criticism (OWS).

For the last half-century, it was taboo in the United States to criticize, debate, or propose changes to the economic system. We could question and alter our educational, transportation, health and other basic systems. However, Cold War anxieties and hysterical anti-communism dictated that the economic system be celebrated. Criticism of capitalism was branded as disloyalty to the United States. Journalists and academics followed the politicians in giving capitalism a free pass. Behind that celebratory veil, a protected capitalism performed ever more poorly for ever more people. As average real wages stopped rising since the 1970s, Americans borrowed more than they could sustain. As flat real wages and rising worker productivity made for huge profits, executives paid themselves astronomical salaries, stock options, and bonuses. Inequality has mushroomed since the 1970s and has contributed considerably to this crisis's depth and duration.

American capitalists took full advantage of their exemption from basic criticism. They widened the distance between employers and employees to produce a new "Gilded Age" now targeted by the 99% vs.1% slogan. It is stunningly effective because it rings so true to most Americans.

The Occupy movement keeps developing and now turns increasingly toward finding solutions for the problems it exposed. One emerging perspective holds that the capitalist economic system itself is the problem and movement to another system is the solution. The goal is not to transition to traditional socialist alternatives (e.g., the old Soviet Union or modern China). Rather, these alternatives too seem flawed systems needing basic change.

The solution for them too is to reorganize production *from the ground up*. Wherever production of goods or services occurs, the workers there should collectively and democratically function as their own board of directors. An exploitative and conflicted capitalism (employer versus employee) should be abolished much as our ancestors abolished slavery (master versus slave) and feudalism (lord versus serf). The solution is a system of *workers' self-directed enterprises*—where those who do the work also design and direct it and distribute its fruits. The basic goal of democracy—that all those affected by any decision participate equally in making it—would finally arrive inside production itself. No longer would a tiny elite minority—major shareholders and the corporate boards of directors they choose — make all the basic decisions: what, how and where to produce and how to use the surpluses/profits. Instead, the workers themselves—in shared democratic partnership with the residential communities interdependent with their enterprises—would make all those decisions.

Only then could we avoid repeating capitalist cycles. Those begin when capital accumulation and competition generate a crisis. When sustained mass suffering follows, movements for reform arise and sometimes succeed. Capitalists use their profits to block reforms and, when unsuccessful, to undo the reforms. This sets the stage for the next period of accumulation and competition and the next crisis: the U.S. pattern since the 1929 crash.

To break such truly vicious cycles, we need now to transform capitalism by internally reorganizing enterprises. Then, those who most need and benefit from reforms would be the self-directed workers who dispose of as well as create the profits of enterprises. No separate class of employers will exist and use the profits to undo the reforms won by workers. Self-directing workers would pay taxes to a state only insofar as it secures those reforms. More basically, our best hope of ending history's legacy of 99% against 1% lies in establishing new enterprises where democratically self-directed workers would no longer distribute incomes in capitalism's grotesquely unequal ways.

Workers' self-directed enterprises are a solution to problems shared by both capitalism and socialism. Establishing workers' self-directed enterprises moves further in the modern democratic movement beyond monarchies and autocracies. Democratizing production in this way can finally take political democracy beyond being merely an electoral ritual facilitating the same old rule by the 1% over the 99%. ❏

Article 10.6

GREETINGS FROM THE NEW ECONOMY
In a race against climate change, a new movement seeks to build a just, sustainable world.

BY ABBY SCHER
July/August 2012

"Are you ready for a new economy? Are you ready for a new politics?" The challenge at the podium came from Gus Speth, the courtly co-founder of the Natural Resources Defense Council, now a professor at Vermont Law School, who is on the board of the newly created New Economics Institute (NEI). The occasion was the founding conference of NEI, held at Bard College in early June, and Speth was making a call for "an economy whose very purpose is not to grow profit…but sustain people and the planet."

NEI is the remade E.F. Schumacher Society, the group based in Massachusetts' Berkshire mountains that promoted the wisdom of the author of *Small Is Beautiful: Economics as if People Mattered* for over 30 years. In honor of this early champion of a sustainable, just economy and the idea that big is not necessarily better, the Society nurtured economic innovations that support community building—community supported agriculture, local currencies, local land trusts.

With the help of the London-based New Economics Foundation, the Schumacher Society rethought what kind of "think and do" tank is needed to transform our fossil fuel-powered, finance-bloated, inegalitarian economy into one that is resilient, just, and sustainable in the environmental and economic transition given true urgency by climate change. And with the help of some deep pockets, it relaunched as NEI and pulled together, all in one place on Bard's rural campus on the Hudson, some of the thinkers and organizers who might have a piece of the puzzle.

People reimagining ownership and work on the job or in the academy, ex-Wall Streeters revealing the secrets of how to curb the power of big finance, community people reclaiming the commons—taking air, water, and land out of the market—and rebuilding local economies from the bottom up, advocates struggling with government to make it responsive, and social scientists who are remaking our economic indicators—they may never have talked with one another before the Strategies for a New Economy conference. But as Bob Massie, the new executive director of NEI said, together they created "raw energy."

Beyond Growth and Finance

The "New Economy" moniker is bubbling around lately, with a meaning recast far from President Bill Clinton's neoliberal usage 20 years ago. The venerable Washington DC-based Institute for Policy Studies has its New Economy Working Group, a partnership with *Yes!* magazine and the 22,000-member Business Alliance for Local Living Economies (BALLE). At the core of the call for a New Economy is an effort to come up with practical alternatives that democratize the control of the economy—including workplaces, finance, and the structure of the firm—in ways that are ecologically sustainable.

The focus on finance—on shrinking a dangerously unstable, extractive banking sector and nurturing an alternative one—is powered by such people as John Fullerton, the former JPMorgan managing director who launched Capital Institute to promote the idea of finance "not as master but as servant" and sees a role for "social impact" investing in the New Economy.

It is in the New Economy movement that you'll hear people talk about how to build a "no-growth" economy that shares more and taxes the earth less, a view promoted in the United States most notably by Boston College professor Juliet Schor. On the board of the new NEI are thinkers like Peter Victor of York University in Toronto, author of 2008's Managing Without Growth: Smaller by Design Not Disaster and Stewart Wallis, head of London's New Economics Foundation, which has been popularizing the no-growth idea for years.

"Even if everybody was to rediscover Keynes, that's not the answer," Wallis told the NEI crowd, referring to the British economist who popularized government investment in the economy during downturns, even if it means running deficits, in order to boost demand and employment. "We can have an economy with high well-being, high social justice" that destroys the planet. "We need a new model, an economy that runs on very different metrics, maximizing returns to scarce ecological resources, maximizing returns [to] human well-being, good jobs."

"We have to move from talking about ourselves as consumers to [regarding ourselves as] stewards." But the New Economy movement is a big tent, and for some growth isn't the question. For Marjorie Kelly, author of *Owning Our Future: The Emerging Ownership Revolution*, and a fellow of the Tellus Institute, the Boston-based think tank focused on sustainability, growth isn't the focus. In a chat at the conference "bookstore," she said,

> The problem is not growth but too much finance. You have the overlap of debt, unemployment, lack of jobs for youth. ... We can't have capital markets run the economy. It has a destructive focus. It's starting to fall apart. That's terrifying. You hold on desperately to what you have as it collapses. But no, you have an alternative. You have the Right, cutting taxes, deregulating. No serious thinker believes that those are the solutions. ...There's an inevitable sorting process. There's some loony ideas and we haven't sorted that out yet. But they said that about democracy.

Following the NEF and Schumacher, the New Economy umbrella also covers those promoting more realistic economic indicators that measure people's well-being and ecological costs, including the Green GDP. It considers which business forms—not just worker-owned companies but also so-called B-Corporations that consider social impact—might be compatible with a just, sustainable economy. It covers those challenging the decontextualized, value-free world of neoclassical economics because, as Massie said, "our current theories have blinded us." In late June, this was the agenda of Juliet Schor's week-long Summer Institute in New Economics at Boston College, where graduate students sat at the feet of

Gar Alperovitz of the University of Maryland, James Boyce of the University of Massachusetts-Amherst, Duncan Foley of the New School, and others.

It's a big tent, and feels a bit like the Progressive Movement of the early 20th century, when many elites and middle-class people began questioning and even challenging how capitalism was organized. Partly because of its high price tag, the Bard gathering was almost entirely white and highly educated, deploring poverty but not necessarily touched by it, yet highly motivated to build a more communal, cooperative economy. How these middle-class reformers will share leadership with low-income immigrants, progressive unions, and co-ops—key social bases for the movement—is a bit of a mystery. It's no mystery, however, that any massive change in the U.S. political economy needs all these sectors pulling toward change.

Andrew Simms, the Brit known for his creative leadership in The Other Economic Summits (which dogged G-7 meetings for years before turning into London's New Economy Foundation), put class and political power on the table when he told the meeting, "When I hear people talk about sustainable capitalism, they are making a strategic error," adding "If we could get where we need to be by writing reports, we would have gotten there." The knowledge that the activists need to raise their game ran through the conference. In his plenary, Massie acknowledged who largely was not represented in the room: unions, communities of color, youth, business. He asked his audience to ask in turn, "How can we work together? How can we make this bigger and make the New Economy a reality?"

Solidarity and Division

It was only April 2009, at University of Massachusetts-Amherst, that the U.S. Solidarity Economy Network held its own sizeable gathering. That brought together people in progressive unions, worker co-ops, credit unions, food co-ops, green jobs initiatives, and even the peace movement. Inspired by the U.S. Social Forum in Atlanta in 2007 and Solidarity Economy movements in Latin America and Quebec, the network was soon celebrating the United Steel Workers' announcement that it would try to take over smaller enterprises for worker ownership, based on the example of Spain's Mondragón cooperatives—an effort slowed by the impact of the economic crisis on the union. Canadian unions reported using their pension funds to support worker ownership.

There is some overlap between the Solidarity Economy and New Economy networks. The NEI conference sought out sustainable business networks and social venture funders while the solidarity framework inspired more lower-income people and people of color. Worker co-ops came to the New Economy gathering at Bard. The green Cleveland co-ops—the complex including industrial laundry and urban farm (see "America Beyond Capitalism," *D&S*, November/December 2011)—received a rousing reception. And NEI board member and plenary speaker Gar Alperovitz is one of worker ownership's most vocal academic champions. But as Donnie Maclurcan, of Australia's Post-Growth Institute asked me at the opening session: "Where is the acknowledgment of the custodians? [Thanking the janitors] is standard in Australia." A participant set up a sign on a picnic table during lunch asking people to come over and talk about race and class. The divide is deep.

Speth was another who took on the divisions in the movements directly but warned the group they had to overcome it:

> Critical here is a common progressive platform. It should embrace a profound commitment to social justice, job creation, and environmental protection; a sustained challenge to consumerism and commercialism and the lifestyles they offer; a healthy skepticism of growth mania and a democratic redefinition of what society should be striving to grow; a challenge to corporate dominance and a redefinition of the corporation, its goals and its management and ownership; a commitment to an array of prodemocracy reforms in campaign finance, elections, the regulation of lobbying; and much more. A common agenda would also include an ambitious set of new national indicators beyond GDP to inform us of the true quality of life in America.

Thinkers like Alperovitz support democratizing our economy by building out our existing network of land trusts, consumer and worker cooperatives, employee stock ownership programs with workers participating in governance, and credit unions—building off institutions crisscrossing the country. He mourns the age of unions as past, noting that more workers are in worker co-ops or ESOPs than private-sector unions. He sees these cooperative endeavors as providing a key base for building the future. He gives a political blueprint calling for redirecting federal, state and local government support toward these enterprises from corporations. This echoes the "cooperative commonwealth" envisioned by some 19th-century populists, and has healthy if long-lost roots in American thought. Markets are left intact but so is government action for the common good.

With a much greater ecological consciousness than many of her peers, Juliet Schor (like Costas Panayotakis in his new book *Remaking Scarcity*) calls for a struggle over our subjectivity and how we define our needs in building a more egalitarian, sustainable economy. While Schor was unable to attend the conference, in some ways she captures the downshifting philosophy of much of the audience better than keynoter Alperovitz. She warns us that capitalism's ability to nimbly create new needs and intensify consumerism needs to be challenged on an ecological and moral basis. Can we remake the common-sense values that are lodged at the core of our current system?

Schor lays out the more explicit vision of what almost seems like a social crusade, yet relies on individual action. She argues we need to remove ourselves from the market, step by step where we can: by working part-time, making do with less disposable cash income, and doing more on our own.. That means everything from cooking to making clothes to home construction. Drawing on the alternative economy movements promoted by the old Schumacher Society, Schor champions local time dollar schemes, freecycle sharing, and barter. These schemes seek to intensify community values by intensifying your web of support with your neighbors. Ultralocal, home-based solar energy production should spread. People should embrace the slow money movement by investing locally through credit unions other other local networks, not through big finance.

Meanwhile, she supports expanding the welfare state so that we are not subject to markets when it comes to our health, to expand living-wage jobs and in protecting the commons.

Slow Money

While the thinkers and policy heads dominated the panels at Bard, in the hallways I met an organic farmer who is a soil activist and writer, a big-city organizer trying to launch a Cleveland-style worker-owned initiative in an impoverished area, an Occupier, a member of a worker coop, and a Rhode Island man hoping to launch a community currency so that impoverished residents can find value in their skills. I also met Frank Nuessle of the Public Banking Institute, which is championing state banks modeled on North Dakota's, and Sean McGuire, Maryland's director of sustainability who championed the Genuine Progress Indicator so the state now measures economic growth with an eye to its social and ecological costs. Attending in force were Transition Woodstock members. These last are part of the international Transition movement begun in the U.K. that tries to encourage communities to downshift and take up resilient, ecologically sound practices so that we respond to climate change in an egalitarian way. NEI's London partner, New Economy Foundation, actively supports the Transition movement.

One of my deepest conversations was with Bonnie Rukin, regional coordinator of Slow Money Maine, which holds events matching people who can give loans or grants to enterprises creating a local sustainable food system. That might mean an organic member-owned restaurant or seaweed harvesters. Inspired by Woody Tasch, the former venture capitalist who founded Slow Money, the Maine group is one of the more successful regional spinoffs. Other people at the conference reported struggling projects in Ohio and Colorado.

"A funder meets a farmer. A farmer meets a legislator. We have a lot of networking time at our meetings," said Rukin, a 62-year-old former organic farmer with a nonprofit background. "We catalyzed the flow of $3 million … and untold amounts of awareness. In terms of hunger needs, we're second in the country. We're on par with Alabama. We want to develop the social fabric."

"We started with 30 people gathering and we're up to 450 people," said Rukin. "They're each given 10 to 15 minutes to tell what they did…then the bell would ring," said Jonathan Lee, a Belfast, Maine Slow Money activist. He describes the scene: "People in the audience are from foundations, government…" Some skilled businesspeople offer their time.

Jonah Fertig, a member of the Sprouts cooperative restaurant funded through Slow Money Maine, said simply, "It's helped us to connect to different resources and people," including fellow "farmers, cooks, food procecessors…"

American Sustainable Business Association

Less explicitly anti-capitalist than many of the alternative economy folks are some of the business-oriented elements of the New Economy movement that wrestle to reform traditional market-based tools so they create incentives toward sustainable, socially just practices.

Or sometimes they just try to create a counterforce to the big-business lobby. "Policies that provide social benefit are called bad for business," David Levine, founding director of the American Sustainable Business Association reported to the Bard gathering. "It was time to ask, 'Bad for whose business?'"

The ASBA formed after the election of President Obama to provide lobbying muscle and build political power for policies that tackle global warming and invest in job growth. "That means showing up before the Energy and Commerce committee and say why regulations are very important for business." It now networks 150 existing local and specialized business associations representing 150,000 members. The New Mexico Green Chamber of Commerce and women's business associations are among their members.

"We can actually produce chemicals that are not toxic. We can produce materials that are recyclable," said Levine. "What are we up against? It's the $200 million budget of the U.S. Chamber of Commerce. While we might not have the money, we can show up and have a voice."

B-Corporations

Being obsessed with profit and growth comes with costs that don't show up in the numbers. Community stakeholders and goals are ignored in corporate ratings, and companies are captive to Wall Street's short-termism. And Wall Street's goals are written into corporate law. A former bond trader came up with a new corporate form, B-corporations, that allows companies to be evaluated by their social performance, not just their economic bottom line. Since 2010, laws allowing B-corps have been enacted in eight states, most recently in Louisiana. Nathan Gilbert's job at B-Lab, a New York-based nonprofit, is to make it spread.

Strategists who think investors will voluntarily make better decisions if they knew the true impact of companies are also creating alternatives like GIIRS, the Global Impact Investing Rating System, to reveal what businesses are doing for the environment, job creation, and job quality.

But only 500 companies are chartered as B-corporations, mostly small firms. "They have $3 billion total capitalization—that's cappuccino money at Apple," said Allen K. White, vice president of Tellus, another speaker. Still, he said, "Ownership does matter. It has a moral and operational quality."

Meanwhile, he pointed out, most of the world's economic activity is controlled by the 1,000 largest corporations, untouched by many of these ideas and local movements. Richard Branson of Virgin may have told Davos, the gathering of the high and mighty, that we are seeing "the end of capitalism," as White noted. And indeed the Solidarity Economy and New Economy movements are debating what should replace it.

The stakes are high. The environmental writer and campaigner Bill McKibben was on hand to give the conference a sense of urgency to curb corporations' destructive power before the imminent damage caused by climate change is irreversible.

"It is a fundamentally altered planet," he told a packed auditorium. Given our interconnection, it's not enough to work in our home communities. "If we don't take care of this large global crisis, we won't realize the future toward which we are all working.

"This is not only a huge practical dilemma but a moral one too," he said, reporting on the dengue fever epidemic he just faced in Bangladesh which he survived when undernourished people died. "Today we learned this spring was the worst spring and the most extreme. Saudi Arabia had the hottest rainstorm recorded on this planet—109 degrees. We're building a science fiction story and I don't know if we can stop it."

"Here's the good news: Most of what we need to do to deal with global warming will also help [people]," he said. With those marching orders, his middle-class reform army filed out. ❑

Sources: Juliet Schor, *True Wealth: How and Why Millions of Americans Are Creating a Time-rich, Ecologically Light, Small-scale, High-satisfaction Economy*, Penguin, 2011; Bill Mckibben, *Eaarth: Making a Life on a Tough New Planet*, New York Times, 2010; Costas Panayotakis, *Remaking Scarcity: From Capitalist Inefficiency to Economic Democracy*, Pluto, 2011; James Gustave Speth, *The Bridge at the Edge of the World: Capitalism, the Environment, and Crossing from Crisis to Sustainability*, Yale UP, 2008; Marjorie Kelly, *Owning Our Future: The Emerging Ownership Revolution*, Berrett-Koehler, 2012; Tim Jackson, *Prosperity without Growth: Economics for a Finite Planet*, Earthscan, 2009; Gar Alperovitz and James Gustave Speth, *America beyond Capitalism: Reclaiming Our Wealth, Our Liberty, and Our Democracy*, Democracy Collaborative/*Dollars & Sense*, 2011; E. F. Schumacher, *Small Is Beautiful: Economics as If People Mattered*, Harper & Row, 1973; Peter Victor, *Managing Without Growth: Smaller by Design Not Disaster*, Edward Elgar Publishing, Inc. 2008; David Brancaccio, "Fixing the Future," pbs.org; The Democracy Collaborative, community-wealth.org; New Economics Institute, neweconomicsinstitute.org; The New Economics Foundation, neweconomics.org; The U.S. Federation of Worker Cooperatives, usworker.coop.

CONTRIBUTORS

Randy Albelda is a professor of economics at the University of Massachusetts-Boston and a *Dollars & Sense* Associate.

William K. Black is executive director of the Institute for Fraud Prevention and teaches economics and law at the University of Missouri at Kansas City.

Sarah Blaskey is a student at the University of Wisconsin-Madison and a member of the Student Labor Action Coalition.

Elissa Dennis is a consultant to nonprofit affordable housing developers with Community Economics, Inc., in Oakland, Calif.

Gerald Friedman is a professor of economics at the University of Massachusetts at Amherst.

Heidi Garrett-Peltier is an economist and research associate at the Political Economy Research Institute at the University of Massachusetts-Amherst.

Phil Gasper teaches at Madison College and writes a column for International Socialist Review.

Amy Gluckman is a former co-editor of *Dollars & Sense*.

Tim Koechlin is a visiting associate professor of economics at Vassar College.

Jonathan Latham is co-founder and executive director of the Bioscience Resource Project, which publishes Independent Science News (independentsciencenews.org).

Arthur MacEwan is professor emeritus of economics at the University of Massachusetts-Boston and is a *Dollars & Sense* Associate.

John Miller is a member of the *Dollars & Sense* collective and professor economics at Wheaton College.

William G. Moseley is a professor of geography at Macalaster College in Saint Paul, Minn.

Robert Pollin teaches economics and is co-director of the Political Economy Research Institute at the University of Massachusetts-Amherst. He is also a *Dollars & Sense* Associate.

Ethan Pollack is a policy analyst at the Economic Policy Institute.

Alejandro Reuss is co-editor of *Dollars & Sense* and an instructor at the Labor Relations and Research Center, UMass-Amherst.

Abby Scher is a sociologist and journalist who was co-editor of *Dollars & Sense* in the 1990s. She is now a *D&S* Associate and an Associate Fellow of the Institute for Policy Studies.

Dan Schneider is a freelance journalist and a member of the *Dollars & Sense* collective.

Katherine Sciacchitano is a former labor lawyer and organizer. She is also a professor at the National Labor College and a freelance labor educator.

Chris Sturr, co-editor of this volume, is co-editor of *Dollars & Sense*.

Jeffrey Thompson is an assistant research professor at the Political Economy Research Institute at the University of Massachusetts-Amherst.

Marjolein van der Veen is an economist who has taught economics in Massachusetts, the Seattle area, and the Netherlands.

Jeannette Wicks-Lim is an economist and research fellow at the Political Economy Research Institute at the University of Massachusetts-Amherst.

Max Fraad Wolff teaches economics at the New School University Graduate Program in International Affairs.

Richard D. Wolff is professor emeritus of economics at the University of Massachusetts-Amherst and author of *Capitalism Hits the Fan: The Global Economic Meltdown and What to Do About It*.

Marty Wolfson teaches economics at the University of Notre Dame and is a former economist with the Federal Reserve Board in Washington, D.C.